Ready-to-Use WRITING PROFICIENCY LESSONS & ACTIVITIES

8th Grade Level

Carol H. Behrman

JOSSEY-BASS
A Wiley Imprint
www.josseybass.com

Published by Jossey-Bass
A Wiley Imprint
989 Market Street, San Francisco, CA 94103-1741 www.josseybass.com

Jossey-Bass books and products are available through most bookstores. To contact Jossey-Bass directly, call our Customer Care Department within the U.S. at (800) 956-7739, outside the U.S. at (317) 572-3993 or fax (317) 572-4002.

Jossey-Bass also publishes its books in a variety of electronic formats. Some content that appears in print may not be available in electronic books.

Library of Congress Cataloging-in-Publication Data
Behrman, Carol H.
Ready-to-use writing proficiency lessons & activities, 8th grade level / Carol H. Behrman.—1st ed.
p. cm.
ISBN: 978-0-7879-6586-0
1. English language—Composition and exercises—Study and teaching (Middle school)—Activity programs—United States. 2. Eighth grade (Education)—United States. I. Title.
LB1631.B377 2003
808'.042'071273—dc21 2003005574

FIRST EDITION

10 9 8 7 6 5 4 3 2 1

DEDICATION

For Patrick, Luke, Matthew, Jonathan, and Rose—write well, my dears!

ABOUT THE AUTHOR

Carol H. Behrman was born in Brooklyn, New York, graduated from City College of New York, and attended Columbia University's Teachers' College, where she majored in education. She married Edward Behrman, an accountant, and moved to Fair Lawn, New Jersey, where they raised three children. They currently reside in Sarasota, Florida. For many years, Mrs. Behrman taught grades five through eight at the Glen Ridge Middle School in New Jersey, where she created a program utilizing a writing process that combined language arts with word-processing instruction. She has written nineteen books, fiction and nonfiction, for children and young adults, and has conducted numerous workshops on the writing process for students, teachers, and aspiring writers. She has served as writer-in-residence at Chautauqua Institution and has been an adjunct lecturer at Seton Hall and New York University's Writing Center.

Mrs. Behrman is also the author of *Ready-to-Use Writing Proficiency Lessons & Activities, 4th Grade Level* (2002), *Writing Skills Problem Solver* (2000), *Writing Activities for Every Month of the School Year* (1997), *Write! Write! Write!* (1995), and *Hooked on Writing!* (1990), all published by The Center for Applied Research in Education.

ABOUT THIS WRITING TESTPREP TEACHING RESOURCE

Ready-to-Use Writing Proficiency Lessons & Activities gives eighth-grade teachers a powerful and effective tool to use when preparing their students for standardized writing tests. This resource provides:

- instruction and extensive guided practice in the mechanics of basic writing skills
- instruction and guided practice in sentence and paragraph writing
- instruction and guided practice in writing the three basic types of essays—informative/expository, narrative, and persuasive—as well as writing letters and stories as called for in standardized tests
- numerous activities in each type of writing as well as simulated testing situations
- examples of state and national guidelines and rubrics and sample student responses to help teachers evaluate student performance

The more than 240 easy-to-use, reproducible activity sheets in this resource are grouped into the following nine sections:

- **Section 1:** The activities in "Choosing the Right Word" help students select the most appropriate word. Homonyms, verbs, adverbs, adjectives, prepositions, nouns, pronouns, similes, metaphors, and words often confused are among the topics covered.
- **Section 2:** The easy-to-complete activities in "Making Mechanics and Usage Work for You" provide a review of capitalization, punctuation, abbreviations, and other pertinent rules of basic writing.
- **Section 3:** "Writing Sentences" contains interesting and age-appropriate activities that help students learn how to write accurate and effective sentences. Some of the topics covered are subjects and predicates, agreement of subject and verb, consistency of tense and number, writing simple and compound sentences, and recognizing incomplete and run-on sentences.
- **Section 4:** The lessons and activities in "Writing Paragraphs" help students to produce a well-constructed paragraph, including using strong topic sentences, effective concluding sentences, and developing the topic in an effective, relevant manner. The steps of the writing process are introduced to aid students in their writing activities.
- **Section 5:** "Essay-Writing Techniques" begins with activities on the prewriting techniques of brainstorming, clustering, and outlining. Students are then taken step by step through the process of producing an essay. Lessons include the use of clear, attention-getting introductory paragraphs; how to develop the topic with effective and relevant examples; and bringing the essay to an effective end with a concluding paragraph. The final activities in this section help students use the writing process to produce three- and

five-paragraph essays. The use of proofreading symbols during the revision process is introduced.

- **Section 6:** The activities in "Writing Informative Essays" give students guided practice in writing essays that convey information, all of which utilize the writing process.
- **Section 7:** Students are encouraged to express their own opinions in "Writing Persuasive Essays." The activities in this section use the writing process to make it easier for students to compose interesting and convincing essays on a variety of topics that are relevant to this grade level.
- **Section 8:** "Narrative Writing" offers activities using the writing process that help students develop competence in writing this type of essay. Included among these narrative activities are imaginative writing projects with instruction and projects for developing story-writing skills such as plotting, characterization, and dialogue.
- **Section 9:** Standardized tests often call for students to convey information or express an opinion in the form of a letter. "Writing Letters" provides students with activities for writing informative and persuasive letters.

Teacher Preparation and Lessons

Teacher lesson plans that offer detailed suggestions for class instruction precede each section of activities. Answer keys are provided where appropriate. The activities in Sections 1 through 3 can be used as part of a language arts program and/or specifically for test preparation. The easy-to-follow directions on all activities make it possible for you to utilize them with entire classes, small groups, or individual students. These basic language skills should be constantly kept in mind and reinforced as students work on the writing sample activities in Sections 4 through 9. You may wish to select skill pages and assign them before students complete a specific assignment or a Practice Test.

Review Tests, Practice Tests, and Standardized Assessment

The review tests at the end of Sections 1 through 3 can be utilized as pretests and/or posttests to assess basic language skills. They can be indicators to you as to which activities should be emphasized and used in complete class instruction, small group work, or individual remediation.

The practice tests at the end of Sections 4 through 9 simulate standardized testing situations by taking the students through the writing process for producing a passage based on prompts. A checklist at the beginning of each test reminds students which skills and techniques are required for each type of writing. Many of these competencies are also referred to on the scoring guide accompanying each test. These scoring guides will help you assess student results. Students may find it helpful to use these guides to assess their own writing as well as the sample student-writing passages provided with the tests. Scores for the sample writing passages and a rationale for each are provided at the end of the Teacher Preparation pages for each section. It may be beneficial for students to read and assign scores to sample passages before proceeding with their own practice tests. Class analysis and discussion of this scoring may help clarify student goals in their own writing.

A good indicator of what is required on standardized writing tests at the eighth-grade level is the National Assessment of Educational Progress (NAEP) writing test. The guidelines for this test succinctly state the objectives for all standardized tests at this level as follows:

- Students should write for a variety of purposes: narrative, informative, and persuasive.
  - ❑ Narrative writing involves the production of stories or personal essays. It encourages writers to use their creativity and powers of observation to develop stories that can capture a reader's imagination.
  - ❑ Informative writing communicates information to the reader to share knowledge or to convey messages, instructions, and ideas. The informative topics in the previous writing assessments required students to write on specified subjects in a variety of formats, such as reports, reviews, and letters.
  - ❑ Persuasive writing seeks to influence the reader to take some action or bring about change. It may contain factual information, such as reasons, examples, or comparisons; however, its main purpose is not to inform, but to persuade. The persuasive topics in previous writing assessments asked students to write letters to friends, newspaper editors, or prospective employers, to refute arguments, or to take sides in a debate.
- Students should write on a variety of tasks and for many different audiences. The writing assessment prompts have presented students with a variety of tasks, such as writing a letter to the editor of a newspaper, offering advice to younger students, reporting to a school committee, and writing a story based on a poem.
- Students should write from a variety of stimulus material. Some of the narrative topics in NAEP writing assessments asked students to write stories in response to photographs, cartoons, or poems. Many of the persuasive topics asked students to write in response to information provided with the assessment, such as newspaper articles, charts, photographs, and reported dialogues. Several of the informative topics asked students to respond to letters, cartoons, or articles.
- Students should generate, draft, revise, and edit ideas and forms of expression in their writing. (NOTE: Some state tests provide written guidelines for students outlining the steps of the writing process and/or multiple sessions in which to complete these tasks.)

Information about the NAEP can be found at www.NAGB.org or at www.nces.ed.gov/nationsreportcard. In this resource, information on standardized testing and on scoring rubrics for the NAEP as well as for several states appears at the beginning of Sections 5 through 9. The scoring guides accompanying the writing practice tests were adapted from the NAEP guidelines. You may wish to compare these guidelines with those for your individual state when scoring students' writing samples.

Ready-to-Use Writing Proficiency Lessons & Activities are also available from Jossey-Bass at the fourth-grade level and the tenth-grade level. The lessons, activities, and sample test items in all three grade-level volumes are invaluable tools for helping students to master basic language and writing skills in preparation for taking standardized tests. Even more important, they will help students develop a sound foundation for becoming proficient writers throughout their lives.

CONTENTS

SECTION 3
WRITING SENTENCES 109

SECTION 4
WRITING PARAGRAPHS 147

SECTION 5
ESSAY-WRITING TECHNIQUES 189

SECTION 6
WRITING INFORMATIVE ESSAYS 231

Section 9

WRITING LETTERS 333

Appendix

PREPARING YOUR STUDENTS FOR STANDARDIZED PROFICIENCY TESTS 361

SECTION 1

CHOOSING THE RIGHT WORD

Teacher Preparation and Lessons

Activities 1-1 through 1-4 focus on words commonly misspelled, while Activities 1-5 through 1-7 focus on words often confused. Activities 1-8 through 1-18 are designed to enlarge students' vocabularies and make their writing more precise. Activities 1-19 through 1-33 concentrate on using the parts of speech correctly. Activities 1-34 through 1-43 help students improve their usage of literal and figurative language. You may wish to use the REVIEW TEST at the end of the section as a pretest and/or as a posttest. Answer keys for this section can be found on pages 6–11.

ACTIVITIES 1-1 through 1-4 review **words commonly misspelled**. Elicit the correct spelling of the following words and write them on the chalkboard: *a lot* (two words), *weird, accurate, accomplish, believe, embarrass, calendar, scissors, disappoint, address, February, handkerchief, really, rhythm, straight.* Point out that the only way to learn how to spell these words is through memorization and usage. Distribute **Activity 1-1 Words Commonly Misspelled (Part One)**. Discuss the spellings and meanings of the words in the boxed material and have students complete the activity. Distribute **Activity 1-2 Words Commonly Misspelled (Part Two).** Discuss the spellings and meanings of the words in the boxed material and have students complete the activity. Distribute **Activity 1-3 Words Commonly Misspelled (Part Three).** Discuss the spellings and meanings of the words in the box and read the directions aloud. When students have completed the activity, have several sentences read aloud for each word. Distribute **Activity 1-4 Words Commonly Misspelled (Part Four)**. Discuss the spellings and meanings of the words in the box and have students complete the activity.

ACTIVITIES 1-5 through 1-7 review **words often confused**. Write the following pairs of words on the chalkboard: *maybe, may be; accept, except; advice, advise; among, between; bring, take; learn, teach.* Elicit the meanings of these words and discuss why they are often confused. Distribute **Activity 1-5 Words Often Confused (Part One)**. Review the words in the box and have students complete the activity. Distribute **Activity 1-6 Words Often Confused (Part Two)**. Read and discuss the spellings and meanings of the words in the box and have the students complete the activity. Distribute **Activity 1-7 Words Often Confused (Part Three)**. Review the words in the box and have the students complete the activity.

ACTIVITIES 1-8 through 1-18 enlarge **students' vocabularies and make their writing more precise.** Activity 1-8 reviews **prefixes.** Write the following words on the chalkboard: *preview, preschool, prepay.* Elicit that *pre* is a **prefix**, and usually means *before.* Ask students to suggest other prefixes and write them on the chalkboard. Distribute **Activity 1-8 Prefixes.** Read the directions and examples together. When students have completed the activity, have several examples of each sentence read aloud.

Activities 1-9 through 1-13 review **suffixes.** Write the following words on the chalkboard: *violinist, typist, artist.* Elicit that *ist* is a **suffix** that means "one who does." Write the suffix *ful* on the chalkboard and elicit a list of words that end with *ful* *(useful, tasteful, beautiful,* etc.). Do the same for *ment.* Distribute **Activity 1-9 Suffixes (Part One)**. Review the words listed in the box and then read the directions together. When students have completed the activity, have several examples of each sentence read aloud. Distribute **Activity 1-10 Suffixes (Part Two)**. Read and discuss the examples of the words using *able* and *ible.* Then have the students complete the activity. Distribute **Activity 1-11 Suffixes (Part Three)**. Read and discuss the examples of the words using *ar, or,* and *er.* Then have the students complete the activity. Distribute **Activity 1-12 Suffixes (Part Four)**. Read and discuss the rules and examples, and have the students complete the activity. Distribute **Activity 1-13 Prefixes and Suffixes.** Read the directions and have the students complete the activity. When completed, have several samples of each read aloud.

Activities 1-14 through 1-16 review **synonyms and antonyms.** Write the following short paragraph on the chalkboard:

My house is small. My room is small, too.
Even my dog, Muffy, is small.

Elicit the repetitive nature of the word *small.* Ask students to suggest other words with the same meaning that could be used. (Elicit that words with the same meaning are called **synonyms.**) Write a list of synonyms for *small* on the chalkboard. Rewrite the paragraph, using some of these new words. Now write the following list of words on the chalkboard: *tired, happy, talk, big.* Have students supply several synonyms for each word. Distribute **Activity 1-14 Synonyms.** Read the directions together. Point out that only the <u>underscored</u> words should be replaced. When students have completed this activity, have several students read their new paragraphs aloud to demonstrate the variety of synonyms that could be used.

Write the following pairs of words on the chalkboard: *last, first; early, late; top, bottom.* Elicit that these are opposites and are called **antonyms.** Distribute **Activity 1-15 Antonyms.** Read the directions together and have students complete the activity. Distribute **Activity 1-16 Synonyms and Antonyms.** Read and discuss the directions. When students have completed these activities, have several examples read aloud for each synonym and antonym.

Activities 1-17 and 1-18 review **homonyms.** Say the word *to* and ask students how it is spelled. Elicit three different spellings: *to, too, two.* Ask for a definition of **homonyms** (words that sound alike but have different meanings). Write the following words on the chalkboard: *not, grate, hire, lessen, aloud, here, mist.* Elicit the meaning of each word. Ask volunteers to write a homonym next to each word and define it. Distribute **Activity 1-17 Homonyms (Part One).** Read the directions together and have the students complete the exercise. Distribute **Activity 1-18 Homonyms (Part Two)**. Read the list of homonyms and discuss their spellings and meanings. Read the directions together and have students complete the activity.

ACTIVITIES 1-19 through 1-33 concentrate on using the **parts of speech correctly**. Write these phrases on the chalkboard: *<u>tall</u> man, <u>blue</u> sky, <u>disgusting</u> sight, <u>winning</u> team, <u>exciting</u> movie.* Ask what the underscored words have in common. Elicit that they are all **adjectives** that modify a noun. Write on the chalkboard: *computer, hair, game, book, song.* Ask students to supply several adjectives for each noun. Activity 1-19 reviews **adjectives.** Distribute **Activity 1-19 Adjectives.** Read the directions and have the students complete the activity. Have several samples for each sentence read aloud.

Write these phrases on the chalkboard: *walk <u>slowly</u>, fight <u>fiercely</u>, fall <u>heavily</u>, whisper <u>softly</u>, arrive <u>late</u>.* Ask what the underscored words have in common. Elicit that each one modifies a verb. Discuss the definition of an **adverb**. Activity 1-20 reviews **adverbs.** Distribute **Activity 1-20 Adverbs**. Read and discuss the rules and examples; then read the directions. When students have completed the activity, have several examples of each sentence read aloud. Distribute **Activity 1-21 Adverbs vs. Adjectives**. Read and discuss the explanation and examples. Then read the directions and have the students complete the activity.

Activity 1-22 reviews **prepositions**. Explain how to use **prepositions** correctly. Write the following sentence on the chalkboard: *I will stop by your house on the way to school.* Elicit that the word *by* is used incorrectly. The sentence should read either *I will stop at your house on the way to school* or *I will pass by your house on the way to school.* Point out that *by* is a preposition and that a preposition shows how a noun or pronoun is connected to another word in the sentence in place, time, or direction. Begin a list of prepositions on the chalkboard, such as *by, from, over, before.* Elicit additional prepositions and add them to the list. Distribute **Activity 1-22 Prepositions.** Read the definition and list of prepositions. Read and discuss the examples of prepositions that are used incorrectly. Then read and discuss the directions, and have students complete the activity.

Activity 1-23 reviews **articles.** Distribute **Activity 1-23 Articles.** Read and discuss the rules and examples. Then have the students complete the activity.

Activities 1-24 through 1-29 review **nouns and pronouns.** Write these words on the chalkboard: *child, country, ball, happiness.* Students will identify these as **nouns.** Elicit the definition of a noun as a name for a person, place, thing, or idea. Note that the examples are **common nouns** and begin with a lowercase letter. Elicit other examples of common nouns. Write on the chalkboard: *Patrick, America, White House.* Elicit that these are **proper nouns** and are always capitalized. Ask students to contribute additional examples of proper nouns. Distribute **Activity 1-24 Common and Proper Nouns.** Read and discuss the rules and examples. Then read the directions and have students complete the activity. Have them read their sentences aloud.

Write these words on the chalkboard: *audience, bunch, team, pack.* Elicit that these terms name groups of people, animals, or things, and are called **collective nouns.** Ask for additional examples of collective nouns. Write on the chalkboard: *shoelace, backpack, high school.* Note that these are called **compound nouns.** Elicit that a compound noun is made up of two or more words used together. Note that these compound words can consist of one word or two words. Elicit additional examples of compound nouns. Distribute **Activity 1-25 Collective and Compound Nouns.** Read and discuss rules and examples. Then read the directions and have students complete the activity. Have them read their sentences aloud.

Explain that **pronouns** take the place of nouns and can serve as subjects or objects of a sentence. They can also show possession. Some pronouns help to point out a specific person, place, or thing. Others are used to ask a question. Distribute **Activity 1-26 Pronouns and Antecedents (Part One)**. Read and discuss the definitions of **pronouns and antecedents,** and have the students complete the activity. Distribute **Activity 1-27 Pronouns and Antecedents (Part Two)**. Read and discuss the rules for **agreement** between pronouns and their antecedents. Discuss the examples for each rule. Be sure students understand why the examples labeled WRONG are incorrect. Read and discuss the directions, and have students complete the activity. Distribute **Activity 1-28 Indefinite Pronouns.** Read and discuss the definition and examples of **indefinite pronouns.** Read the directions and do the first two together. Distribute **Activity 1-29 Personal Possessive Pronouns.** Read and discuss the definition and examples for using **personal possessive pronouns.** Make certain that students understand why the examples labeled WRONG are incorrect. Read the directions and have the students complete the activity.

Activities 1-30 through 1-33 review **verbs.** Effective use of **verbs** is an essential ingredient of good writing and is included in most state assessment rating guidelines. Write these sentences on the chalkboard:

I walk in the yard.

I am in the yard.

Ask students to identify the verbs in these sentences. Elicit the difference between these two verbs (*walk* shows action; *am* shows being). Distribute **Activity 1-30 Verbs (Part One).** Read the examples of action and being verbs. Discuss the directions for completing the activity. When students have finished, have sample sentences read aloud and discussed. Distribute **Activity 1-31 Verbs (Part Two).** Write: *The sun <u>was out</u> in the sky. The sun <u>blazed</u> in the sky.* Point out that <u>blazed</u> is a more vivid or specific action verb that creates a clearer image in the reader's mind. Read and discuss the directions. When students have completed their paragraphs, have samples read aloud. Distribute **Activity 1-32 Verb Tense.** Read and discuss the definitions of verb tenses. Read the directions for Part A. When students have completed this, have the answers read aloud and discussed. Be sure that students fully understand the differences between the various tense forms. Then read and discuss the examples of present and past tense. Ask students to supply the past tenses of other regular verbs, such as *jump, climb, cook, walk.* Read the directions for Part B. When students have finished this activity, have sample sentences read aloud and discussed. Distribute **Activity 1-33 Irregular Verbs.** Explain that sometimes the past tenses of verbs are formed in other ways. Read and discuss the **irregular verbs.** Then have students complete the activity. Encourage students to share their sentences.

ACTIVITIES 1-34 through 1-43 help students improve their usage of **literal and figurative language.** Effective writers know how to make use of sensory language. Ask the class to identify the five senses and list them on the chalkboard. Then elicit examples of words that appeal to each sense and write these on the chalkboard. Examples:

Touch: *sharp, icy, hot, soothing*
Sight: *red, big, tiny, shiny*
Taste: *sweet, sour, spicy, mild*
Sound: *clang, whisper, loud, ring*
Smell: *pungent, putrid, smoky, mouth-watering*

Activities 1-34 and 1-35 teach about **sensory words.** Distribute **Activity 1-34 Sensory Words (Part One).** Read and discuss the examples of sentences using sensory words, and then have students complete the activity. When students have completed their sentences, have several examples of each read aloud. Distribute **Activity 1-35 Sensory Words (Part Two).** Read and discuss the directions. When students have completed their paragraphs, have several read aloud and discussed.

Write the following poem on the chalkboard:

She flung open the shutters and looked upon
A morning as bright as the joy in her heart.
She felt like a flower burst into bloom,
A new life was about to start.

Ask the students to identify the two **similes** in this poem. (*as bright as the joy in her heart, felt like a flower*) Point out that a simile uses the words *as* or *like* to make a comparison. Write on the chalkboard: *as black as* ______. Ask students to complete the phrase. Encourage the use of longer comparisons, such as *black as the heart of a devil.* Follow the same procedure for *as* *sweet as, as big as,* and *as smart as.* Activities 1-36 and 1-37 teach **similes.** Distribute **Activity 1-36 Similes (Part One).** Read and discuss the directions. When students have completed their lists, have several examples read aloud for each simile. Distribute **Activity 1-37 Similes (Part Two).** Read and discuss the directions, and have examples read aloud for each section.

Activities 1-38 and 1-39 explore **metaphors.** Write the following phrases on the chalkboard: *jump the gun, the roar of the crowd, a straight arrow.* Elicit that these are **metaphors** and discuss how metaphors differ from similes. (Metaphors do not use *as* or *like* to compare, but call one thing by the name of another that it cannot possibly be in reality.) Ask for examples of other metaphors and write them on the chalkboard. Distribute **Activity 1-38 Metaphors (Part One).** Read and discuss the directions, and have students complete the activity. Ask students to share and read aloud samples of their metaphors. Distribute **Activity 1-39 Metaphors (Part Two).** Read and discuss the directions. When students have completed the activity, have them share and read aloud samples of their metaphors.

Activity 1-40 teaches about **compound words.** Write the following words on the chalkboard: *mailbox, chalkboard, keyboard, bookcase.* Elicit that each word is made up of two words. Define these as **closed compound words.** Ask students to suggest other examples. Write these words on the chalkboard: *sister-in-law, over-the-counter, counselor-at-law.* Elicit that these are also compound words, but these are **hyphenated.** Ask students to suggest other examples. Write the following words on the chalkboard: *post office, real estate, major general.* Elicit that these compound words consist of two words. Define these as **open compound words.** Ask students to suggest other examples. Distribute **Activity 1-40 Compound Words.** Read and discuss the examples of closed, hyphenated, and open compound words. Note the rule and examples for hyphenating compound words when modifying a noun. Then read the directions and have students complete the activity.

Activity 1-41 covers **double negatives.** Write the following sentence on the chalkboard: *I don't want no spinach.* Elicit that this is a **double negative.** Point out that using a double negative means exactly the opposite of what the writer is trying to say, in this case, *I want spinach.* Elicit other examples of double negatives. Distribute **Activity 1-41 Double Negatives.** Read and discuss the examples, and then have students complete the activity.

Activities 1-42 and 1-43 explore **illiteracies.** Distribute **Activity 1-42 Illiteracies (Part One).** Read and discuss the definition and examples of illiteracies. Then read the directions and have students complete the activity. Distribute **Activity 1-43 Illiteracies (Part Two).** Read and discuss the examples of illiteracies. Then read the directions and have students complete the activity.

ANSWER KEY

1–1. WORDS COMMONLY MISSPELLED (PART ONE)

1. eighth
2. Wednesday
3. believe
4. weird
5. recommend
6. address
7. library
8. familiar
9. bicycle
10. surprise
11. parallel
12. medicine

1–2. WORDS COMMONLY MISSPELLED (PART TWO)

1. foreign
2. twelfth
3. rhythm
4. receive
5. straight
6. whether
7. scissors
8. prejudice
9. government
10. finally

1–3. WORDS COMMONLY MISSPELLED (PART THREE)

Sentences will vary.

1–4. WORDS COMMONLY MISSPELLED (PART FOUR)

1. career
2. physician
3. disappointed
4. February
5. really
6. captain

1–5. WORDS OFTEN CONFUSED (PART ONE)

1. teach
2. advice
3. may be
4. lose
5. Take
6. among
7. learn
8. Maybe
9. bring
10. loose

1–6. WORDS OFTEN CONFUSED (PART TWO)

1. principles
2. capital
3. Capitol
4. dessert
5. already
6. stationery
7. desert
8. principal

1–7. WORDS OFTEN CONFUSED (PART THREE)

1. breathe
2. in
3. sit
4. breath
5. beside
6. rise
7. raise
8. proceed
9. in

1–8. PREFIXES

Sentences will vary.

1–9. SUFFIXES (PART ONE)

Sentences will vary.

1–10. SUFFIXES (PART TWO)

1. likable
2. digestible
3. irritable
4. comfortable
5. acceptable
6. legible
7. breakable
8. believable
9. invisible
10. terrible
11. noticeable

1–11. Suffixes (part three)

Some answers may vary.

1. jeweler
2. calendar
3. lawyer
4. escalator
5. announcer
6. popular
7. professor
8. teacher
9. counselor
10. author
11. officer
12. sugar

1–12. Suffixes (part four)

1. finally
2. plentiful
3. submitted
4. coloring (colorful)
5. shopping
6. biggest
7. happiness
8. slowly
9. actually

1–13. Prefixes and Suffixes

Sentences will vary.

1–14. Synonyms

Possible synonyms are:

loved: enjoyed
happy: thrilled
chosen: picked
friend: pal
first: opening
threw: hurled
hit: smashed
bad: terrible

1–15. Antonyms

Possible antonyms are:

liked: hated
hot: cold
summer: winter
big: small
easy: difficult
old: new
softly: loudly
good: bad
early: late
hot: cold
quickly: slowly
wonderful: terrible
best: worst
always: never

1–16. Synonyms and Antonyms

Part A.

Possible synonyms are:

1. huge
2. smart
3. talk
4. beautiful
5. scare
6. tiny
7. icy
8. easy
9. tasty
10. mix
11. grab
12. happy

Part B.

Possible antonyms are:

1. low
2. thick
3. brave
4. loose
5. hairy
6. soft
7. cold
8. dull
9. dirty
10. ugly
11. simple
12. light

1–17. Homonyms (part one)

1. to
2. too
3. two
4. knot
5. not
6. great
7. grate
8. higher
9. hire
10. allowed
11. aloud
12. missed
13. mist
14. lessen
15. lesson

1–18. HOMONYMS (PART TWO)

1. herd
2. cent
3. hoarse
4. peace
5. rain
6. bury
7. scent

1–19. ADJECTIVES

Part A.

Adjectives and sentences will vary.

Part B.

1. *Adjective:* large; *Noun:* audience
2. *Adjectives:* tall, thin; *Noun:* man
3. *Adjectives:* deep, resounding; *Noun:* voice
4. *Adjectives:* dull, boring; *Noun:* topic
5. *Adjective:* gray-haired; *Noun:* woman
6. *Adjective:* long; *Noun:* speech
7. *Adjective:* happy; *Noun:* moment

1–20. ADVERBS

Possible answers are:

1. softly, loudly, badly
2. slowly, quickly, hungrily
3. sweetly, beautifully
4. really, incredibly
5. happily, sweetly
6. swiftly, quickly
7. patiently, impatiently
8. eagerly, early
9. speedily, quickly
10. sternly, loudly
11. gracefully, lightly
12. fiercely, angrily

1–21. ADVERBS VS. ADJECTIVES

1. b
2. a
3. b
4. a
5. b

1–22. PREPOSITIONS

1. b
2. a
3. b
4. b

1–23. ARTICLES

1. a
2. the
3. a
4. an
5. the
6. the
7. the
8. a
9. The
10. a, the

1–24. COMMON AND PROPER NOUNS

Part A.

The common nouns (c) to be circled and the proper nouns (p) to be underlined are:

1. (c) mall, friend; (p) Aysha, Bonnie
2. (c) mom, brother; (p) Ali
3. (c) kid; (p) Aysha

4. (p) Centertown Mall
5. (c) pest; (p) Aysha, Bonnie, Ali
6. (c) girls, things
7. (c) girls, clothes; (p) Sander's College Shop
8. (c) toy store; (p) Ali
9. (c) idea, book; (p) Bonnie, Ali
10. (c) chair, girls, clothes

Part B.

Sentences will vary.

1–25. Collective and Compound Nouns

Part A.

The collective nouns (col) to be circled and the compound nouns (com) to be underlined are:

1. (col) group
2. (col) flock
3. (col) troop; (com) Boy Scout, den mother
4. (col) audience
5. (col) guys; (com) undershirts
6. (col) crowd, team; (com) ball field, homerun
7. (col) family; (com) housewarming
8. (col) bunch; (com) stepfather

Part B.

Sentences will vary.

1–26. Pronouns and Antecedents (Part One)

1. *pronoun:* it; *antecedent:* bat
2. *pronoun:* she; *antecedent:* Grandma
3. *pronoun:* they; *antecedent:* people
4. *pronoun:* it; *antecedent:* camera
5. *pronoun:* she; *antecedent:* Rose
6. *pronoun:* it; *antecedent:* game
7. *pronoun:* it; *antecedent:* store
8. *pronoun:* he; *antecedent:* Jack
9. *pronoun:* they; *antecedent:* boys

1–27. Pronouns and Antecedents (Part Two)

1. it
2. its (or his or her)
3. they, his (or her)
4. their
5. her, she, their
6. his (or her), it
7. his, It, his
8. me, It, my, its
9. our

1–28. Indefinite Pronouns

1. comes
2. know
3. are
4. agree
5. is
6. happens
7. has
8. are
9. is
10. likes

1–29. Personal Possessive Pronouns

1. his
2. her
3. its
4. my
5. their
6. its (or his or her)
7. his
8. their, ours
9. yours

1–30. VERBS (PART ONE)
Sentences will vary.

1–31. VERBS (PART TWO)
Verbs to be circled are: got, rang, was, said, coming, get, went, looked, saw, moving, walked, coming, said, touched, opened, came, walked, looked, looked, said, walked, went, closed, left, went *(Substitutions will vary.)*

1–32. VERB TENSE
Part A.

1. future
2. past
3. future perfect
4. past perfect
5. present
6. past perfect

Part B.

1. I walked to school.
2. The teacher looked at the class.
3. The dogs barked in the back yard.
4. The pitcher hurled the ball.
5. Our guests knocked at the door.

1–33. IRREGULAR VERBS
Sentences will vary.

1–34. SENSORY WORDS (PART ONE)
Sentences will vary.

1–35. SENSORY WORDS (PART TWO)
Part A.

1. taste
2. smell
3. sight
4. touch
5. sound
6. taste
7. sound
8. sight
9. touch

Part B.
Paragraphs will vary.

1–36. SIMILES (PART ONE)
Answers will vary.

1–37. SIMILES (PART TWO)
Part A.
Answers will vary. Possible similes are: dark as an underground tunnel, scared as a coward in battle, low as a troll's house, hard as flesh hitting rock, painful as a throbbing toothache, small as a baby's closet, confused as a rat in a maze, clever as a professor, famous as a rock star

Part B.
Sentences will vary.

1–38. METAPHORS (PART ONE)
Part A.
Metaphors to be underlined are: blanket of clouds, it had been a breeze, ball was part of his body, perfect work of art, struck out, wrapping Matt in a wet shroud, master of all he surveyed

Part B.
Sentences will vary.

1–39. Metaphors (Part Two)
Sentences will vary.

1–40. Compound Words

1. b	3. b	5. a
2. c	4. c	

1–41. Double Negatives
Sentences may vary slightly from those given here.

1. Scott would not answer any of the teacher's questions.
2. I don't have to do any homework tonight.
3. Jack did not want anything to do with Jill.
4. My brother wouldn't do anything wrong.
5. Don't ever use a double negative.
6. My mom never takes me anywhere.
7. It was hardly worth it.
8. My sister won't do anything to help our mother.

1–42. Illiteracies (Part One)
The illiteracies to be circled followed by correct usage are:

1. ain't—I'm not	3. gonna—going to	5. drownded—drowned
2. brung—brought	4. could of—could have	6. I been—I've been

1–43. Illiteracies (Part Two)

1. b	4. a	7. a
2. a	5. b	
3. a	6. a	

Answers to Review Test

Part One
The answers to Part One appear on the bubble sheet on page 60:

Part Two
The following errors should be circled: a, stopped by, Wensday, libary, bookreport, scene, this here, abscent, freindship, mightn't never

The correct paragraph should be written as follows:

I'll never forget my first meeting with Sam. It was an awfully cold Wednesday in February. I stopped at the school library looking for something easy to read for a book report. A voice asked, "Have you seen this new book by Stephen King?" It was Sam. He had a cold and thought he might be absent the next day. Sam was anxious to find books to read at home. That was the beginning of a great friendship. Sam and I might never have become friends if we hadn't accidentally met that way.

Name ______________________________ Date ______________

1–1. Words Commonly Misspelled (part one)

Misspelled words are like weeds that can ruin your "garden" of writing.

In the word garden below, each flower contains a word that is often misspelled. Look carefully at the correct spelling of each word.

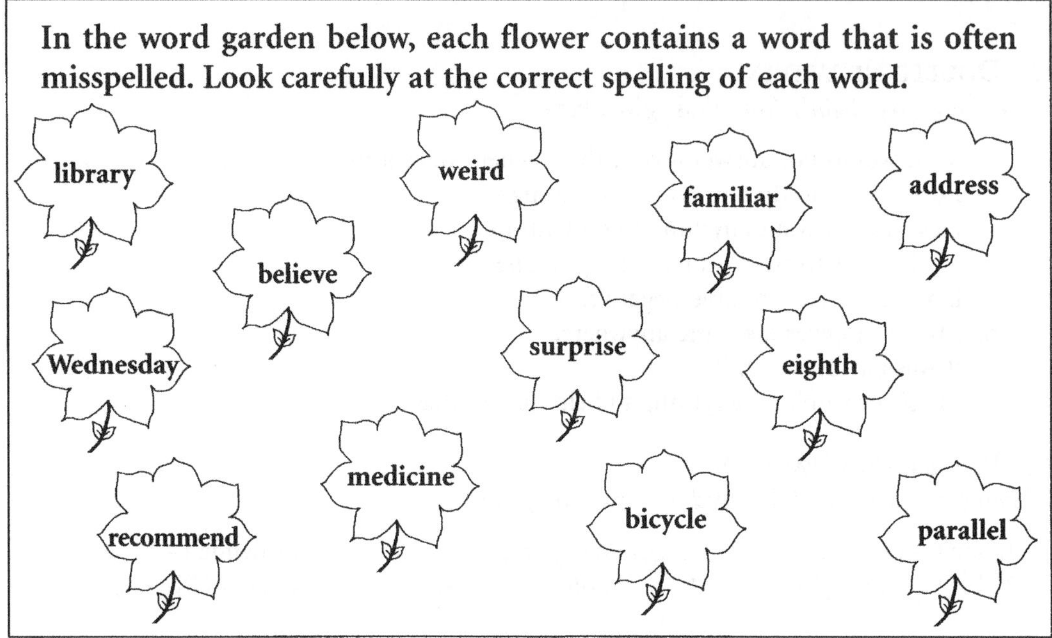

DIRECTIONS: Pluck the correct word from each flower and write it where it belongs in the sentences below. Be sure to avoid "weeds" by copying the correct spelling.

1. Luci is the most popular girl in ______________ grade.
2. Can you come to my house on ______________ after school?
3. Do you ______________ the story that Andy told?
4. It sounded very ______________ to me.
5. Can you ______________ a good restaurant for my birthday party?
6. Do you know the street ______________ of that restaurant?
7. Did you recognize the boy taking books off the shelf in the ______________?
8. That boy seemed ______________ to me.
9. Tony got a new ten-speed ______________ for his birthday.
10. He didn't expect that present, so it was a complete ______________.
11. Lines that go in the same direction are called ______________ lines.
12. The doctor prescribed new ______________ for Mom's arthritis.

Name ______________________________ Date ______________

1–2. WORDS COMMONLY MISSPELLED (PART TWO)

Here are additional words often misspelled.

The words in each flower are often turned into "weeds" by being spelled wrong. Look at the correct spelling of each word.

foreign whether finally rhythm

scissors government

straight prejudice receive twelfth

DIRECTIONS: Pluck the correct word from each flower and write it where it belongs in the sentences below. Avoid "weeds" by copying the correct spelling.

1. Have you ever visited any ______________ countries?
2. ______________ grade is the last year of high school.
3. I enjoy playing drums because I love the ______________.
4. What grade did you ______________ in English last marking period?
5. Don't stop on the way, but go ______________ home after school.
6. Do you know ______________ or not we are having a test today?
7. I need a pair of ______________ to cut this paper.
8. I have no ______________ against anyone who is different from me.
9. The ______________ often passes new laws.
10. I waited and waited, and ______________ got a letter from my friend.

Name ______________________________ Date ______________

1–3. Words Commonly Misspelled (part three)

Here are more words that are often spelled wrong. Memorize the correct spelling.

accidentally	business	anxious	grief
absence	calendar	embarrass	spaghetti
lawyer	probably	disappear	seize
marriage	receipt	achieve	occur

DIRECTIONS: Next to each word below, write a sentence that contains that word. (**Example:** spaghetti—Matt wants meatballs with his spaghetti.) Be sure to spell the word correctly.

1. achieve ______________________________
2. seize ______________________________
3. disappear ______________________________
4. lawyer ______________________________
5. embarrass ______________________________
6. business ______________________________
7. anxious ______________________________
8. calendar ______________________________
9. accidentally ______________________________
10. grief ______________________________
11. absence ______________________________
12. occur ______________________________
13. receipt ______________________________
14. marriage ______________________________
15. probably ______________________________

Name ______________________________ Date ______________

1–4. Words Commonly Misspelled (Part Four)

The words listed in the box below are often misspelled. Memorize the correct spelling.

February	captain	really	possess
restaurant	lightning	abbreviate	career
physician	disappointed		

DIRECTIONS: Can you find the six misspelled words in the paragraph below? Circle each misspelled word. Write these six words *correctly* on the lines below the paragraph.

Carlos always dreamed of having a carreer as a phycisian. He was dissappointed when he had to go to work in a restaurant after high school. He worked hard and saved his money so that some day he might possess enough money to attend college. One day in Febuary, lightning hit the restaurant. Carlos was realy brave. He saved the life of a customer. The man was a rich sea captian. He rewarded Carlos by paying his way through college.

1. ______________________ 4. ______________________

2. ______________________ 5. ______________________

3. ______________________ 6. ______________________

Name ______________________________ Date ______________

1–5. Words Often Confused (part one)

The following are words that writers often confuse.

The verb *lose* means "to suffer the loss of." *(I hope I don't lose my new watch.)*
The adjective *loose* means "not fastened tightly." *(This belt is too loose.)*

The adverb *maybe* means "perhaps." *(Maybe I will pass this test.)*
The words *may be* show chance. *(Tomorrow's test may be difficult.)*

The noun *advice* is something that is given. *(My grandmother always gives me good advice.)*
The verb *advise* shows action. *(My grandmother will advise me what to do.)*

The word *among* is used with more than two things. *(My cousins were among the audience at the concert.)*
The word *between* is used with two things. *(This secret is between you and me.)*

The verb *bring* means "to <u>come here</u> with something." *(Bring the money to me.)*
The verb *take* means "to <u>go there</u> with something." *(Take this food away.)*

The verb *learn* means "to <u>receive</u> information or knowledge." *(I wish I could learn to play the violin.)*
The verb *teach* means "to <u>give</u> information or knowledge." *(My aunt will teach me to play the violin.)*

DIRECTIONS: Fill in the correct word from the pair to complete each sentence.

1. The college professor will ______________ a history course. **(learn, teach)**
2. Friends can often give good ______________. **(advice, advise)**
3. Our classes ______________ harder next year. **(maybe, may be)**
4. Rose was careful not to ______________ her homework. **(lose, loose)**
5. ______________ the dog for a walk in the park. **(Bring, Take)**
6. Brian is ______________ ten students who won science prizes. **(among, between)**
7. Everyone should ______________ to read well. **(learn, teach)**
8. ______________ the game will be rained out tomorrow. **(Maybe, May be)**
9. Please ______________ that book to me. **(bring, take)**
10. The connection to the computer is ______________. **(lose, loose)**

Name ______________________________ Date ______________

1–6. WORDS OFTEN CONFUSED (PART TWO)

Here are more words that are often confused.

The word *already* means "earlier" or "before." *(I have already done it!)*
The term *all ready* means "all are ready." *(The actors are all ready to perform.)*

A *desert* is a dry, sandy place. *(Camels cross the desert.)*
A *dessert* is a sweet course at the end of a meal. *(I had pie for dessert.)*

The word *stationary* means "not moving." *(My mom exercises on a stationary bike.)*
The noun *stationery* is paper for writing. *(Mr. Jones wrote a letter on his business stationery.)*

The noun *principal* means "chief." *(Dr. Corbo is the principal of our school.)*
The noun *principle* means a "rule" or "truth." *(Honesty and truthfulness are two good principles.)*

The noun *capitol* refers to a building. *(Congress meets in the Capitol in Washington.)*
The noun *capital* means a city. *(Washington is the capital of the U.S.)*
The noun *capital* means money. *(Ms. Kerr needs capital to start a business.)*

DIRECTIONS: Fill in the blanks with the correct word from the pair given.

1. My mom teaches me good moral ______________. **(principals, principles)**
2. Did you know that Paris is the ______________ of France? **(Capitol, capital)**
3. The U.S. ______________ has a dome at the top. **(Capitol, capital)**
4. I like ______________ that tastes sweet. **(desert, dessert)**
5. Have you finished that book ______________? **(already, all ready)**
6. Maria wrote a letter on pretty, flowered ______________. **(stationery, stationary)**
7. It is hard to find water in a ______________. **(desert, dessert)**
8. There is a new ______________ at the high school this year. **(principal, principle)**

Name ______________________________ **Date** ______________

1–7. Words Often Confused (Part Three)

Here are additional words that are sometimes confused.

The word *beside* means "by the side of." *(Sit in this chair beside me.)*
The word *besides* means "moreover" or "also." *(I don't like the way this shirt fits, and, besides, it's the wrong color.)*

The verb *proceed* means "to move along." *(Please proceed to write this down.)*
The verb *precede* means "to come before." *(A commercial will precede the movie.)*

The verb *raise* means "to lift up." *(Raise your hand if you know the answer.)*
The verb *rise* means "to get up" or "move upward." *(Do not rise from your chair.)*

The word *in* shows where something is. *(The car is in the garage.)*
The word *into* shows movement from one place to another. *(Go into the garage.)*

The noun *breath means* "air drawn into the lungs." *(Take a deep breath.)*
The verb *breathe* is the act of taking a breath. *(Please breathe deeply.)*

The verb *sit* means "to place oneself." *(Come sit down next to me.)*
The verb *set* means "to put" or "place" something. *(Set this book on the table.)*

DIRECTIONS: Fill in the blanks with the correct word from the pair given.

1. It is so hot today that I can hardly ______________. **(breath, breathe)**
2. Dad is waiting for me ______________ the house. **(in, into)**
3. I need to ______________ down because I am tired. **(sit, set)**
4. The dog's ______________ had an unpleasant smell. **(breath, breathe)**
5. Put the knife ______________ the spoon. **(beside, besides)**
6. Please ______________ from the chair when you speak. **(rise, raise)**
7. This rock is too heavy to ______________ from the ground. **(rise, raise)**
8. The parade will ______________ along Broadway. **(proceed, precede)**
9. I left my books ______________ school. **(in, into)**

Name ______________________________ **Date** ______________

1–8. Prefixes

A *prefix* is placed in front of a word to change its meaning. Here are some common prefixes and their usual meanings.

Dis means "not" or "separate," as in *disappoint* or *disappear.*
Mid means "center," as in *midtown* or *midlife.*
Micro means "small," as in *microchip* or *microscope.*
Non means "not," as in *nonresident* or *nonfat.*
Over means "too much," as in *overcooked* or *overload.*
Post means "after," as in *postwar* or *postscript.*
Trans means "across," as in *transport* or *transatlantic.*
Un means "not," as in *unhappy* or *unwrap.*

DIRECTIONS: Write two sentences containing words with prefixes for *each* prefix below.

1. dis- ______________________________

____

2. mid- ______________________________

____

3. micro- ______________________________

____

4. non- ______________________________

____

5. over- ______________________________

____

6. post- ______________________________

____

7. trans- ______________________________

____

8. un- ______________________________

____

Name ______________________________ Date ______________

1–9. SUFFIXES (PART ONE)

Here are some suffixes that are commonly used at the end of words.

Suffix	Examples	Suffix	Examples
-ist	typist, artist, dentist, pianist, soloist, violinist, organist	*-ful*	useful, careful, tasteful, cheerful, beautiful
-ing	talking, playing, studying, batting, looking, marrying	*-ship*	friendship, courtship, fellowship, citizenship
-ment	excitement, arrangement, agreement, settlement	*-ize*	apologize, organize, criticize, realize

DIRECTIONS: Write ten sentences on the lines below. Each sentence should include at least one word that uses a suffix from the above list. Use the back of this sheet if you need more space for your sentences.

____

____

____

____

____

____

____

____

____

____

____

____

____

____

Name ______________________________ Date ______________

1–10. Suffixes (part two)

Even good spellers sometimes have difficulty knowing whether to use *able* or *ible* at the end of a word. The only way to solve this problem is to memorize the common words below.

Words Using *"able"*	Words Using *"ible"*
available, acceptable, breakable, likable, portable, believable, lovable, laughable, probable, irritable, usable, valuable, bendable, dependable, peaceable, comfortable, noticeable, inflammable	eligible, edible, terrible, horrible, forcible, legible, flexible, sensible, permissible, digestible, admissible, irresistible, predictible, responsible, visible, invisible, collapsible

DIRECTIONS: Fill in the blank with the correct word from the pair given.

1. Matt is popular in school because he is so ____________. **(likible, likable)**
2. This pasta tastes good, but is it ____________? **(digestible, digestable)**
3. When I'm sick, I feel quite ____________. **(irritible, irritable)**
4. This is the most ____________ chair in the room. **(comfortible, comfortable)**
5. The teacher said my essay was not ____________. **(acceptible, acceptable)**
6. My little brother's handwriting is not at all ____________. **(legible, legable)**
7. Be careful not to handle that ____________ vase. **(breakible, breakable)**
8. Luke's excuse for being late was not ____________. **(believible, believable)**
9. Oxygen is in the air, but it is ____________. **(invisible, invisable)**
10. Kim had a ____________ accident yesterday. **(terrible, terrable)**
11. I hope this stain on my shirt is not ____________. **(noticeible, noticeable)**

Name ______________________________ Date ______________

1–11. Suffixes (part three)

Do you know whether to use *ar,* *or,* or *er* at the end of a word? Here is a list of words for you to memorize. These are not all true suffixes, but often misspelled.

1. **Words Using "*ar*"**—beggar, burglar, calendar, caterpillar, cellar, circular, collar, familiar, grammar, liar, particular, peculiar, popular, regular, similar, sugar, vinegar, vulgar
2. **Words Using "*er*"**—announcer, baker, beginner, believer, consumer, employer, jeweler, lawyer, manager, manufacturer, messenger, officer, passenger, prisoner, teacher, traveler, writer
3. **Words Using "*or*"**—actor, author, aviator, behavior, counselor, director, elevator, escalator, humor, governor, minor, motor, neighbor, professor, radiator, senator, supervisor, traitor
4. **Note:** Both *adviser* and *advisor* are correct, although *advisor* is the preferred spelling.

DIRECTIONS: Choose a word from the lists above to complete these sentences.

1. Helen bought a ring from the ____________.
2. The ____________ was opened to the month of March.
3. The ____________ defended her client in court.
4. The elevator was out of order, so Jesse rode the ____________ to the third floor.
5. The radio ____________ had a deep, mellow voice.
6. Paul is ____________ in school because he is nice and friendly.
7. The college ____________ taught a course in science.
8. My ____________, Mrs. Gallo, invited my whole family to dinner.
9. The guidance ____________ at our school tries to be helpful to students.
10. The person who wrote this book is a famous ____________.
11. The traffic ____________ wrote out a ticket for the speeder.
12. My father sweetens his coffee with ____________.

Name ________________________________ Date ______________

1–12. SUFFIXES (PART FOUR)

Here are additional rules to follow when adding suffixes.

1. **When you add a suffix that begins with a vowel to a word that ends with a vowel and consonant, double the final consonant. Examples:** ***shop/shopping, stop/stopping, quit/quitting, big/biggest, rebel/rebellion, submit/submitted, big/bigger, forget/forgettable, hop/hopped.*** **(Note: If the accent does not fall on the last syllable, do not double the final consonant. Examples:** ***shovel/shoveled, color/coloring, enter/entered, label/labeling.*****)**
2. **The suffix** ***ly*** **is used to form an adverb from an adjective. Examples:** ***poor/poorly, sweet/sweetly, slow/slowly.*** **(Note: If the adjective ends in** ***l*****, both** ***l*****'s are kept. Examples:** ***final/finally, real/really, actual/actually, personal/personally, successful/successfully.)***
3. **When a suffix that begins with a consonant is added to a word ending in** ***y*****, the** ***y*** **is usually changed to** ***i*****. Examples:** ***happy/happiness, beauty/beautiful, merry/merriment, bounty/bountiful, plenty/plentiful.***

DIRECTIONS: Fill in the spaces below with a word made by adding a suffix to the word in parentheses. (**Example:** My dad runs his business ______. (successful); **Answer:** successfully)

1. It took three hours to ______________ complete the long assignment. (**final**)
2. Roses are ______________ in the Dawsons' garden. (**plenty**)
3. Kevin ______________ an application for a summer job. (**submit**)
4. Teri bought her little sister a ______________ book. (**color**)
5. I have two brothers who hate to go ______________. (**shop**)
6. Our school is the ______________ building on the block. (**big**)
7. Summer is a time of great ______________ for my family. (**happy**)
8. Tina is playing that song on the piano too ______________. (**slow**)
9. Matt is happy that he is ______________ going to pitch a game. (**actual**)

Name ______________________________ Date ______________

1–13. Prefixes and Suffixes

A. DIRECTIONS: Write a sentence that includes a word using each prefix below.

1. trans- ______________________________
2. dis- ______________________________
3. over- ______________________________
4. dis- ______________________________
5. un- ______________________________

B. DIRECTIONS: Write a sentence that includes a word using each suffix below.

1. -ist ______________________________
2. -ment ______________________________
3. -ful ______________________________
4. -ize ______________________________
5. -able ______________________________
6. -ible ______________________________
7. -er ______________________________
8. -or ______________________________
9. -ar ______________________________
10. -ing ______________________________

Name ______________________________ Date ______________

1-14. Synonyms

DIRECTIONS: Writing can be boring when the same words are used over and over again. Often, other words with the same meaning (synonyms) can be used. The paragraph below contains some repetitious words. These words are underlined. Copy the paragraph, using synonyms for the repetitious words. (Use the dictionary if you need help finding synonyms.)

> **Brad loved to play baseball. Most of all, he loved being in Little League. He was happy to go to the first game of the season, and he was happy when he was chosen to pitch. His friend Pat was chosen as catcher, and his friend Matt was playing first base. Brad wound up and threw the ball to the first batter, who hit a single. Brad then threw the ball to the next guy up. Brad could hardly believe his eyes when the guy hit a homerun. Things looked bad for the home team and the final score was bad. Sadly, Brad's team lost the game.**

(Continue on the back of this sheet, if needed.)

Name ______________________________ Date ____________

1–15. Antonyms

DIRECTIONS: Read the paragraph below. You will notice that some words are underlined. If you substitute an antonym (word that means the opposite) for each of these words, you will end up with a paragraph that means the opposite of the original. Copy the paragraph, but substitute an antonym for each underlined word.

> Erika, who was twelve, liked to cook. One hot summer day, she decided to make dinner for her big family. She found an easy recipe in an old cookbook, and sang softly while she worked. She had a good time preparing the meal. Finishing early, she served a hot meal at exactly six P.M. Her parents and brothers ate quickly because the food tasted wonderful. In fact, everyone said that it was the best meal they had ever eaten. "From now on," said Erika, "I will always cook dinner."

(Continue on the back of this sheet, if needed.)

Name ________________________________ Date ____________

1–16. SYNONYMS AND ANTONYMS

A. DIRECTIONS: Write a **synonym** next to each word.

1. big ____________
2. intelligent ____________
3. speak ____________
4. lovely ____________
5. frighten ____________
6. little ____________
7. cold ____________
8. simple ____________
9. delicious ____________
10. blend ____________
11. seize ____________
12. glad ____________

B. DIRECTIONS: Write an **antonym** next to each word.

1. high ____________
2. thin ____________
3. cowardly ____________
4. tight ____________
5. bald ____________
6. hard ____________
7. hot ____________
8. exciting ____________
9. clean ____________
10. beautiful ____________
11. difficult ____________
12. dark ____________

Name ______________________________________ **Date** ________________

1–17. HOMONYMS (PART ONE)

DIRECTIONS: Homonyms, also known as homophones, are words that sound alike but have different meanings. Complete the following sentences with the correct homonym.

1. Luke goes ____________ Jefferson Middle School. **(to, too, two)**
2. His friend, Jimmy, goes there ____________. **(to, too, two)**
3. Jimmy is ____________ months older than Luke. **(to, too, two)**
4. Luke's father taught him how to tie a sailor's ____________. **(not, knot)**
5. Jimmy does ____________ know how to do it. **(not, knot)**
6. Jimmy is a ____________ friend. **(great, grate)**
7. He has a weird voice that can ____________ on your ear. **(great, grate)**
8. Jimmy has a brother, Mike, in a ____________ grade. **(hire, higher)**
9. Luke's mom is going to ____________ Mike to mow the lawn. **(hire, higher)**
10. Luke is not ____________ to use the riding mower yet. **(aloud, allowed)**
11. Luke is angry, but he tries not to speak angry words ____________. **(aloud, allowed)**
12. Luke ____________ two days of school when he was sick. **(mist, missed)**
13. Today, the rain is falling in a fine ____________. **(mist, missed)**
14. The weather forecaster said the rain will ____________ by evening. **(lessen, lesson)**
15. Luke has to complete the science ____________ for homework. **(lessen, lesson)**

Name ______________________ Date ____________

1–18. Homonyms (Part Two)

There are many homonyms (or homophones) in the English language. Here is a list of some of them.

ant	an insect	*route*	road or path
aunt	your parent's sister	*root*	part of a plant
blue	a color	*weather*	atmospheric condition
blew	past tense of "to blow"	*whether*	if
berry	a small fruit	*pause*	wait
bury	put into the ground	*paws*	the feet of some animals
flu	a contagious disease	*new*	opposite of old
flew	past tense of "to fly"	*knew*	past tense of "know"
herd	a pack of animals	*ceiling*	top of a room
heard	past tense of "to hear"	*sealing*	closing or fastening
piece	part of something	*horse*	an animal
peace	opposite of war	*hoarse*	raspy voice sound
sent	past tense of "to send"	*rain*	water drops
cent	a penny coin	*rein*	a strap on a horse
scent	smell	*reign*	to rule (as a king or queen)

DIRECTIONS: Circle the correct homonym from the pair given.

1. The cowboy saw a ____ of cattle on the plains. **(herd, heard)**
2. I have one ____ left in my piggy bank. **(cent, scent, sent)**
3. Linda's voice sounds ____ because she has a cold. **(horse, hoarse)**
4. It would be wonderful if there was ____ all over the world. **(piece, peace)**
5. The weather report calls for ____ today. **(rain, reign, rein)**
6. The dog will ____ its bone in the yard. **(berry, bury)**
7. There was a strong ____ of roses in the air. **(cent, scent, sent)**

Name ______________________________ Date ______________

1–19. Adjectives

A. DIRECTIONS: Adjectives modify nouns or pronouns. They describe *what kind, how many,* or *which one*. Write a descriptive adjective for each of the following nouns. Then on the back of this sheet write a sentence using that adjective and noun.

Noun	Adjective
1. computer	______________
2. book	______________
3. performer	______________
4. soldier	______________
5. photograph	______________
6. wizard	______________
7. spaceship	______________
8. ocean	______________
9. dessert	______________
10. necklace	______________

B. DIRECTIONS: After each sentence below, list the adjective (or adjectives) and the noun that is modified.

	Adjective(s)	Noun
1. The speaker stood in front of a large audience.		
2. The man was tall and thin.		
3. He spoke in a deep, resounding voice.		
4. The topic was dull and boring.		
5. A gray-haired woman in the back fell asleep.		
6. The long speech seemed to go on forever.		
7. It was a happy moment for all when the speech ended.		

Name ______________________________ Date ______________

1-20. Adverbs

Some adverbs tell more about a verb and answer one of these questions: *where? when? how?* or *to what extent?* Usually (though not always) adverbs end with *ly.*

Examples:	goes *out*	verb: *goes*; adverb (where): *out*
	travel *sometimes*	verb: *travel;* adverb (when): *sometimes*
	speak *softly*	verb: *speak;* adverb (how): *softly*
	go *far*	verb: *go*; adverb (to what extent): *far*

Other adverbs modify adjectives or other adverbs.

Examples:	*too* weak	adjective: *weak;* modifying adverb: *too*
	really smart	adjective: *smart;* modifying adverb: *really*
	very quickly	adverb that is modified: *quickly;* modifying adverb: *very*

DIRECTIONS: Write several adverbs that might be used to modify each underlined word in the following sentences. (**Example:** The mother <u>looked</u> at her baby. Possible adverbs: *lovingly, happily, tenderly*)

1. The pianist <u>played.</u> ______________
2. Andy <u>ate</u> his pizza. ______________
3. The bluebird <u>sang.</u> ______________
4. Shauna is <u>beautiful.</u> ______________
5. The contest winner <u>smiled.</u> ______________
6. The twins <u>ran</u> to the playground. ______________
7. I am <u>waiting</u> for your answer. ______________
8. Bobby <u>came</u> to the party. ______________
9. Pat <u>ran</u> to first base. ______________
10. The teacher <u>spoke</u> to the class. ______________
11. The ballerina <u>danced</u> in "Swan Lake." ______________
12. The dog <u>attacked</u> the mail carrier. ______________

Name ______________________________ Date ______________

1–21. Adverbs vs. Adjectives

Here are some rules that will help you decide when to use an adjective or an adverb.

1. Do not use an adjective to modify a verb.
   WRONG: Carlos did *bad* on his math test.
   RIGHT: Carlos did *badly* on his math test. (adverb *badly* modifies verb *did*)

   WRONG: The pitcher threw the ball *slow.*
   RIGHT: The pitcher threw the ball *slowly.* (adverb *slowly* modifies verb *threw*)
2. Do not use an adjective to modify another adjective.
   WRONG: That is a *real* fine story.
   RIGHT: That is a *really* fine story.

   WRONG: This is an *awful* good meal.
   RIGHT: This is an *awfully* good meal.
3. *Good* is an adjective, as in *Laura did good work on this assignment. Well* is an adverb, as in *Laura works well with others.*
4. *Sure* is an adjective, as in *The outcome of the game is a sure thing. Surely* is an adverb, as in *My team will surely win the game.*

DIRECTIONS: Place a checkmark in front of the correct sentence in each group.

1. ❑ a. My aunt cooked the meal quick.
   ❑ b. My aunt cooked the meal quickly.
2. ❑ a. She is a really good baby.
   ❑ b. She is a real good baby.
3. ❑ a. The old woman walks slow.
   ❑ b. The old woman walks slowly.
4. ❑ a. Luke is a really fine pitcher.
   ❑ b. Luke is a real fine pitcher.
5. ❑ a. My aunt plays the violin good.
   ❑ b. My aunt plays the violin well.

Name ______________________________ **Date** ______________

1–22. Prepositions

Here are the definition of a preposition and some examples.

A preposition is a word that shows how a noun or pronoun is connected to another word in the sentence in place, time, or direction. Here are some common prepositions.

about	away	by	inside	past
above	before	down	near	since
across	behind	during	of	through
after	below	except	off	under
around	beside	for	on	until
as	besides	from	outside	up
at	between	in	over	

Here are some prepositions that are often used incorrectly.

1. *By* means *past* or *by way of.* Never use *by* in place of *at.*
   WRONG: Jane stopped by the library on the way to school.
   RIGHT: Jane stopped at the library on the way to school.
2. *Beside* means *next to. Besides* means *in addition to.*
   WRONG: I have no one to walk to school with beside my brother.
   RIGHT: I have no one to walk to school with besides my brother.
3. You cannot go *over* a place without wings. You can go *to* that place.
   WRONG: I went over Maria's house after school.
   RIGHT: I went to Maria's house after school.
4. Do not use *off* when you mean *from.*
   WRONG: I bought this notebook off my friend.
   RIGHT: I bought this notebook from my friend.

DIRECTIONS: Place a checkmark in front of the correct sentence in each group.

1. ❑ a. I am going over the music store this afternoon.
   ❑ b. I am going to the music store this afternoon.
2. ❑ a. Andy got that bike from his friend.
   ❑ b. Andy got that bike off his friend.
3. ❑ a. Matt has no homework today beside English.
   ❑ b. Matt has no homework today besides English.
4. ❑ a. Jose stopped by my house to see my brother.
   ❑ b. Jose stopped at my house to see my brother.

Name ____ Date ________________

1–23. Articles

The words *the, a, an* are called articles. They are friendly words because they never stand alone. Articles are actually tiny adjectives. They are always combined with nouns.

1. *The* is a definite article. It refers to something specific, to one item in particular, as in: *The horse is in the barn.* (Not any old horse is in the barn, just one particular horse referred to as "*the* horse.")
2. *A* and *an* are indefinite articles. They refer to just one or any one of a thing, as in these sentences:

   I hope that I get an exciting video game for my birthday. (It is not a particular video game, just any one.)

   I saw a horse galloping through the field. (We don't know who this horse is; it's just one horse.)

Note: The article *a* is used before a word that begins with a sounded consonant, such as *horse, holiday, band, computer.* The article *an* is used before a word that begins with a vowel or a silent consonant, such as *honor, hour, elephant, accident.*

DIRECTIONS: Insert an appropriate article (*the, an, a*) in each sentence.

1. We stay at _______ nice hotel when we go to the seashore.
2. We always stay at _______ Regent Hotel when we go to the seashore.
3. Have you found _______ hotel for your family?
4. It will take at least _______ hour to drive there.
5. We expect to arrive exactly at _______ hour of three.
6. We're going to see _______ Teaneck High School band perform on Saturday.
7. We're going to hear _______ best band in the world.
8. Don't look now, but I think there's _______ bug on your arm.
9. _______ insect that bit me was huge.
10. There is _______ game going on at _______ stadium on First Street.

Name ______________________________ Date ______________

1–24. Common and Proper Nouns

Here are the definitions of common and proper nouns and some examples of both.

1. **A noun is the name of a person, place, thing, or idea.**
2. **A common noun** names a person, place, thing, or idea in general, such as: *soldier, village, river.* A common noun starts with a lowercase letter.
3. **A proper noun** names a very specific person, place, thing, or idea, such as: *General Washington, Los Angeles, Potomac River.* A proper noun starts with a capital letter.

A. DIRECTIONS: Circle the common nouns and underline the proper nouns in these sentences.

1. Aysha wanted to go to the mall with her friend Bonnie.
2. Her mom said she had to take her little brother, Ali, along.
3. Aysha groaned, but she agreed to take the kid.
4. They went to the Centertown Mall.
5. Aysha and Bonnie tried to shop, but Ali was a real pest.
6. He kept asking the girls to buy him things.
7. The girls wanted to shop for clothes at Sander's College Shop.
8. Ali kept nagging them to take him to the toy store.
9. Bonnie had the bright idea to buy Ali a book.
10. He sat in a chair and read while the girls tried on clothes.

B. DIRECTIONS: Write five original sentences on the back of this sheet. Each sentence should contain at least one common noun and one proper noun.

Name ______________________________ Date ______________

1–25. Collective and Compound Nouns

Here are two definitions you should know.

1. **A collective noun names a group of people, animals, or things. Examples:** ***crowd, family, litter, herd, group, bundle.***
2. **A compound noun is made up of two or more words. Examples:** ***bookbag, flashlight, doghouse, word processor, den mother.***

A. DIRECTIONS: Circle the collective nouns and underline the compound nouns in these sentences.

1. A group of students went to talk to the principal.
2. The boys spotted a flock of gulls in the sky.
3. Our Boy Scout troop has a terrific den mother.
4. The audience applauded wildly after the performance.
5. Some guys don't like to wear undershirts.
6. The crowd at the ball field cheered when their team got a homerun.
7. The family had a housewarming for the new apartment.
8. Greg's stepfather bought a bunch of roses to bring to the party.

B. DIRECTIONS: Write five sentences on the back of this sheet. Use at least one compound noun and one collective noun in each sentence.

Name ________________________________ Date ______________

1–26. Pronouns and Antecedents (Part One)

Here are two definitions that are important for you to know.

1. **A pronoun is a word that is used in place of a noun. Examples:**
   In place of *this boy*, you could say *he:* See *this boy. He* is my brother.
   In place of *The birds*, you could say *they: The birds* flew overhead. *They* swooped down on the beach.
2. **The noun that the pronoun stands for is called its antecedent. In the examples above, *boy* is the antecedent of *he. Birds* is the antecedent of *they.***

DIRECTIONS: Find the pronouns and their antecedents for each of the following. Write a P above each pronoun and an A above each antecedent.

1. The bat was broken; it was cracked in half.
2. Grandma sat down because she felt dizzy.
3. The people in the car waved as they passed by.
4. Jesse examined the camera and saw that it was broken.
5. Rose is happy because she received high marks in school.
6. The child cannot play that game because it is too complicated.
7. Mrs. Attila shops at the corner store because it is so convenient.
8. Jack told his teacher that he did not do the homework.
9. All the boys are ready now, so they can begin the game.

Name ______________________________ Date ______________

1–27. PRONOUNS AND ANTECEDENTS (PART TWO)

A pronoun must always agree with its antecedent. It must always be clear to whom or what that pronoun refers. Here are some rules that will make it easy to remember which pronoun to use.

1. A pronoun must agree with its antecedent in **person.** The person (or thing) who is speaking is called **first person,** such as *I* or *we.* The person (or thing) spoken to is called **second person,** such as *you.* The person (or thing) spoken about is called **third person,** such as *he, she, it,* or *they.*

   WRONG: When all the performers are ready, *you* can begin the show.
   RIGHT: When all the performers are ready, *they* can begin the show.
2. A pronoun must agree with its antecedent in **number** (singular or plural).
   WRONG: Every student wants to do well on *their* exam.
   RIGHT: Every student wants to do well on *his or her* exam.
3. A pronoun must agree with its antecedent in **gender** (male, female, or neuter).

   WRONG: Dad's new shirt has pearl buttons on *his* cuffs.
   RIGHT: Dad's new shirt has pearl buttons on *its* cuffs.

DIRECTIONS: Write the correct pronouns in the following sentences. Be sure they agree in person, number, and gender with their antecedents.

1. Mark tried to open the window but __________ was stuck.
2. Shauna's cat has a white spot on __________ nose.
3. The captain told the passengers to wear caps when __________ sailed on __________ ship.
4. All the students did well on __________ final exams.
5. The actress told __________ fans that __________ appreciated __________ support.
6. The sign on the door to the dentist's office has __________ name on __________.
7. Matt has a new computer in __________ room. __________ is set up on __________ desk.
8. I want you to give the book back to __________. __________ has __________ name on __________ cover.
9. My brother and I can hardly wait to get __________ presents.

Name ______________________________ Date ______________

1–28. Indefinite Pronouns

An indefinite pronoun names a person, thing, or amount that is not specified.

1. Most indefinite pronouns are *singular*: anybody, anyone, anything, everybody, everyone, everything, nobody, no one, nothing, somebody, someone, something, another, each, either, little, much, neither, one, other.
2. A few indefinite pronouns are *plural*: both, few, many, others, several.

Examples: Everyone comes to Alonzo's parties. *(singular)*
A few friends come to Alonzo's parties. *(plural)*

No one knows how I feel. *(singular)*
Many people know how I feel. *(plural)*

Somebody often leaves papers on the teacher's desk. *(singular)*
A few students leave papers on the teacher's desk. *(plural)*

DIRECTIONS: Fill in the blank in each sentence with a word from the pair given.

1. Nobody important ever ____________ here. **(come, comes)**
2. Many of them ____________ the correct answer. **(know, knows)**
3. Both of them ____________ invited to the party. **(is, are)**
4. How many others ____________ with your idea? **(agree, agrees)**
5. Everybody ____________ going to the game today. **(is, are)**
6. Something weird ____________ whenever I visit you. **(happen, happens)**
7. Each animal ____________ its own cage. **(has, have)**
8. It is sad that so many ____________ homeless. **(is, are)**
9. Someone in your class ____________ cheating. **(is, are)**
10. Neither of the brothers ____________ to study. **(like, likes)**

Name ______________________________ Date ______________

1–29. Personal Possessive Pronouns

Here is a definition of another kind of pronoun.

A personal possessive pronoun shows possession: *my book, your hat, his boots.* The personal possessive pronouns are:

my, mine	**our, ours**
your, yours	**your, yours**
her, hers, his, its	**their, theirs**

Never add an apostrophe and *s* to a personal pronoun, because it already shows possession.

WRONG: This sweater is her's.
RIGHT: This sweater is hers.

WRONG: The dog wagged it's tail.
RIGHT: The dog wagged its tail.

Note: *It's* always stands for *it is.*

DIRECTIONS: Fill in the blanks with a personal possessive pronoun from the list above.

1. Todd says this is not your ball because it is ______________.
2. Maria handed in ______________ test paper.
3. The store closes ______________ doors at 9 P.M.
4. I grabbed ______________ backpack and ran out of the house.
5. All the students raised ______________ hands at the same time.
6. The angry cat arched ______________ back.
7. Mark insisted that it was ______________ turn at bat.
8. The neighbors say the rose bush is in ______________ yard, but we believe it is really in ______________.
9. Do not take anything that is not ______________.

Name ________________________________ **Date** ______________

1–30. VERBS (PART ONE)

A verb shows *action* or *being.*

Here are examples of action verbs: *walk, leap, run, chase, climb, scream, talk, hit, smash, read, play.*

Here are examples of verbs that show being: *is, are, has, have, was, were, feel, believe.*

A. DIRECTIONS: Write five sentences using verbs that show action.

1. ____

2. ____

3. ____

4. ____

5. ____

B. DIRECTIONS: Write five sentences using verbs that show being.

1. ____

2. ____

3. ____

4. ____

5. ____

Name ______________________________ **Date** ______________

1–31. Verbs (part two)

DIRECTIONS: Circle each verb in the story below. Then, rewrite the story, substituting a more vivid, or specific, verb to describe the action wherever possible. **Example:** Substitute *answered* or *grabbed* for *got* in the first sentence.

> **I got the phone when it rang. It was my buddy Jason, who said, "There is a UFO coming to get us." I went outside immediately, looked up, and saw it right away. The huge ship was moving toward the ground. Jason walked from his house to join me as I watched.**
>
> **"It's coming right at us," he said with amazement.**
>
> **At that moment, the ship touched the ground, and a door opened. Two tiny aliens came out and walked toward us. They looked at us with huge black eyes. We looked at them, too, but no one said a word. Then, they walked back to their ship and went inside. After the door closed behind them, the UFO left the ground and went off into space.**

Name ______________________________ Date ______________

1–32. VERB TENSE

The tense of a verb tells when the action occurs.

- **Present Tense means right now, as in** ***I see you now.***
- **Past Tense means before now, as in** ***I saw you yesterday.***
- **Future Tense means any time after now, as in** ***I will see you tomorrow.***
- **Present Perfect Tense means action began in the past and is still continuing (or only recently finished), as in** ***I have seen you five times this week.***
- **Past Perfect Tense means action finished before another past action, as in** ***I had seen you twice before you went away.***
- **Future Perfect Tense means action starts and ends in the future, as in** ***I will have seen you twice before you leave next week.***

A. DIRECTIONS: After each sentence, indicate the tense of the verb (present, past, future, present perfect, past perfect, or future perfect).

1. My family will go on vacation next month.

   ____

2. Matt ran to the ball field quickly.

   ____

3. By this time next month, I will have visited you twice.

   ____

4. Maria has completed five science projects this year.

   ____

5. I see a robin on the oak tree in the yard.

   ____

6. Sean had just finished batting practice when the coach came along.

   ____

Name ______________________________ Date ______________

1–32. VERB TENSE *(continued)*

The most commonly used verb tenses are present and past. The past tense is usually made by adding *d* or *ed* to the present tense. These are called regular verbs. Examples:

> **Present: I *like* the movie I am watching.**
>
> **Past: I *liked* the movie I watched yesterday.**
>
> **Present: I *use* a spoon to eat ice cream.**
>
> **Past: I *used* a spoon to eat ice cream yesterday.**

B. DIRECTIONS: The regular verbs in the sentences below are present tense. On the lines below, rewrite each sentence, changing the verbs to past tense by adding *d* or *ed.*

1. I walk to school.

   ____

2. The teachers look at the class.

   ____

3. The dogs bark in the back yard.

   ____

4. The pitchers hurl the balls.

   ____

5. Our guests knock at the door.

   ____

Name ______________________________ Date ______________

1–33. Irregular Verbs

Sometimes the past tenses of verbs are formed in ways other than adding *d* or *ed.* These are called **irregular verbs,** and they must be memorized. Here are some common irregular verbs:

Present	Past	Present	Past
awake	awoke	get	got
begin	began	give	gave
bite	bit	go	went
blow	blew	grow	grew
break	broke	hide	hid
buy	bought	hold	held
catch	caught	keep	kept
choose	chose	know	knew
come	came	leave	left
dig	dug	lose	lost
do	did	meet	met
draw	drew	pay	paid
fall	fell	ride	rode
fight	fought	sing	sang
fly	flew	sit	sat
forget	forgot	write	wrote

DIRECTIONS: On the following lines, write a sentence using the past tense of each verb below. (You can find the correct word on the list above.)

1. (break) ______________________________
2. (sing) ______________________________
3. (blow) ______________________________
4. (fight) ______________________________
5. (forget) ______________________________
6. (write) ______________________________
7. (give) ______________________________
8. (buy) ______________________________
9. (keep) ______________________________
10. (pay) ______________________________

Name ______________________________ Date ______________

1–34. Sensory Words (part one)

Use of sensory language makes writing more vivid and real.

Look at the three sets of sentences below. The first sentence of each set does not use sensory words. The second one uses sensory words to create a word picture.

Jack is a ten-year-old boy.
Jack is a short, sturdy ten-year-old boy with sparkling brown eyes and a loud, booming voice.

The baby stepped on the sand and laughed.
The golden-haired baby stepped on the soft, squishy sand and laughed loudly.

The deer ran through the woods.
The brown, white-tailed deer ran noiselessly through the dark woods.

DIRECTIONS: Rewrite each sentence below, using sensory words to create word pictures. Add *at least* two sensory words to each sentence. Write your sentences on another sheet of paper.

1. A stranger rang our doorbell and said, "A spaceship has landed."
2. I put on my jacket and followed the man outside.
3. A crowd had gathered under a tree.
4. They were staring at a spacecraft.
5. A door on the ship opened and a creature emerged.
6. The alien looked at the crowd.

Name ______________________________ Date ______________

1–35. Sensory Words (part two)

A. DIRECTIONS: Underline the sensory word in each sentence below. Then write which sense is appealed to (*taste, touch, sight, sound, smell*). **Example:** The sun is bright. (*sight*). **Note:** Some words may appeal to more than one sense.

1. This sauce is too peppery. ______________
2. Hal's basement is musty. ______________
3. He stared at the glowing embers in the fireplace. ______________
4. The seal has smooth skin. ______________
5. Did you hear that woman scream? ______________
6. I love spicy meatballs. ______________
7. The child was frightened by the roaring waves. ______________
8. Stay out of that dark room! ______________
9. My favorite pet is a shaggy dog. ______________

B. DIRECTIONS: Write a short paragraph (four or five sentences) describing your classroom. Use as many sensory words as you can. (Use at least five.)

____

____

____

____

____

____

____

____

____

____

(Continue on the back of this sheet, if necessary.)

Name ______________________ Date ______________

1–36. SIMILES (PART ONE)

DIRECTIONS: Complete the following similes. Instead of using just one word, try creating a simile with an unexpected phrase. (**Example:** as surprised as a toddler feeling sand under his bare feet for the first time) Write your similes on another sheet of paper.

as surprised as ______

as funny as ______

as slippery as ______

as false as ______

as horrified as ______

as dependable as ______

as unpleasant as ______

as colorful as ______

as sharp as ______

as unbelievable as ______

as amazing as ______

as convincing as ______

as comfortable as ______

as elegant as ______

as disgusting as ______

as snobbish as ______

as mischievous as ______

as melancholy as ______

as sad as ______

as slow as ______

as gentle as ______

as painful as ______

as true as ______

as weird as ______

as pesky as ______

as sneaky as ______

as foolish as ______

as desperate as ______

as messy as ______

as warlike as ______

as exciting as ______

as difficult as ______

as perfect as ______

as fearless as ______

as peaceful as ______

as successful as ______

Name ______________________ Date ____________

1-37. Similes (Part Two)

A. DIRECTIONS: Rewrite the following paragraph on another sheet of paper, adding similes to describe each underlined word. (**Example:** The first underlined word is dark. You might write, "as dark as a starless night.")

> **Rose opened her eyes. Where was she? It was dark. She couldn't see a thing. She was scared. She tried to stand up, but the ceiling was low. She banged her head hard. That was painful. Gradually, her eyes became accustomed to the dimness. She was in a walled-in space that was small. How did she get here? Rose was confused. Then she remembered. She was in a spaceship. Last night, she had stowed away. She had been clever, and no one had seen her. Now, she would be the first kid to set foot on Mars. She was going to be famous.**

B. DIRECTIONS: Now write five sentences of your own. Each sentence should contain at least one simile.

1. ______________________________

2. ______________________________

3. ______________________________

4. ______________________________

5. ______________________________

Name ______________________________ **Date** ______________

1–38. METAPHORS (PART ONE)

A. DIRECTIONS: Underline the metaphors in the following paragraph. (**Reminder:** A metaphor is a comparison that *does not* use the word "as" or "like.")

> **Matt was on the pitcher's mound. He stood straight and tall, like a tree. He looked up at the blanket of clouds that covered the sky and hoped it would not rain. He had to win this game. So far, it had been a breeze. Until now, Matt's pitching had been as smooth as silk. He was hot, and knew he could keep going if only the rain held off. The ball was part of his body. He curled his fingers around it and went into his windup. His pitch was a perfect work of art. The crowd roared as the batter struck out. Then the rain came down, wrapping Matt in a wet shroud. It didn't matter. They had won, and Matt was the master of all he surveyed.**

B. DIRECTIONS: Write five original sentences containing metaphors. Choose from the suggestions below, or use your own ideas.

- A sentence describing the taste of some medicine
- A sentence describing a shopping mall
- A sentence telling how you felt when you failed an important test
- A sentence describing your house after your last birthday party
- A sentence describing a singer you admire

____

____

____

____

____

____

____

(Continue on the back of this sheet, if necessary.)

Name ______________________________ Date ______________

1–39. METAPHORS (PART TWO)

DIRECTIONS: Rewrite each sentence, using a metaphor for the underlined word. Begin on the lines below and continue on the back of this sheet, if necessary.

1. The city street was <u>hot</u> on that ninety-degree day in July.
2. The first-grader was <u>happy</u> to be riding home in her neighbor's convertible.
3. It was natural for Britney to be <u>nervous</u> on the first day of summer camp.
4. Look at that <u>nice</u> dress in the department store window!
5. The theater in which the performance took place was <u>dark</u>.
6. Paul's sore hand felt painful and <u>hot</u> when he touched it.
7. According to my mom, my grandmother, who is her mother, is <u>wise</u>.
8. I enjoy the way the other kids look at my best friend, Brad, who is <u>big</u>.
9. In the clubhouse, the football coach <u>gave</u> commands to his team.

Name ______________________________ Date ______________

1–40. Compound Words

A compound word is made up of more than one word.

There are three kinds of compound words.

1. **Closed:** Words are blended together as one: *bookcase* (book + case), *doorman* (door + man), *taxicab* (taxi + cab), *spoonful* (spoon + ful).
2. **Hyphenated:** Examples are *mother-in-law, over-the-counter, hanger-on.*
3. **Open:** These compound words are written as two or more words: *real estate, post office, blood bank, crepes suzettes, department store, police station, half sister.*

Compound words are usually (but not always) hyphenated when they modify a noun. Examples:

Maria works part time at the video store.
Maria is a part-time worker at the video store.

Charles is thirteen years old.
Charles is a thirteen-year-old boy.

DIRECTIONS: Put a checkmark in front of the correctly spelled sentence in each group.

1. ❏ a. I'll look it up in my note book.
   ❏ b. I'll look it up in my notebook.
   ❏ c. I'll look it up in my note-book.

2. ❏ a. Please mail this letter at the post-office.
   ❏ b. Please mail this letter at the postoffice.
   ❏ c. Please mail this letter at the post office.

3. ❏ a. This is a ten year old house.
   ❏ b. This is a ten-year-old house.

4. ❏ a. My mother is working at the bloodbank today.
   ❏ b. My mother is working at the blood-bank today.
   ❏ c. My mother is working at the blood bank today.

5. ❏ a. I like to type on a keyboard.
   ❏ b. I like to type on a key board.
   ❏ c. I like to type on a key-board.

Name ______________________________ Date ______________

1–41. Double Negatives

A double negative is what you get when you combine a negative verb with another negative word to get a sentence that means exactly the opposite of what you intend.

WRONG:	I have not seen nobody.
RIGHT:	I have not seen anybody.
WRONG:	He is not there neither.
RIGHT:	He is not there either.
WRONG:	A liar should not get no respect.
RIGHT:	A liar should not get any respect.

DIRECTIONS: Each sentence contains a double negative. Rewrite each sentence correctly.

1. Scott would not answer none of the teacher's questions. ______________

____

2. I don't have to do no homework tonight. ______________

____

3. Jack did not want nothing to do with Jill. ______________

____

4. My brother wouldn't do nothing wrong. ______________

____

5. Don't never use a double negative. ______________

____

6. My mom never takes me nowhere. ______________

____

7. It wasn't hardly worth it. ______________

____

8. My sister won't do nothing to help our mother. ______________

____

Name ______________________________ **Date** ____________

1–42. ILLITERACIES (PART ONE)

Illiteracies are words and phrases that are incorrect in both spoken and written English. They should *never* be used.

Here are some examples of illiteracies:

The word *brung* should be *brought. (My brother brought in the mail.)*

The word *drownded* should be *drowned. (The swimmer drowned.)*

The word *ain't* should be *isn't* or *aren't.* (*I am not ready to go. Alana isn't my best friend. Jon and Steve aren't going to be on the team.)*

The words *this here* should be *this. (This is a correct sentence.)*

The words *could of* or *couldn't of* should be *could have* or *couldn't have. (Kevin couldn't have been there because he was with me.)*

The word *gonna* should be *going to. (This is going to be an easy activity.)*

The words *I been* should be *I have been. (I have been waiting for ten minutes.)*

DIRECTIONS: Circle the illiteracies in the following sentences. Then write each sentence correctly on the lines.

1. I wish I could go to Abby's party, but I ain't invited. ____________________

   ____

2. I would have brung a nice birthday present for her. ____________________

   ____

3. I was gonna bring this book. ____________________

   ____

4. Abby could of invited me. ____________________

   ____

5. Maybe they are afraid I would have drownded in their pool. ____________________

   ____

6. I been waiting and waiting for an invitation. ____________________

   ____

Name ______________________________ Date ______________

1–43. Illiteracies (Part Two)

The following illiteracies should *never* be used:

Anywheres should be *anywhere. (You are not going anywhere.)*

Nowheres should be *nowhere. (This conversation is going nowhere.)*

Nohow could be *at all. (I can't do this test at all.)*

Goes should never be used in place of *says. (My sister says, "I'm tired." NOT My sister goes, "I'm tired.")*

Alls I know should be *all I know. (All I know is that I did my best.)*

In regards to should be *in regard to* or *regarding. (I'll speak to Mom in regard to my allowance. OR I'll speak to Mom regarding my allowance.)*

Borned should be *born. (My aunt was born in Mexico.)*

Disremember(ed) should be *forget* or *forgot. (I forgot to send you a card.)*

DIRECTIONS: Put a checkmark in front of the correct sentence in each group.

1. ❑ a. Her baby was borned last week.
   ❑ b. Her baby was born last week.
2. ❑ a. The teacher wants to speak to you in regard to your homework.
   ❑ b. The teacher wants to speak to you in regards to your homework.
3. ❑ a. Anna forgot what her mom had told her.
   ❑ b. Anna disremembered what her mom had told her.
4. ❑ a. I can go anywhere I want in my own house.
   ❑ b. I can go anywheres I want in my own house.
5. ❑ a. Alls I know is that I try to do the right thing.
   ❑ b. All I know is that I try to do the right thing.
6. ❑ a. That person is not telling the truth at all.
   ❑ b. That person is not telling the truth nohow.
7. ❑ a. He says, "That is exactly what happened."
   ❑ b. He goes, "That is exactly what happened."

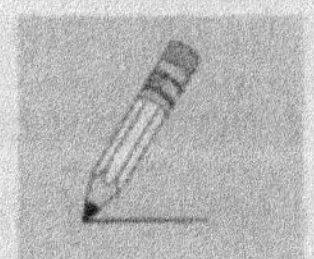

Eighth-Grade Level

Choosing the Right Word Review Test

Review Test: Choosing the Right Word (Part One)

A. DIRECTIONS: Identify the correct tense of the verb in each sentence. Use the Answer Sheet to darken the letter of your choice.

1. Jody goes to the library every Wednesday.
   A. Present B. Past C. Future D. Present Perfect
2. Bobby was disappointed with his grades last year.
   A. Present B. Past C. Future D. Present Perfect
3. I have been to the movies twice this month.
   A. Present B. Past C. Future D. Present Perfect
4. The burglar entered the house through the basement.
   A. Present B. Past C. Future D. Present Perfect
5. Aunt Pia will travel to Europe next summer.
   A. Present B. Past C. Future D. Present Perfect

B. DIRECTIONS: Determine the correct sentence in each group. Use the Answer Sheet to darken the letter of your choice.

6. A. Donna told her mother that she really was not going anywheres.
   B. Donna told her mother that she really was not going anywhere.
   C. Donna told her mother that she realy was not going anywhere.
7. A. She said that she was gonna meet her friend, Sandy.
   B. She said that she was going to meet her freind, Sandy.
   C. She said that she was going to meet her friend, Sandy.
8. A. Her mother remarked that she could have invited Sandy to the house.
   B. Her mother remarked that she could of invited Sandy to the house.
   C. Her mother remarked that she coulda invited Sandy to the house.
9. A. Donna goes, "I can go anywheres I want."
   B. Donna says, "I can go anywhere I want."
   C. Donna says, I can go anywheres I want."
10. A. Donna snuck out of the house and ran strait to the park.
    B. Donna sneaked out of the house and ran strait to the park.
    C. Donna sneaked out of the house and ran straight to the park.
11. A. Sandy was there already, hiding behind a bush.
    B. Sandy was there already hided behind a bush.
    C. Sandy was there all ready hided behind a bush.

Name ______________________________ **Date** ______________

REVIEW TEST: CHOOSING THE RIGHT WORD (PART TWO)

DIRECTIONS: The following paragraph contains **ten** errors in spelling or word usage. Can you find all ten? Circle the mistakes. Then copy the paragraph correctly on the lines below. (Continue on the back of this sheet, if necessary.)

I'll never forget my first meeting with Sam. It was a awfully cold Wensday in February. I stopped by the school libary looking for something easy to read for a bookreport. A voice asked, "Have you scene this here new book by Stephen King?" It was Sam. He had a cold and thought he might be absent the next day. Sam was anxious to find books to read at home. That was the beginning of a great freindship. Sam and I mightn't never have become friends if we hadn't accidentally met that way.

Name ______________________________ Date ______________

Choosing the Right Word

Review Test (Part One): Answer Sheet

Darken the circle above the letter that best answers the question.

1. ○ A ○ B ○ C ○ D
2. ○ A ○ B ○ C ○ D
3. ○ A ○ B ○ C ○ D
4. ○ A ○ B ○ C ○ D
5. ○ A ○ B ○ C ○ D
6. ○ A ○ B ○ C
7. ○ A ○ B ○ C
8. ○ A ○ B ○ C
9. ○ A ○ B ○ C
10. ○ A ○ B ○ C
11. ○ A ○ B ○ C

Choosing the Right Word

KEY TO REVIEW TEST (PART ONE)

1. ● A ○ B ○ C ○ D
2. ○ A ● B ○ C ○ D
3. ○ A ○ B ○ C ● D
4. ○ A ● B ○ C ○ D
5. ○ A ○ B ● C ○ D
6. ○ A ● B ○ C
7. ○ A ○ B ● C
8. ● A ○ B ○ C
9. ○ A ● B ○ C
10. ○ A ○ B ● C
11. ● A ○ B ○ C

SECTION 2

MAKING MECHANICS AND USAGE WORK FOR YOU

Teacher Preparation and Lessons

The activities in Section 2 cover a wide variety of common mechanics and usage skills, concentrating on the understanding and use of correct punctuation. You may wish to use the REVIEW TEST at the end of the section as a pretest and/or as a posttest. Answer keys can be found on pages 65–69.

ACTIVITIES 2-1 through 2-3 help students to form plurals. Write the following pairs of words on the chalkboard: *tiger, tigers; computer, computers; sentence, sentences.* Discuss definitions of **singular** and **plural**. Elicit that a plural is usually formed by adding *s.* Write these words on the chalkboard: *glass, bush, grouch, tax, buzz.* Ask students to supply the plurals and write them on the chalkboard. Point out that words ending with *s, sh, ch, x,* or *z* usually form their plurals by adding *es.* Follow the same procedure with these words: *tomato, echo, hero, mosquito,* and point out that some nouns ending in *o* form plurals by adding *es.* Activities 2-1 through 2-3 review **plurals.** Distribute **Activity 2-1 Plurals (Part One)**. Review the rules for plurals and then read the directions aloud. Distribute **Activity 2-2 Plurals (Part Two)**. Read aloud the examples, and discuss the rules for plurals. **Note:** Emphasize the correct use of apostrophes. Read the directions and have students complete the exercises. Distribute **Activity 2-3 Plurals (Part Three)**. Read and discuss the directions.

ACTIVITIES 2-4 and 2-5 address the rules for **capitalization**. Write the following words on the chalkboard: *Susan, Mr. Jones, America, Italy.* Ask students why these words are **capitalized** and point out that names of people and geographic areas, such as countries, are capitalized. Ask for additional examples and write them on the chalkboard. Distribute **Activity 2-4 Capitalization (Part One)**. Read and discuss the rules and examples. Then have the students complete the activity. Distribute **Activity 2-5 Capitalization (Part Two)**. Read and discuss the rules and examples. Then have the students complete the exercise.

ACTIVITIES 2-6 and 2-7 address rules for **abbreviations**. Write the following abbreviations on the chalkboard: *Sun., Mon., Tues., Wed.* Elicit the days of the week that these represent. Elicit from students the abbreviations for the other days of the week and write them on the chalkboard. Note that most abbreviations are followed by a period. Distribute **Activity 2-6 Abbreviations (Part One)**. Discuss the abbreviations listed and point out where these abbreviations should and should not be used. Then read and discuss the directions, and have the students complete the activity.

Write the following abbreviations on the chalkboard: *adj., adv., Ave., doz., mo., yr.* Have students identify the words that these abbreviations represent. Elicit other common abbreviations and write them on the chalkboard. Distribute **Activity 2-7 Abbreviations (Part Two)**. Discuss some of the abbreviations listed with which students may not be familiar, such as *misc., pop., pp.,* and *bldg.* Read and discuss the directions, and have students complete the activity.

ACTIVITIES 2-8, 2-9, and 2-10 teach usage of **apostrophes.** Write the following words on the chalkboard: *Scott's, isn't.* Elicit that the mark of punctuation used is the apostrophe. Elicit the two uses shown in these examples: to show possession and to show that a letter has been omitted. Elicit that words in the latter category are called **contractions.** Elicit other examples of words using apostrophes in both categories and list them on the board in two columns. Note that a contraction always includes a verb. Distribute **Activity 2-8 Apostrophes (Part One).** Read and discuss the rules and examples for using apostrophes. Then read the directions and have students complete the activity. Distribute **Activity 2-9 Apostrophes (Part Two).** Read and discuss the rules and examples for the use of apostrophes in contractions. Read the directions and have students complete the activity. When students have completed the activity, have several examples of each sentence read aloud. Distribute **Activity 2-10 Apostrophes (Part Three).** Read and discuss the rules for completing this activity, which offers additional practice in the use of apostrophes.

ACTIVITIES 2-11 and 2-12 teach usage of **hyphens.** Distribute **Activity 2-11 Hyphens (Part One).** Read aloud rule #1 regarding the use of hyphens to divide a word between syllables at the end of a line. Read the example. Write several other words on the chalkboard and discuss where they would be divided at the end of a line. Suggest consulting a dictionary when not certain. Read rule #2 regarding the use of hyphens with compound words before nouns. Read the example aloud and elicit other examples. Discuss why the hyphen is not used with the same words after a noun. Read examples aloud and elicit other examples. Read rule #3 regarding the use of hyphens when writing numbers from *twenty-one* to *ninety-nine.* Read rule #4 regarding the use of hyphens in fractions. Read the example aloud and elicit other examples. Read the directions and have the students complete the activity.

Distribute **Activity 2-12 Hyphens (Part Two).** Read the rules and examples. Elicit other examples and write them on the chalkboard. Then read and discuss the directions, and have students complete the activity.

ACTIVITY 2-13 teaches correct use of the **dash.** Distribute **Activity 2-13 Dashes.** Read and discuss the rules for using dashes. Read and be sure students understand the directions before they complete the activity.

ACTIVITIES 2-14 and 2-15 review the use of **end marks.** Write the following three sentences on the chalkboard (without the end marks):

Saturday is the best day of the week because I go to Little League
Will you drive me to the ball field next Saturday
Be quiet

Elicit that these three different types of sentences are called **declarative, interrogative,** and **exclamatory.** Elicit the types of end marks needed after each: period after declarative, question mark after interrogative, and exclamation point after exclamatory. Distribute **Activity 2-14 End Marks (Part One).** Read and discuss the rules and examples. Then read the directions and have students complete the activity. Distribute **Activity 2-15 End Marks (Part Two).** Read and discuss the directions, and have students complete the activity. Be sure students understand that they must capitalize the beginnings of sentences as well as place end marks at the end.

ACTIVITIES 2-16 through 2-20 teach rules about the **comma.** Write the following sentence on the chalkboard: *Bobby's favorite foods are hot dogs pizza and chocolate cake.* Elicit that this sentence is unclear without commas after *hot dogs* and *pizza.* Distribute **Activity 2-16 Commas (Part One).** Read and discuss the definition of and need for commas. Read and discuss the rules regarding the use of commas to separate words in a series or list. Study the examples. Read and discuss the rule for the use of commas to separate phrases in a series, and study the examples. Read the directions and have students complete the activity. Distribute **Activity 2-17 Commas (Part Two)**. Read and discuss the rule and the examples regarding the use of commas with words in apposition. Read and discuss the rule and the examples regarding the use of commas before or after quotations. Read the directions and have students complete the activity. Distribute **Activity 2-18 Commas (Part Three)**. Read and discuss the rule and the examples regarding the use of commas after an introductory word or phrase at the beginning of a sentence. Read and discuss the rule regarding clauses beginning with *which.* Read the directions and have students complete the activity. Distribute **Activity 2-19 Commas (Part Four)**. Read and discuss the rules and examples. Then read the directions and have students complete the activity. Distribute **Activity 2-20 Commas (Part Five)**. Read and discuss the rule and examples regarding the use of commas before conjunctions separating independent clauses. Read and discuss the directions for completing the activity.

ACTIVITIES 2-21 and 2-22 teach rules about using **semicolons**. Write a semicolon (;) on the chalkboard. Elicit that it is made up of a period and a comma. Point out that a semicolon is used for times you want something stronger than a comma but not so final as a period. Distribute **Activity 2-21 Semicolons (Part One)**. Read the description of a semicolon, and read and discuss the rules and examples for using a semicolon. Then read and discuss the directions, and have students complete the activity. Distribute **Activity 2-22 Semicolons (Part Two)**. Read and discuss the additional rule and examples for using semicolons. Read the directions and have students complete the activity.

ACTIVITIES 2-23 and 2-24 teach the rules about using **colons**. Write the following sentence on the chalkboard: *Here's what I want for my birthday: a bike, a football, and a lot of new CDs.* Have students identify the mark that looks like two periods, one on top of the other, as a colon. Point out that the colon is used to prepare the reader for something that follows, in this case a list. Distribute **Activity 2-23 Colons (Part One)**. Read and discuss the rules and examples. Then read the directions and have students complete the activity. Distribute **Activity 2-24 Colons (Part Two)**. Read and discuss the rules and examples. Then read the directions and have students complete the activity.

ACTIVITIES 2-25 through 2-28 teach the correct use of **quotation marks**. Write the following sentence on the chalkboard: *Thomas Jefferson wrote, All men are created equal.* Ask what is missing and elicit that quotation marks should appear around the quote. Write these in the appropriate places. Point out that quotation marks are like bookends that support a quote in between. Distribute **Activity 2-25 Quotation Marks (Part One)**. Read and discuss the rules for using quotation marks around a quote and with some titles. Then read and discuss the directions before having the students complete the activity. Distribute **Activity 2-26 Quotation Marks (Part Two)**. Read and discuss the rules for using quotation marks to set off words that are spoken. Read and discuss the directions, and have students complete the activity.

Write the following sentences on the chalkboard: *Allie said, "Let's go swimming." "Let's go swimming," said Allie.* Elicit the fact that quotation marks are used to set off words that are spoken. Discuss the placement of the comma in each sentence. Distribute **Activity 2-27 Quotation Marks (Part Three)**. Read and discuss the rules for using quotation marks in dialogue. Read and discuss the directions, and have students complete the activity. When students have completed their original drafts, have them read aloud and shared. Distribute **Activity 2-28 Quotation Marks (Part Four)**. Read and discuss the directions for revising and editing the dialogue drafts, and then have the students complete the activity.

ACTIVITY 2-29 teaches the correct usage of **professional titles**. Write the following sentences on the chalkboard:

Mrs. Lester said that Professor O'Hara will speak to the group.
Mrs. Lester said that a professor will speak to the group.

Elicit that the word *professor* is capitalized in the first sentence but not in the second. Point out that titles are capitalized when they come in front of a person's name, but not when they refer to that profession or office in general. Mention that there are several other rules for the use of titles. Distribute **Activity 2-29 Titles**. Read and discuss the rules and examples. Then read the directions and have students complete the activity.

ACTIVITY 2-30 teaches the correct usage of the **slash** and the **ellipsis**. Distribute **Activity 2-30 Slashes and Ellipses**. Read and discuss the rules and examples. Then read and discuss the directions, and have students complete the activity.

ACTIVITY 2-31 teaches the correct usage of **parentheses**. Distribute **Activity 2-31 Parentheses**. Read and discuss the rules for using parentheses. Then read and discuss the directions, and have students complete the activity.

ACTIVITIES 2-32 and 2-33 address how to **avoid misplaced modifiers**. Write the following three sentences on the chalkboard:

The teacher only gave Dave the book.
The teacher gave only Dave the book.
The teacher gave Dave only the book.

Elicit the meaning of each sentence. (In the first sentence, the only thing the teacher did was to give the book to Dave. In the second sentence, the only person the teacher gave the book to was Dave. In the third sentence, the book was the only thing the teacher gave to Dave.) Discuss how the placement of the modifier *only* changed the meaning of the sentence. Discuss the definition of a **modifier** as a word or phrase that tells something about another word or phrase. Distribute **Activity 2-32 Avoiding Misplaced Modifiers (Part One)**. Read and discuss the rules and examples. Then read and discuss the directions, and have students complete the activity. Distribute **Activity 2-33 Avoiding Misplaced Modifiers (Part Two)**. Read and discuss the definition and examples of dangling modifiers. Then read and discuss the directions, and have students complete the activity.

ANSWER KEY

2–1. Plurals (part one)

1. wolves
2. turkeys
3. bushes
4. strawberries
5. chiefs
6. games
7. wives
8. classes
9. beliefs
10. activities
11. pictures
12. valleys
13. butterflies

2–2. Plurals (part two)

1. a
2. b
3. b
4. a
5. b
6. b

2–3. Plurals (part three)

Part A.

The misspelled words are:

1. childs, babys, potatos, beachs, activitys
2. Scoutes, deers, wolfs, buffalos, bodys

Part B.

1. blueberries
2. volcanoes
3. women
4. finches
5. communities
6. valleys
7. heroes
8. swatches
9. indexes
10. arches

2–4. Capitalization (part one)

1. Our new neighbor, Mrs. Smith, said, "I'm glad to meet you."
2. My favorite story is The Wizard of Oz.
3. I am going to my aunt's house in Minnesota for Thanksgiving.
4. Eric's father is Lutheran and his mother is Jewish.
5. We are planning a picnic for the first Sunday of spring.
6. In September, we are going to fly across the Pacific Ocean to Hawaii.

2–5. Capitalization (part two)

The incorrectly capitalized words to be circled are:

1. dear, miss, smith
2. south, Summer
3. South
4. High School
5. jefferson, junior, high
6. navy
7. captain, marcos
8. Grandmother
9. uncle, bill

2–6. Abbreviations (part one)

The incorrect abbreviations to be circled are: Str., Satur., Febr., Aven., CAL, CAL, GA, GA

2–7. Abbreviations (part two)

1. professor
2. Dr.
3. ex.
4. mountain
5. Mt.
6. president
7. Pres.

2–8. APOSTROPHES (PART ONE)

1. Queen's
2. mine
3. wolves'
4. puppy's
5. Matt's
6. your
7. Luke's
8. boys'
9. bride's
10. children's

2–9. APOSTROPHES (PART TWO)

Sentences will vary.

2–10. APOSTROPHES (PART THREE)

1. b
2. b
3. a
4. b
5. c
6. b
7. a
8. c
9. a

2–11. HYPHENS (PART ONE)

1. well-known
2. One-half, twenty-five
3. all-around
4. —
5. brown-haired, blue-eyed
6. water-resistant
7. moth-eaten
8. laugh-ing

2–12. HYPHENS (PART TWO)

1. ex-friend
2. self-confidence
3. 1914-1918
4. ex-president
5. all-rock
6. anti-inflammatory
7. Dowling-Smith
8. ex-marine

2–13. DASHES

1. I know how to cook three things—hamburgers, pancakes, and chili.
2. Mr. Lentini—my favorite teacher—was absent today.
3. Sweet-smelling flowers—roses and lilacs—grow in our garden.
4. Are you sure you have the correct address—235 Maple Road?
5. One emotion stands out above all the rest—love.

2–14. END MARKS (PART ONE)

1. What is your full name?
2. Thomas Jefferson wrote the Declaration of Independence.
3. Ouch! That hurts!
4. The pool opened for the summer the first week in July.
5. Get out of here!
6. Did you raise your hand in class?
7. My new watch is awesome!
8. Isn't my new watch awesome?
9. Andrea just got a new computer.

2–15. END MARKS (PART TWO)

Part A.

This paragraph should be punctuated as follows: Wow! I thought it would be hard to write a paragraph. Now I know that it is not difficult at all. Do you ever have trouble writing paragraphs? Don't worry. Just do it! You'll find it's easy after a little practice. Just be sure to put an end mark at the end of each sentence.

Part B.

This paragraph should be capitalized and punctuated as follows: Do you know what I did last Saturday? I went to the movies with my dad. We saw a new film about invaders from outer space. Wow! It was so exciting! Did you ever see a movie that you wished would never end? That's what this one was like. I wouldn't mind seeing it again. Here's an idea! Do you want to go with me? Would next Saturday be good for you?

2–16. Commas (Part One)

1. Matt has lived in California, Florida, and Arizona.
2. Fruits such as apples, peaches, and bananas are delicious and healthy.
3. The colors of the American flag are red, white, and blue.
4. With a computer you can surf the web, send e-mail, and play awesome games.
5. When I get home I will eat a snack, change my clothes, and go out to play ball.
6. Mrs. Albano grows tomatoes, squash, and pumpkins in her vegetable garden.
7. Jenna bought a sweater with green, white, and black stripes.
8. My baby sister has blue eyes, chubby cheeks, and a sweet smile.
9. Mrs. Ryan's cats are named Tabby, Muffin, Blackie, and Pearl.
10. Presidents I admire are George Washington, John Adams, and John F. Kennedy.

2–17. Commas (Part Two)

Commas should be inserted after the following words in the paragraph: Linda, surprised, over, Ruffles, cat, Linda, smiling, asked, homework, Okay, room, Ruffles, sad, room, sunny,

2–18. Commas (Part Three)

Commas should be inserted after the following words:

1. homework,
2. leave,
3. box, empty,
4. first,
5. note,
6. store, best,
7. However,
8. morning,
9. problem,
10. class,

2–19. Commas (Part Four)

Part A.

1. Did you ever visit Walt Disney World in Orlando, Florida?
2. When I was a baby, my family lived in Austin, Texas.
3. The Declaration of Independence was signed on July 4, 1776.
4. My sister was born on October 5, 1994.

Part B.

Commas should be inserted after the following words: Tampa, August 24, Rochester, In fact, holidays, Your friend,

2–20. Commas (Part Five)

Commas should be inserted before the following words:

1. but
2. or
3. and
4. and
5. so
6. but
7. (*comma is optional before* and)
8. and
9. but
10. so

2–21. SEMICOLONS (PART ONE)

1. a
2. b
3. b
4. a
5. b
6. a

2–22. SEMICOLONS (PART TWO)

1. b
2. b
3. a
4. b
5. b
6. b

2–23. COLONS (PART ONE)

Colons should be inserted after the following words:

1. problem:
2. rule:
3. names:
4. items:
5. rule:
6. home:
7. trip:
8. meeting:
9. *Top:*

2–24. COLONS (PART TWO)

Colons should be inserted in the following places:

1. words:
2. NOTICE:
3. Madam:
4. 6:30
5. 7:10
6. us:
7. 6:30
8. 7:30

2–25. QUOTATION MARKS (PART ONE)

1. "Once upon a midnight dreary" is from a poem by Poe.
2. Sophie's favorite pop song is "I'll Be There Soon."
3. In his essay, Matt wrote, "Our generation will be great."
4. There's a funny article called "Kids Today" in the school newspaper.
5. Have you read the poem "Annabel Lee"?
6. "I Wanna Hold Your Hand" is a famous Beatles song.

2–26. QUOTATION MARKS (PART TWO)

1. a
2. b
3. b
4. b
5. a

2–27. QUOTATION MARKS (PART THREE)

Dialogue will vary.

2–28. QUOTATION MARKS (PART FOUR)

Revised dialogue will vary.

2–29. TITLES

1. doctor
2. President
3. Sr.
4. Governor
5. grandparents
6. Uncle
7. mayor
8. Dad
9. Dr.

2–30. SLASHES AND ELLIPSES

Sentences will vary.

2–31. PARENTHESES

Parentheses should appear around the following phrases:

1. (1-800-444-GAME)
2. (it is guaranteed to be accurate)
3. (a) (b) (c)
4. (whoever they are)
5. (She is my cousin.)
6. (NASA)
7. (pages 140 to 155)

2–32. Avoiding Misplaced Modifiers (part one)

1. Adam was able to stay for nearly the whole party.
2. The museum is closed to visitors for alterations.
3. Luke has just enough money to buy a sled.
4. The child doesn't even know how to button his jacket.

2–33. Avoiding Misplaced Modifiers (part two)

Sentences will vary. Some possible answers are:

1. I examined the calendar that was hanging on the wall.
2. When I turned on the light, the bulb exploded.
3. As Max was driving down the street, the car got a flat tire.
4. When Mrs. Perillo was 90 years old, her family found her cooking a turkey.
5. I petted the dog that was licking my hand.
6. Walking to the side of the house, Alison saw a light go on.

Answers to Review Test

Part One

The answers to Part One appear in the bubble sheet on page 108.

Part Two

The following errors should be circled:

My (aunt) Eva ((She's) my (mothers) sister) is my favorite relative. Yesterday, she came to our (house,) and asked me, "Do you want to take a trip with me to (los angeles.) You and I can visit many (well known) (parks.) I am so excited! Here are some things I (mustnt) forget to (pack) my camera, my hair (dryer) and my two (diarys.) We are leaving (Thursday) November 5.

The correct paragraph should be written as follows:

My Aunt Eva (she's my mother's sister) is my favorite relative. Yesterday, she came to our house and asked me, "Do you want to take a trip with me to Los Angeles? You and I can visit many well-known parks." I am so excited! Here are some things I mustn't forget to pack: my camera, my hair dryer, and my two diaries. We are leaving on Thursday, November 5.

Name ______________________________ Date ______________

2–1. PLURALS (PART ONE)

Most plurals are formed by adding *s*. There are some exceptions.

1. **Add *es* to nouns that end with *ch, sh, s,* or *x*. Examples:** ***watch/watches; bush/bushes; loss/losses; fox/foxes; class/classes***
2. **Nouns ending in *y* preceded by a consonant usually change the *y* to *ie*, then add *s* to form a plural. Examples:** ***activity/activities; library/libraries; strawberry/strawberries; butterfly/butterflies***
3. **Nouns ending in *y* preceded by a vowel usually add an *s* without changing the final *y*. Examples:** ***attorney/attorneys; turkey/turkeys; valley/valleys***
4. **When a word ends with a single *f*, the plural is often made by changing the *f* to a *v* and adding *es*. Examples:** ***wife/wives; calf/calves; wolf/wolves; thief/thieves; loaf/loaves.*** **(Note: Some words ending in *f* just add *s* for the plural, as in *belief/beliefs; chief/chiefs; handkerchief/handkerchiefs.*)**

DIRECTIONS: Fill in the blank in each sentence with the plural of the word in parentheses.

1. We saw three ______________ on our camping trip to Yosemite. **(wolf)**
2. Jesse's grandmother roasted two ______________ last Thanksgiving. **(turkey)**
3. Yesterday, I spotted a squirrel hiding in the ______________. **(bush)**
4. Craig's favorite dessert is ______________ with cream. **(strawberry)**
5. The tribal ______________ held a meeting in the lodge. **(chief)**
6. Annie likes to play computer ______________ after dinner. **(game)**
7. Did you know that King Henry VIII of England had six ______________? **(wife)**
8. How many ______________ do you have before lunch, Sally? **(class)**
9. Paul likes to study the ______________ of different religions. **(belief)**
10. In July and August, Pat enjoys summer ______________ at camp. **(activity)**
11. There are two framed ______________ of horses in my room. **(picture)**
12. There are many mountains and ______________ in Colorado. **(valley)**
13. While biking, I saw brightly colored ______________ in the fields. **(butterfly)**

Name ______________________________ Date ______________

2–2. Plurals (Part Two)

Here are additional rules for forming plurals.

1. Most nouns that end in *o* form plurals by adding *s*. Examples: *radio/radios; rodeo/rodeos; piano/pianos; banjo/banjos; solo/solos; stereo/stereos.*
2. Nouns ending in *o* preceded by a consonant often add *es* to form plurals. Examples: *buffalo/buffaloes; hero/heroes; mosquito/mosquitoes; volcano/volcanoes; potato/potatoes.*
3. Some nouns have irregular plurals and need to be memorized. Examples: child/children; deer/deer; sheep/sheep; foot/feet; goose/geese; man/men; woman/women; mouse/mice; tooth/teeth.

Note: Never use an apostrophe to form a plural! Apostrophes are used in contractions (*can't, isn't*) or to show possession, as in the examples below:

Computers is the plural of *computer*, as in *My family owns two computers.*

Computer's means "belonging to the computer," as in *This computer's modem is broken.*

Boys is the plural of *boy*, as in *Three boys are playing basketball.*

Boy's means "belonging to the boy," as in *That boy's shirt is torn.*

DIRECTIONS: Place a checkmark next to the correct sentence in each group.

1. ❑ a. Have you ever heard the song called "Dueling Banjos"?
   ❑ b. Have you ever heard the song called "Dueling Banjoes"?
2. ❑ a. All of Jason's friend's are coming to his party next Wednesday.
   ❑ b. All of Jason's friends are coming to his party next Wednesday.
3. ❑ a. I was bitten by mosquitos at the lake, and the spots are still sore.
   ❑ b. I was bitten by mosquitoes at the lake, and the spots are still sore.
4. ❑ a. I saw two deer in the woods today, but they fled when they noticed me.
   ❑ b. I saw two deers in the woods today, but they fled when they noticed me.
5. ❑ a. Lee loves mashed potatos with gravy and can even cook it himself.
   ❑ b. Lee loves mashed potatoes with gravy and can even cook it himself.
6. ❑ a. The shepherd in the hills of Peru took care of his flock of sheeps.
   ❑ b. The shepherd in the hills of Peru took care of his flock of sheep.

Name ______________________________ Date ______________

2-3. Plurals (part three)

A. DIRECTIONS: Five plural words are spelled wrong in each paragraph below. Circle the misspelled words.

1. Mr. and Mrs. Clark are our neighbors. The Clarks have three childs. Mark is my age, but the twins, Andy and Randy, are just babys. Our families like to hang out and do things together. We have barbecues on the patio with hot dogs and french-fried potatos. Sometimes, we go to beachs during the summer. I always enjoy activitys with the Clarks, and we are lucky that they live next door.

2. Last month, I went on a camping trip with the Boy Scoutes. We did lots of interesting things. We went on long hikes in the woods and saw deers and wolfs. One night, as we sat around a campfire, we heard a thundering noise. Our leader told us that it was a herd of buffalos going by. The only thing I did not like about the trip were the vicious mosquitoes. We all came home with painful bites on our bodys.

B. DIRECTIONS: Write the correct plural form next to each word below.

1. blueberry ______________
2. volcano ______________
3. woman ______________
4. finch ______________
5. community ______________
6. valley ______________
7. hero ______________
8. swatch ______________
9. index ______________
10. arch ______________

Name ______________________________ Date ______________

2–4. Capitalization (Part One)

Follow these rules for capitalization.

Always capitalize:

1. The first word in a sentence: *This is a sentence.*
2. The pronoun "I": *Do you think I am smart?*
3. The first word of a direct quotation: *She said, "Please excuse me."*
4. Proper nouns such as names of people: *Jason and Craig are brothers.*
5. Proper nouns and adjectives used for geographic areas: *Nebraska, Mississippi River, Pakistan, American, French.*
6. Names of religions and religious groups: *Catholic, Muslim, Hindu, Jewish.*
7. National and local holidays: *Halloween, Labor Day, Thanksgiving.*
8. The main words in a title: *Harry Potter and the Sorcerer's Stone.*
9. Days of the week and months of the year: *Sunday, Monday, March.* (<u>Do not</u> capitalize the seasons: *spring, summer, fall, winter.*)

DIRECTIONS: On the back of this page, rewrite these sentences with correct capitalization.

1. our new neighbor, mrs. smith, said, "i'm glad to meet you."
2. My favorite story is <u>the wizard of oz.</u>
3. I am going to my aunt's house in minnesota for thanksgiving.
4. eric's father is lutheran and his mother is jewish.
5. we are planning a picnic for the first sunday of spring.
6. in september, we are going to fly across the pacific ocean to hawaii.

Name ________________________________ Date ____________

2–5. Capitalization (Part Two)

Here are more rules for capitalization.

Always capitalize:

1. **Each word in the greeting of a letter:** ***Dear Jenna, My Dear Sirs, Dear Friend,***
2. **The first word in the closing of a letter:** ***Yours truly, Very truly yours, Your friend,***
3. **Names of schools or colleges:** ***Columbia University, Central High School.*** **(Do not capitalize these words when they are not used with a specific name:** ***the high school I attend, my brother's college.)***
4. **Titles or positions of people when they refer to specific persons:** ***Captain Smith, President Kennedy, Dr. Sanchez.*** **(Do not capitalize these titles when they are used in general or preceded by a possessive pronoun:** ***my doctor, a major in the army, the first president.*****)**
5. **Directions when they refer to specific geographic areas:** ***the Middle East, the American West.*** **(Do not capitalize directions when they do not refer to specific areas:** ***traveling west on Route 80, Georgia is north of Florida.*****)**

DIRECTIONS: Circle the words that are not capitalized correctly in these sentences.

1. I received a letter that began, "dear miss smith:".
2. My family will be touring the south this Summer.
3. We will begin by traveling South on Route 95.
4. I can hardly wait to go to High School.
5. I now attend jefferson junior high.
6. My neighbor is a captain in the U.S. navy.
7. His name is captain marcos.
8. I like to visit my Grandmother.
9. I think uncle bill is coming to dinner.

Name ________________________________ Date ______________

2–6. ABBREVIATIONS (PART ONE)

Here are common abbreviations.

1. Days of the week: *Sun., Mon., Tues., Wed., Thurs., Fri., Sat., Sun.*
2. Months: *Jan., Feb., Mar., Apr.,* (May, June, and July are not abbreviated), *Aug., Sept., Oct., Nov., Dec.*
3. States of the U.S.: Your post office can provide you with the correct postal abbreviations for each state. Here are a few of them:

Alabama	AL	California	CA	Florida	FL
Alaska	AK	Colorado	CO	Georgia	GA
Arizona	AZ	Connecticut	CT	Hawaii	HI
Arkansas	AR	Delaware	DE	Idaho	ID

Note: These abbreviations are used on letters and envelopes. Do not abbreviate when referring to the state in a sentence. It should be "I visited New York in April." NOT "I visited NY in April."

DIRECTIONS: Circle the incorrect abbreviations in the following letter. Then write the letter correctly on the back of this sheet.

106 Thornton Str.
Atlanta, GA 15467
Satur. Febr. 3, 2003

Miss Jane Doe
56 Philips Aven.
Los Angeles, CAL 56897

Dear Jane,

We are sad since you moved to CAL. All your friends here in GA miss you a lot. We hope you return to GA soon.

Your friend,
Sarah

Name ____ Date ________________

2–7. Abbreviations (Part Two)

Here are some other common abbreviations. Almost all end with periods.

ave.	avenue	ex.	example	Pres.	President
anon.	anonymous	ft.	foot, feet	Prof.	Professor
apt.	apartment	gal.	gallon	pt.	pint
asst.	assistant	Gen.	General	qt.	quart
atty.	attorney	Gov.	Governor	Rd.	Road
bldg.	building	in.	inches	Rev.	Reverend
Capt.	Captain	Jr.	junior	Sen.	Senator
co.	company	lb.	pound	Sgt.	Sergeant
cont.	continued	Maj.	Major	Sr.	Senior
dr.	doctor	misc.	miscellaneous	St.	Street; Saint
dept.	department	Mt.	Mount, Mountain	supt.	superintendent
doz.	dozen	oz.	ounces	vs., v.	versus, opposing
etc.	and so forth	p., pp.	page, pages	yd.	yard

Note: Abbreviations are never used as words by themselves. They always go along with other words or names, as in:

This is the street where I live. I live at 55 Elm St.

My uncle is a captain in the army. My uncle's name is Capt. Al Sanchez.

My apartment is on the third floor. I live in Apt. 3A.

DIRECTIONS: Fill in the blanks below with a correct abbreviation; however, if the word should not be abbreviated, spell it out in full instead.

1. My father is a ______________ at the State College.
2. Last week, ______________ Patel examined me at his office.
3. Did you figure out ______________ #3 on the test?
4. Some day, I'm going to climb to the top of a ______________.
5. ______________ Everest is a very high peak.
6. Do you think the ______________ of the country is doing a good job?
7. My favorite historical person is ______________ Abraham Lincoln.

Name ______________________________ Date ______________

2–8. Apostrophes (Part One)

Here are rules for using apostrophes.

> **1. An apostrophe can be used to show possession by someone or something.**
>
> ***Adam's*** **coat is on the chair. (The coat belongs to Adam.)**
>
> **The** ***teacher's*** **desk is at the front of the room. (The desk belongs to the teacher.)**
>
> **2. Put the apostrophe** ***after*** **the** ***s*** **in plural words.**
>
> **I found Ms. Alcada in the** ***teachers'*** **cafeteria. (The cafeteria is for** ***teachers*****—plural.)**
>
> **The** ***students'*** **test papers are in a folder. (The test papers are for** ***students*****—plural.)**
>
> **3. Do not use an apostrophe with personal possessive pronouns—*my, mine, your, yours, her, hers, its, our, ours, your, yours, their, theirs.*** **These already show possession without the apostrophe.**
>
> **The kitten was looking for** ***its*** **litter box.**
>
> **That CD is** ***hers.***
>
> ***Ours*** **is much better than** ***theirs.***

DIRECTIONS: Complete the following sentences by inserting the correct word.

1. The ________________ crown is on her head. (The crown belongs to the Queen.)
2. This pen is ________________. (This pen belongs to me.)
3. The ________________ howling was eerie. (The howling belongs to the wolves.)
4. I love my ________________ cute face. (The face belongs to the puppy.)
5. ________________ team is the best in the league. (The team belongs to Matt.)
6. This is ________________ book. (The book belongs to you.)
7. ________________ brother is in the air force. (The brother belong to Luke.)
8. The ________________ locker room is down the hall. (The locker room belongs to the boys.)
9. The ________________ flowers are beautiful. (The flowers belongs to the bride.)
10. This is the ________________ playroom. (The playroom belongs to the children.)

Name ______________________________ Date ______________

2–9. Apostrophes (Part Two)

Here are more rules for using apostrophes.

The apostrophe is used to show that one or more letters have been left out. These are called *contractions.* Some common contractions are: *I'm* (I am), *I'd* (I would; I had), *I'll* (I will), *you'll* (you will), *you'd* (you would; you had), *you're* (you are), *he'll* (he will), *he's* (he is), *she'll* (she will), *she'd* (she would), *it's* (it is), *it'll* (it will), *we've* (we have), *we'd* (we would), *we're* (we are), *they'll* (they will), *they're* (they are), *who's* (who is; who has), *who'd* (who would), *that'll* (that will), *that's* (that is; that has), *let's* (let us), *aren't* (are not), *can't* (cannot), *didn't* (did not), *shouldn't* (should not), *there's* (there is; there has), *what's* (what is; what has), *that's* (that is; that has).

> *He's* going to do well in the basketball tryouts.
>
> (*He's* stands for *he is.* The apostrophe takes the place of the *i* in *is.*)
>
> *It's* going to rain today.
>
> (*It's* stands for *it is.* The apostrophe takes the place of the *i* in *is.*) Note: *It's* always stands for *it is.* If *it is* does not make sense in the sentence, use *its.*
>
> I *can't* help how I feel.
>
> (*Can't* stands for *cannot.* The apostrophe takes the place of the *n* and the *o* in *not.*)

DIRECTIONS: Write a sentence using each of the following contractions.

1. (they're) ______________________________
2. (it's) ______________________________
3. (I've) ______________________________
4. (she's) ______________________________
5. (won't) ______________________________
6. (doesn't) ______________________________
7. (hasn't) ______________________________
8. (who'll) ______________________________
9. (couldn't) ______________________________
10. (what's) ______________________________

Name ______________________________ Date ______________

2–10. APOSTROPHES (PART THREE)

DIRECTIONS: Put a checkmark in front of the correct sentence in each group below.

1. ❑ a. Luis' father is a lawyer.
   ❑ b. Luis's father is a lawyer.

2. ❑ a. Shaunas dog is wagging it's tail.
   ❑ b. Shauna's dog is wagging its tail.
   ❑ c. Shauna's dog is wagging it's tail.

3. ❑ a. Tino's team has already won two pennants.
   ❑ b. Tinos team has already won two pennant's.
   ❑ c. Tinos' team has already won two pennants.

4. ❑ a. I dont always agree with my parents' rules.
   ❑ b. I don't always agree with my parents' rules.
   ❑ c. I don't always agree with my parent's rules.

5. ❑ a. Sarah's mother said that shes sick today.
   ❑ b. Sarahs mother said that she's sick today.
   ❑ c. Sarah's mother said that she's sick today.

6. ❑ a. A skunks scent is its defense against enemies.
   ❑ b. A skunk's scent is its defense against enemies.
   ❑ c. A skunk's scent is it's defense against enemies.

7. ❑ a. My mother's doctor couldn't see her yesterday.
   ❑ b. My mothers doctor couldn't see her yesterday.
   ❑ c. My mother's doctor couldnt see her yesterday.

8. ❑ a. The two brother's scores aren't the same.
   ❑ b. The two brothers scores arent the same.
   ❑ c. The two brothers' scores aren't the same.

9. ❑ a. Ellen's kitten couldn't find its litter box.
   ❑ b. Ellen's kitten couldn't find it's litter box.
   ❑ c. Ellens kitten couldn't find its litter box.

Name ______________________________________ **Date** ________________

2–11. Hyphens (part one)

Here are rules for using hyphens.

1. **Hyphens are used to divide a word between syllables at the end of a line.**

   When I do my homework, I'll be care-

   ful to read directions and check each prob-

   lem to be sure it is correct.

Note: It is always best *not* to divide a word at the end of a line. When necessary, divide only between syllables. Consult a dictionary if you are not sure.

2. **Hyphens are used in compound words *before* nouns.**

   Matt Damon is a *well-known* actor.

   I have a *strong-willed* sister.

Note: If the description comes *after* the noun, don't use a hyphen.

   The actor Matt Damon is *well known.*

   My sister is *strong willed.*

3. **Hyphens are used when writing numbers *twenty-one* to *ninety-nine.***
4. **Hyphens are used when spelling out fractions, as in *one-half* or *two-thirds.***

DIRECTIONS: Insert a hyphen where necessary in the following sentences. Be careful! Some may not need hyphens.

1. This book was written by a well known author.
2. One half of fifty is twenty five.
3. Tony's dad was an all around great athlete in college.
4. Uncle Seth likes his steak well done.
5. That brown haired and blue eyed boy is my cousin Jonathan.
6. The raincoat is made of water resistant material.
7. I'm not going to wear that moth eaten sweater!
8. Last night, I watched a show on TV that was so funny I couldn't stop laugh ing.

Name ________________________________ Date ______________

2–12. Hyphens (part two)

Here are more rules for using hyphens.

1. **Hyphens are used when adding *some* prefixes to words such as *anti-inflammatory.* Hyphens are almost always used after the prefixes *ex, self,* and *all.***

self-starter	*ex-athlete*	*all-around*
self-supporting	*ex-president*	*all-knowing*
self-satisfied	*ex-marine*	*all-seeing*

2. **Hyphens are used between places, years, times, numbers, pages, etc., that mark time limits in place of the word *to.***

   I will be in eighth grade during the 2003-2004 school year.

   Our assignment is to read pages 135-150.

   The library is open Monday-Saturday, 9 A.M.-9 P.M.

3. **Hyphens are used in double last names.**

   My math teacher is Ms. Sanchez-Smith.

   Mr. Ferrar married Ms. Perillo, and her last name became Perillo-Ferrar.

DIRECTIONS: Insert a hyphen where necessary in the following sentences.

1. Sally and I had a fight yesterday and she is now my ex friend.
2. I wish I had more self confidence.
3. The First World War lasted from 1914 1918.
4. My Uncle Fred is the ex president of his company.
5. I like to listen to our local all rock radio station.
6. Mrs. Hernandez must take an anti inflammatory for her arthritis.
7. My sister got married and her new last name is Dowling Smith.
8. My brother, Tino, is proud to be an ex marine.

Name ______________________________ **Date** ______________

2–13. Dashes

Here are rules for using dashes.

1. **Dashes set off ideas that are separate from the main sentence. They are similar to commas, but interrupt the sentences more forcefully and emphasize the additional thought, as in these examples.**

   Uncle Paul—a wild and funny guy—is my dad's younger brother.
   The New York Giants—my favorite team—are not doing well this season.
   Alison O'Connor—a really annoying person—sits next to me in class.

2. **Dashes can also be used to introduce a word—or group of words—you want to emphasize, as in these examples.**

   Patrick needs one thing to make his life complete—a new bike.
   At the supermarket, I ran into the person I least wanted to see—Brad Somers.
   Do you have everything you need for the trip—your sleeping bag, a change of clothing, and your camera?

DIRECTIONS: Rewrite these sentences on the lines below, inserting dashes where needed.

1. I know how to cook three things hamburgers, pancakes, and chili.

   ____

   ____

2. Mr. Lentini my favorite teacher was absent today.

   ____

   ____

3. Sweet-smelling flowers roses and lilacs grow in our garden.

   ____

   ____

4. Are you sure you have the correct address 235 Maple Road?

   ____

   ____

5. One emotion stands out above all the rest love.

   ____

   ____

Name ______________________________ Date ______________

2-14. End Marks (Part One)

Here are rules for using end marks.

The *period,* the *question mark,* and the *exclamation point* are like STOP signs on a highway. They tell the reader to come to a halt.

1. The period marks the end of a declarative sentence. Every sentence that is a statement should end with a period, as in:

   Abraham Lincoln was president during the Civil War.
   My brother and I attend Midtown Middle School.
   Hold the dog's leash tightly.

2. The question mark shows the end of an interrogative sentence (a sentence that asks a question), as in:

   Do you know who was president during the Civil War?
   What school do you attend?
   Are you holding the dog's leash tightly?

3. The exclamation point marks the end of a sentence that expresses strong feelings or forceful commands, as in:

   State your name immediately!
   I'm hungry!
   Grab that leash!

DIRECTIONS: Insert the correct punctuation mark at the end of each sentence.

1. What is your full name
2. Thomas Jefferson wrote the Declaration of Independence
3. Ouch That hurts
4. The pool opened for the summer the first week in July
5. Get out of here
6. Did you raise your hand in class
7. My new watch is awesome
8. Isn't my new watch awesome
9. Andrea just got a new computer

Name ______________________________ Date ______________

2-15. End Marks (part two)

A. DIRECTIONS: Without end marks, a paragraph can be confusing to the reader. Punctuate the following paragraph. Insert periods, question marks, and exclamation points where needed.

> **Wow I thought it would be hard to write a paragraph. Now I know that it is not difficult at all Do you ever have trouble writing paragraphs Don't worry Just do it You'll find it's easy after a little practice Just be sure to put an end mark at the end of each sentence**

B. DIRECTIONS: The next paragraph is a bit more difficult. There are no capital letters to show where each sentence begins. Rewrite the paragraph correctly on the lines below. Capitalize the beginning of each new sentence. Put a period, question mark, or exclamation point at the end of each sentence.

> **Do you know what I did last Saturday I went to the movies with my dad we saw a new film about invaders from outer space wow it was so exciting did you ever see a movie that you wished would never end that's what this one was like I wouldn't mind seeing it again here's an idea do you want to go with me would next Saturday be good for you**

____

____

____

____

____

____

____

____

(Continue on the back of this sheet, if necessary.)

Name ______________________________ Date ______________

2–16. Commas (Part One)

Here are three rules for using commas.

Commas are generally used to separate words or phrases in a sentence to make their meaning clearer. Putting a comma in the wrong place can make a sentence as confusing as using no comma at all, so it is important to know the rules regarding this mark of punctuation.

1. A comma is used to separate *words* in a series or list.

   Mike, Ethan, and Alex are coming to my party.
   My hobbies are basketball, hockey, and computer games.

2. Do not use a comma before the first word in a list or after the last word in a list.

   WRONG: *I had, soup, pasta, and cookies, for dinner.*
   RIGHT: *I had soup, pasta, and cookies for dinner.*

3. Commas are used to separate *phrases* in a series.

   Julio has two books, three pens, and one notebook.
   I looked for my mom in the house, on the porch, and in the garden.

DIRECTIONS: Insert commas where needed to separate words or phrases in a series.

1. Matt has lived in California Florida and Arizona.
2. Fruits such as apples peaches and bananas are delicious and healthy.
3. The colors of the American flag are red white and blue.
4. With a computer you can surf the web send e-mail and play awesome games.
5. When I get home I will eat a snack change my clothes and go out to play ball.
6. Mrs. Albano grows tomatoes squash and pumpkins in her vegetable garden.
7. Jenna bought a sweater with green white and black stripes.
8. My baby sister has blue eyes chubby cheeks and a sweet smile.
9. Mrs. Ryan's cats are named Tabby Muffin Blackie and Pearl.
10. Presidents I admire are George Washington John Adams and John F. Kennedy.

Name ______________________________ Date ______________

2–17. Commas (part two)

Here are two additional rules for using commas.

4. Use commas to enclose a word or phrase that follows a noun (or pronoun) to identify or describe it. This is called a word (or phrase) in apposition.

   Mr. Malloy, my English teacher, is fond of Shakespeare's plays.

   This wastebasket, filled to the top, must be emptied.

Note that if you leave out the words in apposition, the sentences would still be complete.

5. Use a comma before (or after) a quotation, as in the following dialogue:

   My mother asked, "Do you have a lot of homework today?"

   "Not much," I told her.

Note: Do not use a comma if there is a question mark or exclamation point at the end of the quote, as in *"Are you coming?" she asked.*

DIRECTIONS: Insert commas where needed in the following paragraph.

Linda looking surprised opened the door. "I told you I was coming" I reminded her. I walked into the living room and saw Ruffles Linda's cat on the couch. Linda smiling plopped down next to the cat and asked "What would you like to do?" "Let's do our homework" I suggested. "Okay" Linda replied. "Let's go to my room" she suggested. Linda got up from the couch. Ruffles looking sad meowed. Linda's room bright and sunny was a perfect place to do homework. "Should we work on Math first?" I asked. "Right!" she exclaimed.

Name ______________________ **Date** ____________

2–18. COMMAS (PART THREE)

Be sure to use commas correctly with phrases and clauses.

6. Use a comma after an introductory phrase at the beginning of a sentence to separate it from the main part of the sentence.

   When I saw my school photo, I laughed out loud.

   If you want to get good grades, study hard.

   After you get to the stadium, wait for me.

   As usual, Cliff overslept.

7. Use commas around clauses beginning with *which.*

   The bus, which was usually late, came on time today.

   The concert, which started at 7 P.M., did not end until 9.

DIRECTIONS: Insert commas in the following sentences to separate the introductory clause from the rest of the sentence.

1. After I finish my homework I usually watch TV.
2. Before you leave put on your coat.
3. My e-mail box which is almost never empty had no messages today.
4. If you get there first wait for me.
5. After reading the note Gail turned pale.
6. The Main Street Video Store which is the one I like best is a mile from my home.
7. However that's the one at which I shop.
8. In the morning Mrs. Cole met with Tony about his report.
9. When you finally finish that problem show it to me.
10. By the end of the class we should get back our tests.

Name ______________________________ Date ______________

2–19. Commas (part four)

Here are rules 8, 9, 10, and 11 for using commas.

8. Use a comma between a city and state, as in: *Philadelphia, Pennsylvania.*
9. Use a comma between a date number and year, as in: *June 6, 2003.*
10. Use a comma after the greeting in a friendly letter, as in: *Dear Aunt Jane,*
11. Use a comma after the closing in a letter, as in: *Yours truly,*

A. DIRECTIONS: Insert commas where they belong in the following sentences.

1. Did you ever visit Walt Disney World in Orlando Florida?
2. When I was a baby my family lived in Austin Texas.
3. The Declaration of Independence was signed on July 4 1776.
4. My sister was born on October 5 1994.

B. DIRECTIONS: Insert commas where they belong in the following friendly letter.

87 Hamilton Road
Tampa Florida
August 24 2003

Dear Kurt,

I hope you are happy in your new home. What is it like to live in Rochester New York? I am sad that you live so far away. In fact everyone here misses you. When you come back to visit for the holidays don't forget to call me.

Your friend
Jonathan

Name ______________________________ Date ____________

2–20. COMMAS (PART FIVE)

Here is rule 12 for using commas.

12. A comma may be used to separate independent clauses joined by conjunctions such as *and, but, or, so.* **Examples:**

Each student writes two book reports a month, and the teacher chooses the best to be published in the school magazine.

Patrick ran as fast as he could, but he came in third in the race.

Finish your homework assignment every day, or you will fall behind in your work.

Tom seemed hungry, so his mother served an extra portion of meat.

Exception to the rule: The comma may be omitted before *and* if the clauses are short and have the same subject. It is always best to use the comma before *but, so, or.* **Examples:**

Jesse overslept and he was late to school.

The story was interesting and it was true.

I tried, but I did not succeed.

DIRECTIONS: Insert commas where they belong in the following sentences.

1. It was a cloudy day but we went to the beach anyway.
2. Do as I say or you will be sorry!
3. Rose practiced the piano every day and her teacher was amazed at her progress.
4. The campers hiked to the top of the hill and the other campers were waiting for them.
5. There was a severe snowstorm so school was canceled.
6. Jamie waited for an hour but the bus never came.
7. Tommy worked hard and he passed the course.
8. Use a comma after the greeting in a letter and use it also between a city and state.
9. My cousin went to Washington, D.C. but he did not see the White House.
10. Bonnie overslept on Monday morning so she was late to school.

Name ______________________________ Date ______________

2–21. Semicolons (Part One)

Think of a semicolon (;) as being stronger than a comma, but not so strong as a period. Here are some rules for the use of semicolons.

1. Use a semicolon to separate independent clauses not joined by a conjunction (such as *and*).

   Each clause can stand as a separate sentence; the semicolon brings them closer together.

   English class meets at one o'clock; science is at two.

Note: In the examples above, each of the clauses on either side of the semicolon could be a complete sentence.

2. Use a semicolon between independent clauses (each of which could stand alone as a sentence) if they are joined by such words as *however, also, besides, indeed, otherwise, therefore, in fact, meanwhile, furthermore, for example, for instance, for this reason, in addition, nevertheless, on the other hand,* and *yet,* as in these examples:

   I would like to visit you; however, I have a cold.

   He is not a nice person; in fact, he is the grouchiest person I know.

Note: Do not use the semicolon if the clauses are joined by a conjunction such as *and* or *but,* as: *He is not a nice person and he is the grouchiest person I know.*

DIRECTIONS: Put a checkmark in front of the correctly punctuated sentence in each group.

1. ❑ a. Jenny loves ice cream; her favorite flavor is vanilla.
   ❑ b. Jenny loves ice cream, her favorite flavor is vanilla.
2. ❑ a. I like cookies; and I also like cake.
   ❑ b. I like cookies and I also like cake.
3. ❑ a. Sam is ready, however, he is waiting for Jamie.
   ❑ b. Sam is ready; however, he is waiting for Jamie.
4. ❑ a. Mom doesn't want me to watch that program; furthermore, it's on too late.
   ❑ b. Mom doesn't want me to watch that program, furthermore, it's on too late.
5. ❑ a. Carlos dropped his books, they landed with a thud.
   ❑ b. Carlos dropped his books; they landed with a thud.
6. ❑ a. I got here first; therefore, I should get the seat in front.
   ❑ b. I got here first, therefore, I should get the seat in front.

Name ______________________________ Date ______________

2–22. Semicolons (Part Two)

Here is an additional rule for using semicolons.

> 3. Use a semicolon in a series of three or more when commas are used as part of the listed items.
>
> *Sheila's three pets are Barney, the frog; Marlon, the cat; and Bumbles, the rabbit.*
>
> *My brother's friend, Alex; my cousin, Colin; and another cousin, Randy, are all coming to the party.*

DIRECTIONS: Place a checkmark in front of the correctly punctuated sentence in each group.

1. ❑ a. Adam, the lawyer, Santiago, the doctor, and Alan, the carpenter, belong to the same bowling club.
   ❑ b. Adam, the lawyer; Santiago, the doctor; and Alan, the carpenter, belong to the same bowling club.
2. ❑ a. The meeting was attended by Julie, the president, Adam, the vice-president, Sam, the secretary; and Joe, the treasurer.
   ❑ b. The meeting was attended by Julie, the president; Adam, the vice-president; Sam, the secretary; and Joe, the treasurer.
3. ❑ a. My three best friends are Maria, the brunette; Renee, the redhead; and Tasha, the blonde.
   ❑ b. My three best friends are Maria, the brunette; Renee, the redhead, and Tasha, the blonde.
4. ❑ a. I'm too tired to go to the restaurant, furthermore, I'm not hungry.
   ❑ b. I'm too tired to go to the restaurant; furthermore, I'm not hungry.
5. ❑ a. Sandy is rich, however, he dresses quite plainly.
   ❑ b. Sandy is rich; however, he dresses quite plainly.
6. ❑ a. Marsha wants to go to the party; and so does Anita.
   ❑ b. Marsha wants to go to the party, and so does Anita.

Name ____ **Date** ________________

2–23. Colons (part one)

A colon (:) is used to prepare the reader for something that follows. Think of a colon as a ramp inviting you to continue onto the road.

1. A colon introduces a word or phrase that explains or illustrates the preceding sentence. *Joe has a problem: to remain at the party or to leave.* Note: The statement before the colon should be able to stand by itself. (*Joe has a problem.*)
2. A colon may introduce a list. *Here is what you will need for school: pens, pencils, rulers, and notebooks.*
3. A colon is used to separate the title from the subtitle of a book.

   Poet of the Sacred: The Life of William Blake

   Life on the Edge: My Four Months as a Homeless Person

DIRECTIONS: Insert colons where they belong in the following sentences.

1. Here is Ethan's problem how to pass his geometry course.
2. This is the golden rule Do unto others as you would have them do unto you.
3. I have four favorite boys' names Matt, Jon, Luke, and Pat.
4. My shopping list contains these items milk, bread, orange juice, and cheese.
5. Remember this rule Honesty is the best policy.
6. Do these things when you get home walk the dog and finish your homework.
7. Pack these items for our trip one pair of jeans, two shirts, and three pairs of socks.
8. We have several items to discuss at today's student government meeting the dress code, the cafeteria food, and upcoming assembly programs.
9. Jeni's favorite book is *Make It to the Top Ten Keys to Financial Success.*

Name ______________________________ Date ______________

2–24. Colons (part two)

Here are some more rules for the use of the colon.

> **4. A colon may replace a comma before a long quotation.** ***Abraham Lincoln said: Fourscore and seven years ago our fathers brought forth on this continent a new nation, conceived in liberty, and dedicated to the proposition that all men are created equal.*** **Note: Quotation marks are not used with a long, direct quotation, such as this.**
>
> **5. A colon is used after the greeting in a business letter.** ***Dear Mr. Harrison:***
>
> **6. A colon is used between hours and minutes.** ***10:30 A.M.*** **or** ***2:45 P.M.***
>
> **7. A colon is used to separate a heading or an introductory label from the words that follow it.** ***HELP WANTED: babysitter; CAUTION: wet paint; IMPORTANT NOTICE: This shop will be closed on Election Day.***

DIRECTIONS: Insert colons where they belong in the following sentences.

1. The article concluded with these words The sort of person you will become is determined by how you live your everyday life and the ways in which you treat your fellow human beings.
2. The sign on the front door read, "IMPORTANT NOTICE We will be closed until further notice."
3. Dear Sir or Madam is an appropriate beginning for many business letters.
4. I usually wake up at 6 30 in the morning.
5. My dad always begins his daily exercise workout at 7 10 A.M.
6. The Declaration of Independence tells us We hold these truths to be self-evident, that all men are created equal, that they are endowed by their Creator with certain unalienable rights, that among these are life, liberty, and the pursuit of happiness.
7. My mom puts the baby to sleep at 6 30 every evening.
8. The library opens at 9 and closes at 7 30 Monday through Friday.

Name ____ Date ________________

2–25. Quotation Marks (part one)

Quotation marks are sociable. They never travel alone, but are always found in pairs: one at the beginning and one at the end. "__________"

1. **Quotation marks are used to set off words that are quoted. The quotation mark is preceded by a comma when the quote comes midway or at the end of a sentence. When the quote comes at the beginning of a sentence, the comma is placed before the closing quotation mark, as in these examples:**

   William Shakespeare wrote, "All the world's a stage."

   "All the world's a stage," wrote William Shakespeare.

2. **Quotation marks are used around titles of TV programs, songs, short stories, articles, essays, and poems:**

   "Get Happy" is my favorite song.

   Have you read "The Raven" by Edgar Allan Poe?

DIRECTIONS: Place quotation marks and commas where they belong in these sentences.

1. Once upon a midnight dreary is from a poem by Poe.
2. Rose's favorite pop song is I'll Be There Soon.
3. In his essay, Matt wrote Our generation will be great.
4. There's a funny article called Kids Today in the school newspaper.
5. Have you read the poem Annabel Lee?
6. I Wanna Hold Your Hand is a famous Beatles song.

Name ______________________________ Date ______________

2-26. Quotation Marks (part two)

Quotation marks are used to set off words that are spoken.

1. Put quotation marks at the beginning and end of each speech.
2. When the quote comes at the beginning of a sentence, a comma is placed before the closing quotation mark. If the quote comes midway or at the end of a sentence, a comma is placed before the first quotation mark.

   "I'm ready to leave now," Martha said.

   Martha said, "I'm ready to leave now."
3. A question mark or exclamation point can be used instead of the comma where appropriate.

   "Where are you?" Lilith asked.

   "Here I come!" shouted Mark.

DIRECTIONS: Place a checkmark in front of the sentence in each group that uses quotation marks and related punctuation correctly.

1. ❑ a. "Hi," said Jon, opening the door.
   ❑ b. "Hi" said Jon, opening the door.
   ❑ c. Hi, said Jon, opening the door.

2. ❑ a. In his letter, Mike wrote "I miss everyone at Fairview Junior High.
   ❑ b. In his letter, Mike wrote, "I miss everyone at Fairview Junior High."
   ❑ c. In his letter, Mike wrote "I miss everyone at Fairview Junior High."

3. ❑ a. "Is your mother home"? asked the man.
   ❑ b. "Is your mother home?" asked the man.
   ❑ c. "Is your mother home," asked the man.

4. ❑ a. "Run! Patrick shouted when the ball smashed the window.
   ❑ b. "Run!" Patrick shouted when the ball smashed the window.
   ❑ c. "Run!", Patrick shouted when the ball smashed the window.

5. ❑ a. Rubbing her eyes, Samantha said, "I'm tired."
   ❑ b. Rubbing her eyes, Samantha said "I'm tired."
   ❑ c. Rubbing her eyes, Samantha said, "I'm tired.

Name ______________________________ Date ______________

2–27. Quotation Marks (part three)

It's fun to write conversations between people. When writing dialogue, be sure to follow these rules.

1. **Put quotation marks at the beginning and end of each speech.**
2. **Begin a new paragraph every time someone different begins to speak.**

Joe looked all around the room. He called out, "Where's my brother?"

"Here I am," Luis shouted from the den.

"Hurry up! Dinner's ready!" Joe told him.

DIRECTIONS: Write some cool conversation. Below is the beginning of a conversation between Matt and Jonathan. Continue with this dialogue, adding *at least* eight more lines. You can include some action during the dialogue as is done at the beginning. This is just a draft, so concentrate on getting your thoughts down on paper; don't worry about spelling and grammar, except for the use of quotation marks and accompanying punctuation. Indent at the beginning of each paragraph and when someone begins to speak.

Matt saw Jonathan ahead on his way to school. "Hey, Jonathan," he called in a loud voice.

Jonathan stopped to wait. "Hi!" he said.

____

____

____

____

____

____

____

(Continue on the back of this sheet, if necessary.)

Name ______________________________ Date ______________

2–28. Quotation Marks (part four)

A. DIRECTIONS: You are going to revise and edit the dialogue you wrote in Activity 2-27. First, read this boxed material, which you will use as guidelines.

1. **Did you add at least eight more lines?**
2. **Can you think of more interesting dialogue to add?**
3. **Did you begin a new paragraph each time someone different begins to speak?**
4. **Did you indent at the beginning of each paragraph?**
5. **Are there quotation marks at the beginning and end of each speech?**
6. **Are commas placed where they belong?**
7. **Are there any words you are not sure how to spell? (Consult a dictionary.)**

B. DIRECTIONS: Using the above guidelines, write your revised dialogue here. When your dialogue is as good as you can make it, write your final copy on another sheet of paper.

____

____

____

____

____

____

____

____

____

____

(Continue on the back of this sheet, if necessary.)

Name ______________________________ Date ______________

2–29. Titles

Here are six rules for using titles.

1. Capitalize official titles or positions when they come in front of a person's name.

   Captain John Smith — *Vice President Marjorie Castro*
   Judge Alan Wong — *Governor Mark Wright*

2. Capitalize important titles when they refer to a *specific person* even if that person's name is not mentioned.

   The President of France visited Washington, D.C., last week.
   Give this medal to his honor, the Mayor.

3. Capitalize official titles when they are used without the person's name if you are speaking or writing directly to that person.

   I want to thank Your Majesty for this great honor.
   I am writing to you, Governor, to tell you that you are a hero to me.

4. Do not capitalize titles when they do not refer to a specific person.

   There will be an election for mayor next November.
   I must call a doctor because Steven is sick.

5. Capitalize the titles of family members when they are used with their names, or when you are speaking or writing to them directly. Also, capitalize these titles if you are speaking about them without using their names.

   Uncle Josh, Cousin Bette, Aunt Heidi
   Thanks for the birthday present, Grandma.
   Did you know that Mom and Dad have been married fifteen years?

   But do not capitalize these titles when speaking in general.

   Does your grandmother live in Florida?
   I think Jon's father is a lawyer.

6. Capitalize abbreviations of titles before or after someone's name.

   Dr. Roger Rabbitt — *Lt. Alison Prinn*
   Martin Luther King, Jr. — *Roger Rabbitt, M.D.*

Name ______________________________ Date ______________

2–29. TITLES *(continued)*

DIRECTIONS: Circle the correct title from the pair given in the sentences below.

1. That office is occupied by a ______. **(doctor, Doctor)**
2. Write a letter to ______ Grimm. **(president, President)**
3. This package is addressed to Joe Bingham, ______. **(sr., Sr.)**
4. Yes, ______, I will mail this letter for you. **(Governor, governor)**
5. Many kids' ______ live in Florida. **(grandparents, Grandparents)**
6. My favorite relative is ______ Paul. **(uncle, Uncle)**
7. Our town will elect a new ______ in November. **(mayor, Mayor)**

8 ______, please let me go skiing on Saturday. **(dad, Dad)**

9. Brian made an appointment to see ______ Larson. **(dr., Dr)**

Name ______________________________ Date ____________

2–30. Slashes and Ellipses

Here are the rules for using slashes and ellipses.

1. A **slash** (/) shows a choice between two words or phrases.

   Every student should write his/her name at the top of the paper.

   Here is the May/June agenda for our club.

2. An **ellipsis** consists of three dots (. . .). It is used inside a quote to show that you have omitted some words.

   In his letter, Jake wrote, "I'm having a great time here. Yesterday, I saw a movie . . . and stayed up late."

A. DIRECTIONS: On the lines below, write three sentences using a slash.

____

____

____

____

____

____

B. DIRECTIONS: On the lines below, write three sentences using an ellipsis.

____

____

____

____

____

____

Name ________________________________ Date ______________

2–31. Parentheses

Parentheses are like two arms placed around a gift to the sentence. Here are some rules to follow when using parentheses.

1. Parentheses are placed around a word or group of words to show that something is extra or explanatory to the main subject.

   A sentence may be interrupted with parentheses (like these) to add something extra.

   Read Chapter 4 (pages 20-37) for homework.

2. When a sentence is used in parentheses *inside* another sentence, do not use capital letters or periods for the enclosed sentence.

   My Aunt Alison (you met her at my party) is coming to visit on Sunday.

3. When a sentence is placed in parentheses *after* a complete sentence, capitalize the first letter and use a period, question mark, or exclamation point.

   The new kid in class thinks he is so great. (He is mistaken.)

4. Use parentheses around the abbreviation of an organization after its full name.

   Have you heard of the Society for the Prevention of Cruelty to Animals (SPCA)?

5. Use parentheses to show numbers or letters that show divisions.

   Today, the club will discuss: (a) appointing a holiday party committee, (b) how to get new members, and (c) setting a date for the next meeting.

DIRECTIONS: Insert parentheses where they belong in the following sentences.

1. Our toll free number 1-800-444-GAME is easy to remember.
2. This map it is guaranteed to be accurate will lead us to the treasure.
3. Some of the items I need to buy for school are a two notebooks, b a ruler, and c three ballpoint pens.
4. The Smith family whoever they are will move in next door tomorrow.
5. I would like you to meet Tanya. She is my cousin.
6. Dad works for the National Aeronautics and Space Administration NASA.
7. Turn to Chapter 8 pages 140 to 155 in your math book.

Name ______________________________ Date ______________

2–32. Avoiding Misplaced Modifiers (part one)

Remember these rules to avoid misplaced modifiers.

A modifier is a word or phrase that tells something about another word. The modifier must be in the right place in the sentence to show which word it is modifying; otherwise, it can seem to be attaching itself to a different word. This can give the sentence a completely different meaning, as in these examples.

I almost saw the whole game.
(I came close to seeing the game, but did not do so.)
I saw almost the whole game.
(I saw most of the game but not the whole thing.)

I only want Sam to go with me.
(The only thing I want is for Sam to go with me.)
I want only Sam to go with me.
(Sam is the only person I want to go with me.)
I want Sam to only go with me.
(I want Sam to go with only me and no one else.)

I went to see the team play with my father.
(Did the team really play with your father? This sentence should read: *I went with my father to see the team play.*)

She hung the jacket on a hanger so it wouldn't get creased.
(So the hanger wouldn't get creased? This sentence could read: *So as not to crease the jacket, she hung it on the hanger.*)

DIRECTIONS: Place each modifier where it belongs in the sentence. (Rewrite each sentence completely on the line below or use another sheet of paper.)

1. **(nearly)** Adam was able to stay for the whole party.

 ____

2. **(to visitors)** The museum is closed for alterations.

 ____

3. **(just)** Luke has enough money to buy a sled.

 ____

4. **(even)** The child doesn't know how to button his jacket.

 ____

Name ____ **Date** ________________

2–33. Avoiding Misplaced Modifiers (Part Two)

Here are more rules to keep in mind to avoid misplaced modifiers.

A misplaced modifier at the beginning of a sentence is called a *dangling modifier.* It can cause confusion, especially if the modifier is a clause containing a word that ends in *ing,* as in the following examples.

WRONG: *While talking to a neighbor, the dog ran off.* (Was the dog really talking to a neighbor?)
RIGHT: *The dog ran off while I was talking to a neighbor.*

WRONG: *Walking down the aisle, the stage looked empty.* (Can a stage walk down the aisle?)
RIGHT: *Walking down the aisle, I looked at the empty stage.*

WRONG: *Running to second base, the ball was caught by the shortstop.* (Was the ball really running?)
RIGHT: *Running to second base, I stopped when the shortstop caught the ball.*

DIRECTIONS: On the back of this page, rewrite each sentence correctly.

1. Hanging on the wall, I examined the calendar.
2. Turning on the light, the bulb exploded.
3. Driving down the street, the car got a flat tire.
4. At the age of 90, Mrs. Perillo's family found her cooking a turkey.
5. Licking my hand, I petted the dog.
6. Walking to the side of the house, a light went on.

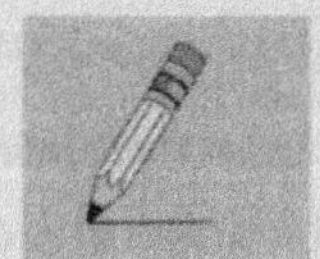

Eighth-Grade Level

Mechanics and Usage Review Test

Review Test: Mechanics and Usage (Part One)

DIRECTIONS: Decide which sentence is punctuated correctly in each group. Use the Answer Sheet to darken the letter of your choice.

1. A. My friend, Linda had a birthday party on Friday December 3.
   B. My friend Linda had a birthday party, on Friday December 3.
   C. My friend, Linda, had a birthday party on Friday, December 3.

2. A. Luke's dad, Jack Smith won an Olympic medal when he was twenty-four.
   B. Luke's dad, Jack Smith, won an Olympic medal when he was twenty-four.
   C. Luke's dad, Jack Smith, won an Olympic medal when he was twenty four.

3. A. I like to visit, Washington D.C., I also like to go to Orlando, Florida.
   B. I like to visit Washington, D.C.; I also like to go to Orlando Florida.
   C. I like to visit Washington, D.C.; I also like to go to Orlando, Florida.

4. A. When I go to Tony's house, I always eat his mom's delicious apple pie.
   B. When I go to Tony's house I always eat his moms delicious apple pie.
   C. When I go to Tonys house, I always eat his mom's delicious apple pie.

5. A. We have two cats, three dogs and a hamster.
   B. We have two cats three dogs, and a hamster.
   C. We have two cats, three dogs, and a hamster.

6. A. Andy's father said, "Its time to go to bed."
   B. Andys father said "It's time to go to bed."
   C. Andy's father said, "It's time to go to bed."

7. A. Is Rose's father coming to the party on Thursday, February 1.
   B. Is Rose's father coming to the party on Thursday, February 1?
   C. Is Rose's father coming to the party on Thursday February 1?

8. A. I love Aunt Bonnie, she is the nicest person I know?
   B. I love Aunt Bonnie she is the nicest person I know.
   C. I love Aunt Bonnie; she is the nicest person I know.

9. A. Jordan's favorite foods are pizza, hot dogs, and hamburgers.
   B. Jordans favorite foods are pizza, hot dogs, and hamburgers.
   C. Jordan's favorite foods are, pizza, hot dogs and hamburgers.

10. A. Here is Adam's problem, how to get his teacher's attention.
    B. Here is Adam's problem; how to get his teachers attention.
    C. Here is Adam's problem: how to get his teacher's attention.

Name ______________________________ Date ______________

REVIEW TEST: MECHANICS AND USAGE (PART TWO)

DIRECTIONS: The following paragraph contains thirteen errors in punctuation or word usage. Can you find all thirteen? Circle the mistakes. Then copy the paragraph correctly on the lines below.

> **My aunt Eva (She's my mothers sister) is my favorite relative. Yesterday, she came to our house, and asked me, "Do you want to take a trip with me to los angeles. You and I can visit many well known parks. I am so excited! Here are some things I mustnt forget to pack my camera, my hair dryer and my two diarys. We are leaving on Thursday November 5.**

____

____

____

____

____

____

____

____

____

____

____

____

____

Name ______________________________ Date ______________

Mechanics and Usage

Review Test (part one): Answer Sheet

Darken the circle above the letter that best answers the question.

1. ○ A ○ B ○ C
2. ○ A ○ B ○ C
3. ○ A ○ B ○ C
4. ○ A ○ B ○ C
5. ○ A ○ B ○ C
6. ○ A ○ B ○ C
7. ○ A ○ B ○ C
8. ○ A ○ B ○ C
9. ○ A ○ B ○ C
10. ○ A ○ B ○ C

Mechanics and Usage

Key to Review Test (Part One)

	A	B	C
1.	○	○	●
2.	○	●	○
3.	○	○	●
4.	●	○	○
5.	○	○	●
6.	○	○	●
7.	○	●	○
8.	○	○	●
9.	●	○	○
10.	○	○	●

SECTION 3

WRITING SENTENCES

Teacher Preparation and Lessons

The ability to write and recognize a complete sentence is the basic building block of written expression. A common thread in the scoring of writing samples for the various state and national assessment tests is the student's ability to exhibit control over sentence boundaries. When guiding students through the activities in this section, it is important to keep in mind that this is the primary goal. You may wish to use the REVIEW TEST at the end of the section as a pretest and/or posttest. Answer keys for this section can be found on pages 113-117.

ACTIVITIES 3-1, 3-2, and 3-3 help students recognize a sentence as a complete thought with a **subject** and **predicate**. Write the following sentence on the chalkboard: *Mrs. Cohen bakes delicious cakes.* Point out that this is a complete sentence because it has a subject and predicate. Elicit that the subject is *Mrs. Cohen* and the predicate is *bakes delicious cakes.* Elicit that the subject contains a noun or pronoun (*Mrs. Cohen*) and the predicate contains a verb (*bakes*). Point out that this is always true even in longer sentences. Write on the chalkboard: *Mrs. Cohen, my neighbor, bakes delicious cakes for every holiday of the year.* Elicit that the subject in this sentence is *Mrs. Cohen, my neighbor* and the predicate is *bakes delicious cakes for every holiday of the year.* Distribute **Activity 3-1 Subjects and Predicates.** Read and discuss the definitions and examples of subjects and predicates. Read the directions and have students complete the activity.

Look at the chalkboard: *Mrs. Cohen, my neighbor, bakes delicious cakes for every holiday of the year.* Elicit that *Mrs. Cohen* is the main noun that describes the subject. Point out that this is called the **simple subject.** The simple subject and all the words that go with it (*Mrs. Cohen, my neighbor*) are called the **complete subject.** Elicit that the verb in this sentence is *bakes.* Point out that this is called the **simple predicate**, and the rest of that sentence (*baked delicious cakes for every holiday of the year*) is the **complete predicate.** Distribute **Activity 3-2 Simple and Complete Subjects.** Read and discuss the definitions and examples of simple and complete subjects. Read and discuss the directions, and have students complete the activity. Distribute **Activity 3-3 Simple and Complete Predicates** and repeat the procedure.

ACTIVITY 3-4 teaches about sentences with **one subject and one verb.** Distribute **Activity 3-4 Sentences with One Subject and One Verb.** Read and discuss the definitions and examples. Then read and discuss the directions, and have students complete the activity.

ACTIVITIES 3-5 and 3-6 teach about sentences with **more than one subject and more than one verb.** Write the following sentences on the chalkboard: *Red is a color. Red and blue are colors.* Elicit that the second sentence has more than one subject (*Red and blue*) which are joined by a conjunction (*and*). Point out that this is called a **compound subject.** Distribute **Activity 3-5 Sentences with Compound Subjects.** Read and discuss the definition and examples of compound subjects. Read and discuss the directions, and have students complete the activity. Have students share their sentences aloud. Distribute **Activity 3-6 Sentences with Compound Predicates.** Read and discuss the directions, and have students complete the activity. Have students share their sentences aloud.

ACTIVITIES 3-7 and 3-8 review **subject and verb agreement**. Write the following sentences on the chalkboard: *The lion roars. The lions roar.* Elicit that the subject in the first sentence is singular. Point out that verbs must agree with subjects in number, so a singular subject takes a singular verb. Elicit that the subject in the second sentence is plural, so it takes a plural verb. Elicit verbs that might follow these subjects (use the chalkboard): *The man* ________. *The men* ________. *The student* ________. *All the students* ________. *Allie's brother* ________. *Allie's brother and sister* ________. Distribute **Activity 3-7 Subject–Verb Agreement: Number.** Read and discuss the rule and examples. Then read and discuss the directions, and have students complete the activity.

Write the following sentences on the chalkboard:

I am going to write a great story.
You are going to write a great story.
He is going to write a great story.

Elicit that the subjects in these sentences differ in person. Point out that a first-person subject (*I*) takes a first-person verb (*am*), a second-person subject (*You*) takes a second-person verb (*are*), and a third-person subject (*He*) or (*She*) takes a third-person verb (*is*). Distribute **Activity 3-8 Subject–Verb Agreement: Person**. Read and discuss the rule and examples. Then read and discuss the directions, and have students complete the activity. When done, have students read their sentences aloud.

ACTIVITIES 3-9, 3-10, and 3-11 deal with **dependent and independent clauses.** Write these sentences on the chalkboard:

Our plane is departing at 5 P.M.
Although many seats are empty.
Although many seats are empty, our plane is departing at 5 P.M.

Elicit that the first example is a complete sentence. The second sentence is not, even though it contains a subject noun (*seats*) and a predicate verb (*are*). Elicit that each of these sentences becomes part of the third sentence. Point out that they are now called **clauses.** *Our plane is departing at 5 P.M.* is called an **independent clause** because it can stand alone as a sentence. *Although many seats are empty* is called a **dependent clause** because it cannot stand alone. Distribute **Activity 3-9 Dependent and Independent Clauses (Part One)**. Read and discuss the definitions and examples. Read and discuss the directions, and have students complete the activity. Distribute **Activity 3-10 Dependent and Independent Clauses (Part Two).** Read and discuss the rule and examples. Read and discuss the directions, and have students complete the activity. Distribute **Activity 3-11 Dependent and Independent Clauses (Part Three)**. Follow the same procedure as for the previous two activities.

ACTIVITY 3-12 reviews **simple sentences.** Write the following sentences on the chalkboard: *The bus arrived. The bus from Carson City arrived at the station three hours late.* Identify the complete subject of the first sentence as *The bus* and the complete predicate as *arrived.* Identify the complete subject of the second sentence as *The bus from Carson City.* Identify the complete predicate of this sentence as *arrived at the station three hours late.* Point out that both of these are called **simple sentences** even though one is short and the other is long, since both sentences contain one complete subject and one complete predicate. Distribute **Activity 3-12 Simple Sentences**. Read and discuss the definition and examples. Then read and discuss the directions, and have students complete the activity.

ACTIVITY 3-13 reviews **compound sentences**. Write the following sentence on the chalkboard: *I got a new bike and my brother did, too.* Elicit that these are two independent clauses connected by the conjunction *and*. Point out that this is called a **compound sentence** and the conjunction connects two equally important ideas. Distribute **Activity 3-13 Compound Sentences.** Read and discuss the definition and examples. Read and discuss the directions, and have students complete the activity.

ACTIVITIES 3-14, 3-15, and 3-16 deal with **complex sentences.** Distribute **Activity 3-14 Complex Sentences (Part One)**. Read and discuss the definition and examples. Read and discuss the directions, and have students complete the activity. Distribute **Activity 3-15 Complex Sentences (Part Two)**. Read and discuss the rules and examples. Read and discuss the directions, and have students complete the activity. When done, have students read their sentences aloud. Point out that there is more than one way to correctly combine these clauses into a complex sentence. Distribute **Activity 3-16 Simple, Compound, and Complex Sentences.** Read and discuss the review. Then read and discuss the directions, and have students complete the activity. Students might read their sentences aloud.

ACTIVITIES 3-17 and 3-18 review the **four types of sentences.** Write these sentences on the chalkboard:

I can do this difficult problem now.
Can I do this difficult problem now?
I'll do it!
Do it now!

Describe these as **declarative, interrogative, exclamatory,** and **imperative sentences.** Discuss how each one falls into its category and the end mark for each. Distribute **Activity 3-17 Declarative, Interrogative, Exclamatory, and Imperative Sentences (Part One)**. Read and discuss the definitions. Read and discuss the directions, and have students complete the activity. Distribute **Activity 3-18 Declarative, Interrogative, Exclamatory, and Imperative Sentences (Part Two).** Read and discuss the directions, and have students complete the activity. You may want to have students read their sentences aloud.

ACTIVITIES 3-19 and 3-20 review **sentence fragments.** Write the following on the chalkboard:

Anita's audition at the modeling school last week.
Traveling from city to city every time his father's job changed.

Point out that even though these phrases are long, they are not sentences because neither one expresses a complete thought. Read them aloud to the class, as their incomplete nature will be even more evident orally. Ask what happened at Anita's audition—there is no predicate. Point out that the second sentence lacks both a subject and a predicate. Ask who (subject) was traveling and what happened (predicate). Elicit ways of making these into complete sentences (such as *Anita's audition at the modeling school last week went well. Joey traveled from city to city every time his father's job changed.*) and write the results on the chalkboard. Distribute **Activity 3-19 Recognizing Sentence Fragments (Part One).** Read and discuss the definition and examples. Read and discuss the directions, and have students complete the activity. Distribute **Activity 3-20 Recognizing Sentence Fragments (Part Two)**. Read and discuss the rule and examples. Then read and discuss the directions, and have students complete the activity.

ACTIVITY 3-21 deals with **run-on sentences**. Write the following sentences on the chalkboard:

The weather is great, it is a perfect day for a picnic.
Alan slung his pack over his shoulder, he began to climb up the hill.

Ask what is wrong with these sentences. Elicit that each sentence fails to stop when the thought is complete, but continues to express two complete thoughts. Point out that this is called a **run-on sentence.** Elicit several ways in which these run-on sentences could be corrected. For example, the first sentence could be rewritten as two sentences: *The weather is great. It is a perfect day for a picnic.* The second sentence could read: *Alan slung his pack over his shoulder. He began to climb up the hill.* Write these on the chalkboard. Point out that these complete thoughts could be connected with a conjunction, as *The weather is great, and it is a perfect day for a picnic.* Distribute **Activity 3-21 Recognizing Run-on Sentences.** Read and discuss the definition and examples. Read the directions and have students complete the activity.

ACTIVITIES 3-22 and 3-23 review the most important rules and problems in writing sentences. They help to solidify the proper construction of a sentence in the minds of the students. Distribute **Activity 3-22 Do's and Don'ts for Writing Sentences (Part One)**. Read and discuss the rules and cautions. Read the directions and have students read their sentences aloud. Distribute **Activity 3-23 Do's and Don'ts for Writing Sentences (Part Two)**. Read the directions and have students complete the activity.

ANSWER KEY

3–1. Subjects and Predicates

1. The test is very easy.
2. The computer is a very useful tool.
3. Dogs make wonderful pets.
4. Tony's clock always has the correct time.
5. My brother goes to college.
6. The runner jogs every day at the same time.
7. This pen writes in red ink.
8. These horses ran in the third race.

3–2. Simple and Complete Subjects

1. *(circled)* cousin; *(underlined)* My cousin Patrick
2. *(circled)* bat; *(underlined)* The bat with the initials DJ
3. *(circled)* cousin; *(underlined)* Valerie's cousin who lives in Alaska
4. *(circled)* movie; *(underlined)* The long, boring movie on TV
5. *(circled)* kitten; *(underlined)* The black-and-white kitten from next door
6. *(circled)* store; *(underlined)* The cool, new music store in the shopping center
7. *(circled)* children; *(underlined)* The barefooted children

3–3. Simple and Complete Predicates

1. *(circled)* barks; *(underlined)* barks when he hears the mail carrier
2. *(circled)* play; *(underlined)* play exciting games on their computer
3. *(circled)* dropped; *(underlined)* dropped a book while running to school
4. *(circled)* played; *(underlined)* played for the Veterans' Day parade last year
5. *(circled)* was; *(underlined)* was a great general and president
6. *(circled)* salutes; *(underlined)* salutes the American flag every morning
7. *(circled)* tells; *(underlined)* tells the most exciting story I ever read

3–4. Sentences with One Subject and One Verb

1. *Subject:* band; *Verb:* played
2. *Subject:* friend; *Verb:* eats
3. *Subject:* man; *Verb:* walks
4. *Subject:* man; *Verb:* walks
5. *Subject:* dinosaur; *Verb:* stands
6. *Subject:* Uncle Bernie; *Verb:* lives
7. *Subject:* Uncle Bernie; *Verb:* lives

3–5. Sentences with Compound Subjects

Part A.

1. Jaime and his brother
2. Alicia or Jenny

3. The two girls and their friends
4. Hamburgers, hot dogs, and pizza
5. Two men and three women

Part B.
Sentences will vary.

3–6. SENTENCES WITH COMPOUND PREDICATES

Part A.

1. danced and sang
2. eagerly watched and waited for the letter carrier
3. snapped her fingers and whistled a tune
4. whispered and laughed all through the performance
5. jogs every morning and rides her bike every afternoon

Part B.
Sentences will vary.

3–7. SUBJECT–VERB AGREEMENT: NUMBER

1. need
2. are
3. was
4. work
5. were
6. lives
7. are
8. were

3–8. SUBJECT–VERB AGREEMENT: PERSON

Sentences will vary.

3–9. DEPENDENT AND INDEPENDENT CLAUSES (PART ONE)

1. *(circled)* I failed the test; *(underlined)* because I was not prepared
2. *(circled)* I arrived at school on time; *(underlined)* Although I woke up late
3. *(circled)* I remember the fun I had last summer; *(underlined)* whenever I hear a certain tune
4. *(circled)* Elena is not allowed to watch TV; *(underlined)* until she finishes her homework
5. *(circled)* the audience grew quiet; *(underlined)* As soon as the show began
6. *(circled)* The United States of America became a nation; *(underlined)* after the Revolutionary War
7. *(circled)* Mark failed the test; *(underlined)* because he was not prepared
8. *(circled)* they lost the game; *(underlined)* Although the team had worked hard for days
9. *(circled)* my friend, Alicia, drove up and gave me a ride; *(underlined)* While I was waiting for the bus
10. *(circled)* please get me some potato chips; *(underlined)* As long as you are up

3–10. DEPENDENT AND INDEPENDENT CLAUSES (PART TWO)

1. I failed the test because I was not prepared.
2. Maria bought a new dress because she was going to a party.

3. I'm not ready because I woke up late.
4. I want to be a violinist because I love music.
5. I can't buy that jacket because I haven't enough money.

3–11. Dependent and Independent Clauses (part three)

1. a	3. b	5. a
2. b	4. a	6. b

3–12. Simple Sentences

1. *(circled)* The butterfly; *(underlined)* fluttered on the windowpane
2. *(circled)* My family; *(underlined)* had a picnic of sandwiches and salads in Central Park
3. *(circled)* My brother, my sister, and all my aunts and uncles; *(underlined)* were there
4. *(circled)* I; *(underlined)* bought a new scanner and printer for my computer
5. *(circled)* My favorite author; *(underlined)* has written three books
6. *(circled)* The monkey in the zoo; *(underlined)* is jumping from bar to bar
7. *(circled)* Cal and Hal; *(underlined)* are my best buddies
8. *(circled)* The room; *(underlined)* contained two tables and one desk
9. *(circled)* Robins and gulls; *(underlined)* are easy to identify
10. *(circled)* The baby; *(underlined)* gurgled and clapped his hands

3–13. Compound Sentences

1. Anna went to the park and she rode her bicycle there.
2. The delivery person knocked at the door, but there was no answer.
3. I wish I could go to the costume party, but I don't have anything appropriate to wear.
4. We can go shopping today, or we can do it tomorrow.
5. I want a hamburger for lunch and I want ketchup on it.

3–14. Complex Sentences (part one)

1. *(underlined)* you should exercise daily; *(circled)* If you want to have strong muscles
2. *(underlined)* My dad always works out at the gym; *(circled)* before he comes home from work
3. *(underlined)* you are strengthening your leg muscles; *(circled)* When you ride your bike each day
4. *(underlined)* he forces himself to run three miles each day; *(circled)* Although Mark would rather watch TV
5. *(underlined)* Thomas Jefferson was opposed to slavery; *(circled)* even though he owned slaves himself
6. *(underlined)* Jason became close friends with a boy; *(circled)* whom he met at sports camp

7. *(underlined)* Marla stayed in her seat; *(circled)* because she didn't know the bell had rung
8. *(underlined)* he keeps his eye on the pitcher; *(circled)* Whenever my brother watches a baseball game
9. *(underlined)* Rose would have gotten an A in Spanish; *(circled)* If she had completed her homework
10. *(underlined)* You don't have to finish your dinner; *(circled)* since you don't feel well

3–15. COMPLEX SENTENCES (PART TWO)

1. I studied hard each day because I wanted to do well on the test. **(OR)** Because I wanted to do well on the test, I studied hard each day.
2. You will find it easier to do well if you just relax. **(OR)** If you just relax, you will find it easier to do well.
3. Whenever I get upset, my mom can usually calm me down. **(OR)** My mom can usually calm me down whenever I get upset.
4. I'll meet you in the hall after the swim meet. **(OR)** After the swim meet, I'll meet you in the hall.

3–16. SIMPLE, COMPOUND, AND COMPLEX SENTENCES

Part A.

1. simple
2. simple
3. complex
4. simple
5. compound
6. complex
7. complex
8. complex
9. simple

Part B.

Sentences will vary.

3–17. DECLARATIVE, INTERROGATIVE, EXCLAMATORY, AND IMPERATIVE SENTENCES (PART ONE)

1. exclamation point
2. period
3. question mark
4. exclamation point
5. question mark
6. exclamation point
7. period
8. exclamation point
9. question mark
10. period

3–18. DECLARATIVE, INTERROGATIVE, EXCLAMATORY, AND IMPERATIVE SENTENCES (PART TWO)

Sentences will vary.

3–19. RECOGNIZING SENTENCE FRAGMENTS (PART ONE)

1. complete
2. fragment
3. fragment
4. complete
5. fragment
6. fragment
7. fragment
8. complete
9. fragment

3–20. Recognizing Sentence Fragments (part two)

Sentences will vary slightly. Here are examples.

1. I was feeling sad, when suddenly my dog, Jack, climbed onto my lap.
2. Leaving school one afternoon, Josh walked into a wild blizzard.
3. We lived in Dayton two years ago in a house on the west side of town.
4. Meeting my next-door neighbor at the supermarket, I said, "Hello."
5. Working hard and having a vision of your future is a formula for success.

3–21. Recognizing Run-on Sentences

1. Alison broke her leg skiing. Now she has to wear a cast and use crutches.
2. Today is May first. Your calendar is on the wrong page.
3. Dad's new car has leather seats and a moon roof. It is really cool.
4. I am looking forward to our class trip. We are going to Washington, D.C.
5. Abbie got a dog for her birthday. It is a mixed breed.

3–22. Do's and Don'ts for Writing Sentences (part one)

Sentences will vary.

3–23. Do's and Don'ts for Writing Sentences (part two)

Sentences may vary slightly. Here are examples.

1. We had a substitute because the teacher was sick.
2. These portions of steak are very tough.
3. After the salute to the flag in the auditorium, we sang the national anthem.
4. *This sentence is correct.*

Answers to Review Test

Part One

The answers to Part One appear on page 145.

Part Two

The only correct sentence is: There are many serious problems. *Here is a rewritten paragraph. (Other forms are possible.)*

The first Earth Day was celebrated on April 22, 1970. It was the idea of Gaylord Nelson, a senator from Wisconsin. Afterwards, more and more people started becoming concerned about the environment and misuse of the world's resources. There are many serious problems with the air we breathe, the water we drink, and the food we eat. It is time for us to pay attention to our beautiful Earth and try to preserve a healthy, safe environment for future generations. What can you do to help? Taking part in community trash cleanups and sorting items to be recycled are a few helpful activities.

Name ______________________________ Date ______________

3–1. Subjects and Predicates

Be sure your sentences are complete thoughts.

> **A sentence is a complete thought that contains a subject and a predicate. The subject tells *who* or *what* is doing the action. The predicate tells what the subject is doing or gives more information about the subject.**
>
> Examples: *The audience applauded.*
> Subject: *audience;* predicate: *applauded.*
>
> *The dog wagged its bushy tail.*
> Subject: *dog;* predicate: *wagged its bushy tail.*

DIRECTIONS: Combine each subject in column A with a predicate from column B to make a complete sentence. Write these sentences on the lines below.

A	B
1. The test	always has the correct time.
2. The computer	jogs every day at the same time.
3. Dogs	writes in red ink.
4. Tony's clock	is very easy.
5. My brother	make wonderful pets.
6. The runner	is a very useful tool.
7. This pen	ran in the third race.
8. These horses	goes to college.

1. ______________________________
2. ______________________________
3. ______________________________
4. ______________________________
5. ______________________________
6. ______________________________
7. ______________________________
8. ______________________________

Name ______________________________ Date ______________

3–2. Simple and Complete Subjects

Know the difference between a simple subject and a complete subject.

1. A simple subject is the main noun or pronoun that names the subject. It is usually one word and tells who or what the sentence is about.
2. The complete subject consists of the simple subject and all the words that go with it. Examples:

   A tall, good-looking stranger knocked on the door.
   Simple subject: *stranger*
   Complete subject: *A tall, good-looking stranger*

   The dog with the broken leg limped into the vet's office.
   Simple subject: *dog*
   Complete subject: *The dog with the broken leg*

DIRECTIONS: Circle the simple subject and underline the complete subject in each sentence.

1. My cousin Patrick likes to help his dad mow the lawn.
2. The bat with the initials DJ belongs to me.
3. Valerie's cousin who lives in Alaska flew south to visit her family.
4. The long, boring movie on TV put Hank's grandfather to sleep.
5. The black-and-white kitten from next door rubbed against my ankle.
6. The cool, new music store in the shopping center will be closing soon.
7. The barefooted children were running along the beach.

Name ______________________________ Date ______________

3–3. Simple and Complete Predicates

Know the difference between a simple predicate and a complete predicate.

1. A simple predicate is the main verb of the sentence.
2. The complete predicate includes the simple predicate and all the words that go with it. Examples:

   Mom laughs at all of Dad's corny jokes.
   Simple predicate: *laughs*
   Complete predicate: *laughs at all of Dad's corny jokes*

   I ran after the ball as fast as I could.
   Simple predicate: *ran*
   Complete predicate: *ran after the ball as fast as I could*

DIRECTIONS: Circle the simple predicate and underline the complete predicate in each sentence.

1. Our dog barks when he hears the mail carrier.
2. Jonathan and his brother play exciting games on their computer.
3. Martin dropped a book while running to school.
4. The marching band played for the Veterans' Day parade last year.
5. George Washington was a great general and president.
6. The class salutes the American flag every morning.
7. This book tells the most exciting story I ever read.

Name ______________________________ Date ______________

3–4. Sentences with One Subject and One Verb

Here is how to write an easy sentence.

The easiest kind of sentence to write contains just one subject and one verb.

Sheri went to the store. (Subject: *Sheri;* verb: *went)*

Pat likes his teacher. (Subject: *Pat;* verb: *likes)*

Many sentences that seem longer still contain only one subject and one verb, as in:

Tall, beautiful, blue-eyed Sheri went to the video store in the mall.

My second cousin, Pat, likes his friendly new history teacher.

Despite the extra descriptive words, each of these sentences has just one subject ***(Sheri, Pat)*** **and one verb (*went, likes*).**

DIRECTIONS: Circle the one subject and underline the one verb in each sentence.

1. The band played in the parade.
2. My best friend, Frieda, eats lots of fruit like apples, pears, and bananas.
3. The old man walks slowly.
4. The poor old man from around the corner usually walks slowly and carefully.
5. The largest dinosaur in the museum stands in a room by itself.
6. Uncle Bernie lives on Elm St.
7. My favorite relative, Uncle Bernie, lives in a big house at the end of Elm St.

Name ______________________________ **Date** ______________

3–5. Sentences with Compound Subjects

Keep this rule in mind.

A compound subject contains more than one subject joined by a conjunction (*and, or*), as in:

Lions, tigers, and bears can be found in the zoo.
Compound subject: *Lions, tigers, and bears*

Paul, Raymundo, and Sean made the first team.
Compound subject: *Paul, Raymundo, and Sean*

A. DIRECTIONS: Underline the compound subjects in these sentences.

1. Jaime and his brother both got bikes for Christmas.
2. Either Alicia or Jenny will get the prize.
3. The two girls and their friends walked to the movie theater.
4. Hamburgers, hot dogs, and pizza are my favorite choices for lunch.
5. Two men and three women entered the shop at the same time.

B. DIRECTIONS: Write five sentences below. Each sentence should contain a compound subject.

____

____

____

____

____

____

____

____

Name ______________________________ Date ______________

3–6. Sentences with Compound Predicates

Keep this rule in mind.

> A compound predicate contains two or more verbs (simple predicates) joined by a conjunction (*and, or, but*), as in:
>
> *Our dog slipped through the back door and ran away.*
> Compound predicate: *slipped through the back door and ran away*
>
> *The mountain goats leaped and skipped over the craggy rocks.*
> Compound predicate: *leaped and skipped over the craggy rocks*

A. DIRECTIONS: Underline the compound predicates in these sentences.

1. The people in the chorus danced and sang.
2. The soldier's wife eagerly watched and waited for the letter carrier.
3. Anita snapped her fingers and whistled a tune.
4. The rude audience whispered and laughed all through the performance.
5. Kelly jogs every morning and rides her bike every afternoon.

B. DIRECTIONS: Complete each sentence below with a compound predicate.

1. My favorite activities are ______________________________

____

2. In the morning, ______________________________

____

3. In the summer, my family ______________________________

____

4. The animals in the forest ______________________________

____

5. A spaceship from a distant star ______________________________

____

Name ______________________________ **Date** ______________

3–7. Subject–Verb Agreement: Number

The verb in a sentence must agree with the subject in number.

1. **A singular subject takes a singular verb.**
   My cat likes a sunny spot.
   Singular subject: ***cat;*** **singular verb:** ***likes***

   My cat likes all the sunny spots in the garden.
   Don't be confused by "sunny spots." The subject ***(cat)*** **is still singular, and so is the verb (*****likes*****).**
2. **A plural subject takes a plural verb.**
   My cats like sunny spots.
   Plural subject: ***cats,*** **plural verb:** ***like***
3. **Note: Collective nouns such as** ***band, crowd, gang, family, bunch, set, audience,*** **etc., are usually followed by a singular verb, as in:** ***My family loves vacations.***

DIRECTIONS: Complete these sentences by circling the correct verb from the pair given.

1. These old guitars ______ to be restrung. **(need, needs)**
2. Bobby and his friends ______ going to a jazz concert. **(is, are)**
3. A bowl of apples ______ on the table. **(was, were)**
4. My brothers ______ in a supermarket after school. **(work, works)**
5. The rooster and the hen ______ in the barnyard. **(was, were)**
6. A family of rabbits ______ in our garden. **(live, lives)**
7. The girl in red and the boy in brown ______ coming this way. **(is, are)**
8. The people in the cast of the play ______ great. **(was, were)**

Name ______________________________ Date ______________

3–8. Subject–Verb Agreement: Person

A subject and verb must agree in person.

1. **A first-person subject takes a first-person verb: *I am very happy.* (First person refers to the person speaking.)**
2. **A second-person subject takes a second-person verb: *You are very happy.* (Second person refers to the person spoken to.)**
3. **A third-person subject takes a third-person verb: *She is very happy. Jeremy is very happy.* (Third person is the person, place, or thing spoken about.)**

DIRECTIONS: Write:

- Two sentences using a first-person subject.
- Two sentences using a second-person subject.
- Two sentences using a third-person subject.

____

____

____

____

____

____

____

____

____

____

____

____

(Continue on the back of this sheet, if necessary.)

Name ______________________________ Date ______________

3–9. Dependent and Independent Clauses (Part One)

Keep these rules in mind.

> **A clause is a group of words containing a subject and a predicate. The following sentence contains two different types of clauses: *Whenever you are ready, we can leave.***
>
> 1. **A clause that can stand alone as a sentence is called an independent clause. In the sentence above, *we can leave* can stand alone and is, therefore, an independent clause.**
> 2. **A clause that cannot stand alone as a sentence is called a dependent or subordinate clause. In the example above, *Whenever you are ready* cannot stand on its own and is, therefore, a dependent clause.**
> 3. **Words that are often used to introduce dependent clauses are: *who, whoever, which, what, whether, when, where, how, if, that, after, although, as, as much as, as long as, because, before, since, so that, than, though, unless, until, whenever, while.***

DIRECTIONS: Circle the independent clauses and underline the dependent clauses in the following sentences.

1. I failed the test because I was not prepared.
2. Although I woke up late, I arrived at school on time.
3. Whenever I hear a certain tune, I remember the fun I had last summer.
4. Elena is not allowed to watch TV until she finishes her homework.
5. As soon as the show began, the audience grew quiet.
6. The United States of America became a nation after the Revolutionary War.
7. Mark failed the test because he was not prepared.
8. Although the team had worked hard for days, they lost the game.
9. While I was waiting for the bus, my friend, Alicia, drove up and gave me a ride.
10. As long as you are up, please get me some potato chips.

Name ______________________________ Date ______________

3–10. Dependent and Independent Clauses (Part Two)

Keep this rule in mind.

> **A dependent clause is a group of words with a subject and predicate that cannot stand alone as a sentence. Sometimes dependent clauses can be misplaced and make a sentence confusing.**
>
> WRONG: *I was sick was the reason why I didn't go to the party.*
> RIGHT: *I didn't go to the party because I was sick.*
>
> WRONG: *The reason I am not going to school is because I am sick.*
> RIGHT: *I am not going to school because I am sick.*
>
> **Note:** ***The reason why*** **and** ***the reason is because*** **are often misused and should be reworded.**

DIRECTIONS: Rewrite each sentence correctly on the lines below.

1. I was not prepared was the reason I failed the test.

 ____

 ____

2. Maria bought a new dress. Because she was going to a party.

 ____

 ____

3. The reason why I'm not ready is because I woke up late.

 ____

 ____

4. I love music is the reason why I want to be a violinist.

 ____

 ____

5. I haven't enough money is the reason why I can't buy that jacket.

 ____

 ____

Name ______________________________ Date ______________

3–11. Dependent and Independent Clauses (Part Three)

Keep this rule in mind.

> **Do not attach dependent clauses to sentences with words that cause confusion, as in these examples.**
>
> WRONG: *Although Maya studied hard caused her to fail the test.*
> RIGHT: *Although Maya studied hard, she failed the test.*
> RIGHT: *Maya studied hard but she failed the test.*
>
> WRONG: *In trying to fix the chair another leg broke.*
> RIGHT: *When I tried to fix the chair, another leg broke.*
> RIGHT: *Another leg broke when I tried to fix the chair.*

DIRECTIONS: Put a checkmark next to the correct sentence in each group.

1. ❑ a. Although I rushed to get ready, I was late.
   ❑ b. Although I rushed to get ready was why I was late.

2. ❑ a. In doing Mark's homework there was difficult problems.
   ❑ b. There were difficult problems in Mark's homework.

3. ❑ a. I was sick caused me to have a fever.
   ❑ b. I had a fever because I was sick.

4. ❑ a. By using a new ball, our team won the game.
   ❑ b. By using a new ball helped our team win the game.

5. ❑ a. My only hope is to pass the test.
   ❑ b. My only hope is I will pass the test.

6. ❑ a. Even though Chang did his best was a surprise to fail the test.
   ❑ b. Even though Chang did his best, he failed the test.

Name ______________________________ Date ______________

3–12. Simple Sentences

Remember these rules about simple sentences.

1. **A simple sentence is made up of one complete subject and one complete predicate. The sentence could be short:** ***Hansel jumped.*** **Or the sentence could be long:** ***That poor boy, Hansel, jumped out of the witch's oven.***
2. **As long as it contains just one complete subject and one complete predicate, it is a simple sentence. Even if the subject and/or the predicate are compound, it is still a simple sentence, as in these examples:**

   My brother and sister are teenagers.

   My brother is playing ball and eating a banana.

   My brother and sister are eating and laughing.

DIRECTIONS: Circle the complete subject and underline the complete predicate in each sentence.

1. The butterfly fluttered on the windowpane.
2. My family had a picnic of sandwiches and salads in Central Park.
3. My brother, my sister, and all my aunts and uncles were there.
4. I bought a new scanner and printer for my computer.
5. My favorite author has written three books.
6. The monkey in the zoo is jumping from bar to bar.
7. Cal and Hal are my best buddies.
8. The room contained two tables and one desk.
9. Robins and gulls are easy to identify.
10. The baby gurgled and clapped his hands.

Name ______________________________ Date ______________

3–13. Compound Sentences

Remember these rules about compound sentences.

A compound sentence is made up of two or more independent clauses. Each clause is a simple sentence that could stand alone.

1. If the clauses are short, they are joined by a conjunction such as *and, but,* or *or,* as in these examples: *The game was short and our team won. Stop laughing or you'll choke on your food.*
2. For longer clauses, use a comma in addition to the conjunction, as in: *Jon invited me to his birthday party, and I told him I would come. I wanted to ride my bike to Marla's house, but I didn't know the way.*

Note: If you are not sure whether to use the comma and conjunction or the conjunction alone, you are always safe in using both.

3. Occasionally, a colon (:) can be used when the second part of the compound sentence explains the first, as in: *This is my plan: we are going to pool our money for Mom's present.*

DIRECTIONS: Combine the two simple sentences into one compound sentence.

1. Anna went to the park. She rode her bicycle there.

   ____

   ____

2. The delivery person knocked at the door. There was no answer.

   ____

   ____

3. I wish I could go to the costume party. I don't have anything appropriate to wear.

   ____

   ____

4. We can go shopping today. We can do it tomorrow.

   ____

   ____

5. I want a hamburger for lunch. I want ketchup on it.

   ____

   ____

Name ______________________________ Date ______________

3–14. Complex Sentences (part one)

A complex sentence contains an independent clause and a dependent clause. Each clause consists of a subject and a predicate. The dependent clause often begins with a conjunction. It is called a subordinating conjunction because it introduces the less important, dependent clause, as in the following example.

Although I'm very hungry, I won't be able to eat until later.

The independent clause in this sentence is *I won't be able to eat until later.* (This can stand on its own as a sentence.).

The dependent clause is *Although I'm very hungry.* (This cannot stand on its own as a sentence.)

Note: If a dependent clause comes at the beginning of a sentence, it should be followed by a comma, as in the example above.

DIRECTIONS: Underline the independent clause and circle the dependent clause in each of the following complex sentences.

1. If you want to have strong muscles, you should exercise daily.
2. My dad always works out at the gym before he comes home from work.
3. When you ride your bike each day, you are strengthening your leg muscles.
4. Although Mark would rather watch TV, he forces himself to run three miles each day.
5. Thomas Jefferson was opposed to slavery even though he owned slaves himself.
6. Jason became close friends with a boy whom he met at sports camp.
7. Marla stayed in her seat because she didn't know the bell had rung.
8. Whenever my brother watches a baseball game, he keeps his eye on the pitcher.
9. If she had completed her homework, Rose would have gotten an A in Spanish.
10. You don't have to finish your dinner since you don't feel well.

Name ______________________________ Date ______________

3–15. Complex Sentences (part two)

A complex sentence consists of an independent clause and a dependent clause. The dependent clause usually begins with a conjunction or a preposition.

Some conjunctions often used with dependent clauses are: *if, although, unless, because, though,* as in these examples:

Although I am on a diet, I will eat cake on my birthday.

Independent clause: *I will eat cake on my birthday*

Dependent clause: *Although I am on a diet*

Mara's little sister is allowed to attend the party if she behaves.

Independent clause: *Mara's little sister is allowed to attend the party*

Dependent clause: *if she behaves*

Prepositions such as *after, before, while, until,* and adverbs like *when, whenever, how, where, why* can also be used to introduce the dependent clause, as in these examples:

Before you leave school, be sure to check your locker.

You can eat this sandwich whenever you feel hungry.

DIRECTIONS: Combine each set of two clauses into a complex sentence on the lines below.

1. Because I wanted to do well on the test. I studied hard each day.

   ____

   ____

2. You will find it easier to do well. If you just relax.

   ____

   ____

3. Whenever I get upset. My mom can usually calm me down.

   ____

   ____

4. I'll meet you in the hall. After the swim meet.

   ____

   ____

Name ______________________________ Date ______________

3–16. Simple, Compound, and Complex Sentences

Remember these types of sentences.

1. **A simple sentence is made up of one complete subject and one complete predicate:** ***I walk my dog in the park every morning.***
2. **A compound sentence is made up of two or more independent clauses:** ***I walk my dog in the park and I always keep him on a leash.***
3. **A complex sentence contains an independent clause and a dependent clause:** ***Whenever I walk my dog, I always keep him on a leash.***

A. DIRECTIONS: Next to each sentence, write whether it is *simple, compound,* or *complex.* (**Example:** *Before you say a word, listen to me.* complex)

1. It is easy to recognize a simple sentence. ____________
2. It is more difficult to identify a complex sentence. ____________
3. Whenever I am sad, I think about my blessings. ____________
4. The tiny bud burst open into a beautiful and colorful flower. ____________
5. Jack climbed into the spaceship and they took off. ____________
6. Besides our own sun, there are many other stars in the universe. ____________
7. I can get this homework done if you will help me. ____________
8. Even though Mia and Rose are different, they are best friends. ____________
9. Matt went to New York to see his cousin, Pat. ____________

B. DIRECTIONS: On the lines below, write one simple sentence, one compound sentence, and one complex sentence.

____

____

____

____

____

Name ______________________________ Date ______________

3–17. Declarative, Interrogative, Exclamatory, and Imperative Sentences (Part One)

Use these four types of sentences and their end marks correctly.

1. **A declarative sentence makes a statement. It is followed by a period.** ***(This sentence makes a statement. A good writer knows how to express his or her ideas.)***
2. **An interrogative sentence asks a question. It is followed by a question mark.** ***(Is this sentence making a statement? Does a good writer know how to express his or her ideas?)***
3. **An exclamatory sentence expresses strong feelings or emotions. It is followed by an exclamation point.** ***(I hate making statements! My ideas are great!)***
4. **An imperative sentence makes a request or gives a command. If it is a mild request, it can be followed by a period. If it is an urgent request or strong command, it should be followed by an exclamation point.** ***(I would like you to make a statement now. Make that statement now!)***

DIRECTIONS: Insert the correct punctuation (period, question mark, or exclamation point) at the end of each sentence.

1. Begin immediately
2. I would like to stay up until midnight on New Year's Eve
3. What time will you go to sleep that night
4. Give me that book, or else
5. When do you expect to finish reading that book
6. I'm so excited I can hardly breathe
7. I'll be happy when I finish this problem
8. Get that fly ball
9. Do you think you can catch that high fly ball
10. I can catch it without any problem

Name ______________________________ Date ______________

3–18. Declarative, Interrogative, Exclamatory, and Imperative Sentences (Part Two)

DIRECTIONS: On the lines below, write two declarative sentences, two interrogative sentences, two exclamatory sentences, and two imperative sentences. Be creative!

____

____

____

____

____

____

____

____

____

____

____

____

____

____

____

____

____

____

____

(Continue on the back of this sheet, if necessary.)

Name ______________________________ Date ______________

3–19. Recognizing Sentence Fragments (Part One)

Avoid sentence fragments in your writing.

A sentence that does not express a complete thought is not really a sentence. It is called a sentence fragment. Usually, this is because it is missing either the subject or the main verb, as in these examples:

WRONG: *Standing in the rain.* (This is a fragment because the subject is missing.)

RIGHT: *The lost boy is standing in the rain.*

WRONG: *A boy who was in my class last year.* (This is a fragment because the main verb is missing.)

RIGHT: *A boy who was in my class last year suddenly appeared in the hall.*

DIRECTIONS: Next to each sentence below, write *complete* if it is a complete sentence, or write *fragment* if it is not a complete sentence.

1. Mike is doing his best to succeed. ______________
2. Logging onto the Internet and getting information. ______________
3. Wizards and magicians using strange spells. ______________
4. Tying a strong knot is not easy. ______________
5. Although I have been trying to learn for a long time. ______________
6. Stopping at my friend's house. ______________
7. My aunt who lives in Argentina. ______________
8. Training my dog is my favorite hobby. ______________
9. Ghosts and goblins coming to our house on Halloween. ______________

Name ______________________________ Date ______________

3–20. Recognizing Sentence Fragments (Part Two)

Avoid sentence fragments in your writing.

The word *fragment* means a broken piece. A fragmented sentence is broken because it is missing an important part—either a subject or a predicate verb. Both these things must be present to complete the thought (and the sentence, too). Here are some ways that sentences are sometimes fragmented and how to fix them.

1. Do not use a dependent clause as a sentence.

   WRONG: *Alex used to go to Midtown Junior High. From which he transferred here.* (The first sentence is correct, but the second is only a fragment.)

   RIGHT: *Alex transferred here from Midtown Junior High.*

2. Avoid starting a sentence one way and then changing construction.

   WRONG: *A girl in my class who because she got the flu and missed a week of classes failed the test.*

   RIGHT: *A girl in my class failed the test because she got the flu and missed a week of classes.*

DIRECTIONS: On the back of this sheet, rewrite the fragmented sentences correctly.

1. I was feeling sad. When suddenly, my dog, Jack, climbed onto my lap.
2. Leaving school one afternoon and walked into a wild blizzard.
3. We lived in Dayton two years ago. Our house being on the west side of town.
4. Meeting my next-door neighbor at the supermarket.
5. This is a formula for success. Working hard and having a vision of your future.

Name ______________________________ Date ______________

3–21. Recognizing Run-on Sentences

Know when to rewrite to avoid run-on sentences.

A sentence is called a run-on sentence when it continues past the point where it should stop, as in these examples:

I went shopping last week, the stores were so crowded that I didn't buy anything.

I took my bike out of the garage, the wheel had gotten bent and I couldn't ride it.

1. An end mark (period, question mark, exclamation point) signals the end of a complete sentence. Each complete thought in the examples above should have an end mark.

   I went shopping last week. The stores were so crowded that I didn't buy anything.

   I took my bike out of the garage. The wheel had gotten bent and I couldn't ride it.

2. A conjunction could be used to combine the two clauses in each sentence.

   I went shopping last week, but the stores were so crowded that I didn't buy anything.

   I took my bike out of the garage, but the wheel had gotten bent and I couldn't ride it.

DIRECTIONS: On the back of this sheet, rewrite each run-on sentence. Use an end mark or a conjunction.

1. Alison broke her leg skiing, now she has to wear a cast and use crutches.
2. Today is May first, your calendar is on the wrong page.
3. Dad's new car has leather seats and a moon roof, it is really cool.
4. I am looking forward to our class trip, we are going to Washington, D.C.
5. Abbie got a dog for her birthday, it is a mixed breed.

Name ______________________________ Date ______________

3–22. Do's and Don'ts for Writing Sentences (Part One)

Keep these rules in mind.

1. DO the following when writing sentences:
   - Be sure the sentence contains a subject and a predicate with a verb.
   - Be sure the sentence expresses a complete thought.
   - Use an end mark (period, question mark, or exclamation point) at the end of each sentence.
2. DON'T do the following:
   - Write fragmented sentences.
   - Write run-on sentences.

DIRECTIONS: Write these different kinds of sentences.

1. Write a simple sentence that contains one subject and one predicate.

____

____

____

2. Write a compound sentence that contains two independent clauses connected by a conjunction.

____

____

____

3. Write a complex sentence that contains one independent clause and one dependent clause.

____

____

____

4. On the back of this sheet, write one declarative sentence, one interrogative sentence, one exclamatory sentence, and one imperative sentence.

Name ______________________________ Date ______________

3–23. Do's and Don'ts for Writing Sentences (Part Two)

Keep these additional rules in mind.

3. DO the following when writing sentences:
   - Be sure that the subject and verb always agree.

     My brother likes to play board games.

     My brother and sister like to play board games.

     I am going to travel four hundred miles.

     We are going to travel four hundred miles.

4. DON'T do the following:
   - Write a dependent clause as a complete sentence.

     WRONG: *While I was putting out the garbage yesterday.*

     RIGHT: *While I was putting out the garbage yesterday, I slipped and fell.*

     RIGHT: *I slipped and fell while I was putting out the garbage yesterday.*
   - Attach dependent clauses to sentences with words that cause confusion.

     WRONG: *When getting a haircut made Jenny feel like a different person.*

     RIGHT: *Getting a haircut made Jenny feel like a different person.*

     RIGHT: *Jenny felt like a different person when she got a haircut.*

DIRECTIONS: Write each sentence correctly on the back of this sheet.

1. Because the teacher was sick was the reason we had a substitute.
2. These portions of steak is very tough.
3. After the salute to the flag in the auditorium.
4. Either Sean, Brad, or Mario scores the run.

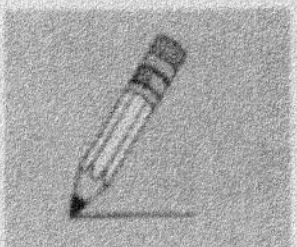

Eighth-Grade Level

Writing Sentences Review Test

REVIEW TEST: WRITING SENTENCES (PART ONE)

A. DIRECTIONS: Decide if each sentence below is a fragment, a run-on sentence, or if the sentence is written correctly. Then on the Answer Sheet, darken **A** for fragment, **B** for run-on, or **C** if the sentence is correct.

1. Watching from the outfield as the ball sails through the air and over the fence.
2. Seth's father is in the U.S. Army, he is a captain.
3. The girl is sad.
4. Rachel's bike is broken, she needs a new one.
5. When June comes each year and everyone is excited about summer vacation.
6. The Declaration of Independence written in 1776.
7. Good citizens care about their neighbors, their communities, and their country.
8. Recommended by doctors as necessary to a patient's health.
9. Basketball is Brian's favorite sport, and skiing is a close second choice.
10. With final exams coming up in a week, the students in Mr. Lapin's class.

B. DIRECTIONS: Decide the correct end mark—period (.), question mark (?), or exclamation point (!)—for the end of each of the following sentences. Then, on the Answer Sheet, darken **A** for period (.), **B** for question mark (?), or **C** for exclamation point (!).

11. Sarah is happy because her birthday party was a tremendous success
12. What a great pet you have
13. Did the teacher say that this project must be completed in two days
14. How many dimes are needed to make three dollars
15. Get out of here right now
16. I wonder whether or not I will become a doctor some day
17. Do you ever wake up in the morning and wish you could stay in bed all day
18. Watch out for that speeding car
19. Isn't Rose coming with us to the beach tomorrow
20. When the furniture arrives, will you know how to put it together

Name ______________________________ Date ______________

REVIEW TEST: WRITING SENTENCES (PART TWO)

DIRECTIONS: The following paragraph contains eight errors in sentence construction. Circle the sentences that are incorrect. Then rewrite the complete paragraph correctly on the lines below.

> The first Earth Day celebrated on April 22, 1970. The idea of Gaylord Nelson, a senator from Wisconsin. Afterwards, more and more people becoming concerned about the environment and misuse of the world's resources. There are many serious problems. With the air we breathe, the water we drink, and the food we eat. A time to pay attention to our beautiful Earth. Trying to preserve a healthy, safe environment for future generations. What can you do to help. Taking part in community trash cleanups, sorting items to be recycled.

____

____

____

____

____

____

____

____

____

____

____

____

Name ______________________________ Date ______________

Writing Sentences

Review Test (Part One): Answer Sheet

Darken the circle above the letter that best answers the question.

1. ○ A ○ B ○ C
2. ○ A ○ B ○ C
3. ○ A ○ B ○ C
4. ○ A ○ B ○ C
5. ○ A ○ B ○ C
6. ○ A ○ B ○ C
7. ○ A ○ B ○ C
8. ○ A ○ B ○ C
9. ○ A ○ B ○ C
10. ○ A ○ B ○ C
11. ○ A ○ B ○ C
12. ○ A ○ B ○ C
13. ○ A ○ B ○ C
14. ○ A ○ B ○ C
15. ○ A ○ B ○ C
16. ○ A ○ B ○ C
17. ○ A ○ B ○ C
18. ○ A ○ B ○ C
19. ○ A ○ B ○ C
20. ○ A ○ B ○ C

Writing Sentences

Key to Review Test (Part One)

	A	B	C
1.	●	○	○
2.	○	●	○
3.	○	○	●
4.	○	●	○
5.	●	○	○
6.	●	○	○
7.	○	○	●
8.	●	○	○
9.	○	○	●
10.	●	○	○
11.	●	○	○
12.	○	○	●
13.	○	●	○
14.	○	●	○
15.	○	○	●
16.	●	○	○
17.	○	●	○
18.	○	○	●
19.	○	●	○
20.	○	●	○

SECTION 4

WRITING PARAGRAPHS

Teacher Preparation and Lessons

Recognizing and writing paragraphs is a necessary prerequisite to essay writing. The acquisition of paragraph writing skills helps students to organize their thinking as well as their writing, and to be able to communicate thoughts and ideas clearly to the reader. These skills are an important component of the writing process in both state and national standardized assessment tests for writing. The PRACTICE TEST assesses students' ability to apply their knowledge of language and writing skills. The rubric and student samples can be used to assist in assessing students' writing. Answer keys for this section are found on pages 152–155.

ACTIVITIES 4-1 and 4-2 are designed to help students **organize paragraphs**. Write the following short paragraph on the chalkboard:

> *My last birthday was a never-to-be forgotten day. I was in my room trying to cool off when the doorbell rang. Mom called me down and told me to look out the window. There were all of my friends with balloons, stuff for the beach, and all the food we could ever eat. That birthday was definitely the best one yet.*

Point out that, like a story, a paragraph has a beginning, middle, and end. Elicit that the opening sentence introduces the subject. Tell the class that this is called the topic sentence. Ask what the last sentence does and elicit that it brings the story to an end. Tell the class that this is called the concluding sentence. Point out that the sentences in the middle develop the topic. Distribute **Activity 4-1 Organizing a Paragraph (Part One)**. Read and discuss the paragraph description, and read and discuss the directions. Then have the students complete the activity. Distribute **Activity 4-2 Organizing a Paragraph (Part Two)**. Read the directions, and have students complete the activity.

ACTIVITIES 4-3 and 4-4 help students develop a **topic sentence**. Distribute **Activity 4-3 Writing a Topic Sentence (Part One)**. Read and discuss the rule and examples. Read and discuss the directions for finding the topic sentences, and discuss the results. Then read and discuss the directions for completing the activity. Have students share their topic sentences by reading them aloud.

Write the following pairs of sentences on the chalkboard:

> *Our class went on a trip.*
> *You won't believe what happened on our class trip!*
>
> *Here is what happened the last time I baby-sat.*
> *Have you ever had a disaster when baby-sitting?*

Point out that each sentence introduces the subject of a paragraph and is a topic sentence. Ask which sentence in each pair does a better job of getting the reader's attention, and point out that a topic sentence not only introduces the subject, but, preferably, should do so in an interesting way. Distribute **Activity 4-4 Writing a Topic Sentence (Part Two)**. Read and discuss the suggestions and examples for writing a good topic sentence. Then read and discuss the rules for completing the activity. Have students read their paragraphs aloud when completed.

ACTIVITIES 4-5 and 4-6 deal with writing a **concluding sentence**. Distribute **Activity 4-5 Writing a Concluding Sentence (Part One)**. Read and discuss the definition and purpose of a concluding sentence and the example. Read and discuss the directions for completing the activity. When done, have students read their concluding sentences aloud. Distribute **Activity 4-6 Writing a Concluding Sentence (Part Two)**. Read and discuss the restatement of topic and concluding sentences. Read and discuss the directions for completing the activity. When done, have students read their topic and concluding sentences aloud.

ACTIVITIES 4-7 and 4-8 help students **develop a topic**. Distribute **Activity 4-7 Developing the Topic (Part One)**. Read and discuss the description of a complete paragraph. Read and discuss the directions for indicating the parts of the paragraph, and have students compare their results. Then read and discuss the directions for writing the original paragraph. When this activity has been completed, collect the papers and read some of the paragraphs aloud, followed by a discussion of how successfully these paragraphs are developed. Distribute **Activity 4-8 Developing the Topic (Part Two)**. Read and discuss the directions for completing the paragraphs. Collect the papers and read several paragraphs aloud, followed by a discussion of how successfully the topics are introduced, developed, and concluded.

ACTIVITIES 4-9 and 4-10 are designed to help students **use tense consistently**. Distribute **Activity 4-9 Using Tense Consistently (Part One)**. Read the directions and example. Discuss where the change of tense takes place and why this is confusing. Read and discuss the directions for the next part of the activity and compare results. When the activity has been completed, collect the papers and read several samples aloud, followed by a discussion about the consistency of tense in each. Distribute **Activity 4-10 Using Tense Consistently (Part Two)**. Read the example and discuss why the change of tense is correct. Then read the directions for the rest of the activity. When the activity has been completed, have students share their results by reading their paragraphs aloud.

ACTIVITY 4-11 reviews using **pronouns consistently**. Distribute **Activity 4-11 Using Pronouns Consistently**. Read and discuss the rule and example. Then read the directions for completing the activity and discuss the students' results.

ACTIVITIES 4-12, 4-13, and 4-14 reinforce students' use of **transitional words and phrases**. Write the following sentences on the chalkboard: *I heard someone knocking and flew downstairs to open the door. It was stuck.* Elicit that the last part sounds choppy and awkward because there is no connection. Point out that the most beautifully expressed ideas in the world will not be convincing unless the reader can move easily from one thought to another. These thoughts need to be connected. Ask students how they could connect these sentences, and write appropriate suggestions on the chalkboard, such as:

I heard someone knocking and flew downstairs to open the door, but it was stuck.
I heard someone knocking and flew downstairs to open the door. Unfortunately, it was stuck.

Distribute **Activity 4-12 Using Transitional Words and Phrases (Part One).** Read the paragraph aloud twice. The first time, read it as written. The second time, read it with the transitional words and phrases omitted. Discuss how these words and phrases make the paragraph less choppy and easier to comprehend. After the students have listed the transitional words and phrases in the paragraph, ask the class to suggest additional ones that everyone can add to the list. Then read and discuss the directions for completing the activity. When done, have several students read their examples aloud and discuss. Distribute **Activity 4-13 Using Transitional Words and Phrases (Part Two)**. Discuss the organization of the transitional words and phrases, and ask for examples of how they can be used. Ask students if they can make any additions to the list. Then read and discuss the directions for completing the activity. When it has been completed, have several examples of each type read aloud. Distribute **Activity 4-14 Using Transitional Words and Phrases (Part Three)**. Read and discuss the list of the most common transitional words and phrases. Read and discuss the directions, and have students complete the activity. Have several samples of each completed paragraph read aloud.

ACTIVITIES 4-15 and 4-16 deal with **staying on the subject**. Distribute **Activity 4-15 Staying on the Subject (Part One)**. Read aloud the paragraph and discuss where it begins to change subject and why an abrupt change in focus is confusing. Read the directions and have students complete the activity. Distribute **Activity 4-16 Staying on the Subject (Part Two)**. Read aloud the paragraph and discuss where it changes focus and why this is confusing. Read the directions for completing the activity. When done, have the answers read aloud and discussed. Be sure students understand where the change of subject occurs and why it is incorrect.

ACTIVITY 4-17 helps students to **avoid irrelevant details**. Distribute **Activity 4-17 Avoiding Irrelevant Details**. Read aloud the paragraphs and ask students to identify the irrelevant details that take the reader's attention away from the subject. Compare the rewritten paragraph with the original and discuss why it is better. Then read and discuss the directions, and have students complete the activity.

ACTIVITIES 4-18 and 4-19 deal with using **variety in sentence length**. Distribute **Activity 4-18 Using Variety in Sentence Length (Part One)**. Read aloud the two paragraphs. Discuss why the second paragraph is preferable and why using only short sentences makes a paragraph awkward and choppy. Point out that a variety of sentences, short and long, helps make the writing more flowing and easier to read. Read and discuss the directions, and have students complete the activity. When done, collect the papers and read several examples aloud to discuss. Distribute **Activity 4-19 Using Variety in Sentence Length (Part Two)**. Read and discuss the directions and two paragraphs. Point out that a paragraph containing only long, involved sentences can be just as boring as one with short, choppy ones. Discuss why the revised paragraph holds the reader's interest better. Read and discuss the directions for completing the activity. When done, collect the papers and read a selection to be discussed, with special emphasis on variety in sentence length.

ACTIVITIES 4-20 and 4-21 deal with using **variety in sentence structure**. Write the following sentences on the chalkboard:

> *I went to the jazz concert with my uncle.*
> *There was a lot of traffic along the way, but we arrived in time for the opening act.*
> *Although our seats were far back, we were able to enjoy all the exciting performances.*

Elicit that the first sentence is a simple sentence and contains one independent clause. Elicit that the second sentence is a compound sentence containing more than one independent clause. Discuss the third sentence, which is a complex sentence containing one independent clause and one dependent clause. Point out that these three sentences can be combined to produce a paragraph that contains all three kinds of sentence structure. Distribute **Activity 4-20 Using Variety in Sentence Structure (Part One).** Read and discuss the definitions and examples. Then read the directions and have students complete the activity. Distribute **Activity 4-21 Using Variety in Sentence Structure (Part Two).** Read and discuss the definitions. Read and discuss the directions, and have students complete the activity. When done, have several examples read aloud.

ACTIVITY 4-22 deals with using **variety in sentence type.** Distribute **Activity 4-22 Using a Variety of Sentence Types.** Read and discuss the definitions and examples of sentence types. Then read and discuss the directions, and have students complete the activity. When done, have several examples read aloud.

ACTIVITIES 4-23, 4-24, and 4-25 involve students in **using the writing process.** First, review the parts of a paragraph and write them on the chalkboard as follows: *topic sentence, developing the topic, concluding sentence.* Discuss the purpose and structure of each part. Distribute **Activity 4-23 Using the Writing Process: Prewriting.** Discuss the directions for choosing a topic. Guide students through making the topic choice and writing a brief description. Read the next directions and discuss how this task will make the actual writing of the paragraph easier by providing a topic sentence, making a list to develop the topic, and deciding upon a concluding sentence. When completed, collect the papers and read several samples aloud. Lead a discussion about how well these responses prepare the writer, and how they might be improved. Return the papers, and ask students to make any changes or additions that seem necessary as a result of the discussion.

Distribute **Activity 4-24 Using the Writing Process: Writing the First Draft.** Read aloud and discuss the directions. Be sure students understand that this is just a first draft, not the final product. Encourage them to concentrate on getting their thoughts on paper without being too concerned about spelling or grammar. Distribute **Activity 4-25 Using the Writing Process: Revising and Writing the Final Copy.** Read and discuss all the suggestions for revising. Encourage students to make revisions on their draft copies. Discuss the advantages of using proofreading symbols and give each student a copy of page 360 containing proofreading symbols. Read the directions for completing the activity. Be sure students understand that this is their final copy.

Practice Test: Writing Paragraphs

Distribute the practice test. Explain that when they take tests, students should read and follow directions carefully. Read the directions together and make sure students understand what is required of them. Review the **writing process** by reading and discussing the four steps outlined in the directions. Also, read and discuss the **checklist for revising and editing the first draft.** Make a list of proofreading marks available and encourage students to use them wherever they may be helpful when revising.

The sample student responses can be helpful to the students in learning to recognize writing weaknesses and strengths, and applying this knowledge to their own writing. These can be read and discussed either before or after the test. The students should be encouraged to assign their own ratings from the scoring guide before being told the actual ratings that these responses received.

The sample student paragraphs A and B are rated a 2 and a 5, respectively. Although **paragraph A** begins with a clear topic sentence, the information that follows is not developed.

The response is too brief to offer any evidence of an organizational pattern. Limited vocabulary obscures meaning, as do frequent errors in basic punctuation. This paragraph is rated a 2. **Paragraph B** focuses on the topic with ample supporting examples and is logically structured and organized. The writing exhibits some variety in sentence structure and good, mature word choices. With rare exceptions, sentences are complete. With few exceptions, the paper follows the conventions of punctuation, capitalization, and spelling, and minor errors do not interfere with understanding. This paragraph is rated a 5.

ANSWER KEY

4–1. ORGANIZING A PARAGRAPH (PART ONE)

It is fun to spend a hot summer day at the seashore. The trip there would be uncomfortable if our car was not air-conditioned. When we arrive, we spread our blanket on the sand close to the ocean's edge. I spend most of the day in the water riding the waves. The hot dogs and soft drinks we buy on the boardwalk have a special flavor. We get home at the end of the day, tired, covered with sand, but happy.

4–2. ORGANIZING A PARAGRAPH (PART TWO)

Mike O'Hara was a passenger on the first voyage from Earth to Venus. NASA had decided to send one thirteen-year-old. They wanted to test the effect of space travel on adolescents. There was a nationwide search that lasted two months. Mike was chosen for his intelligence, character, and health. The trip made Mike famous, and his life was never the same again.

4–3. WRITING A TOPIC SENTENCE (PART ONE)

Part A.

The topic sentences to be circled are:

1. A famous American writer was born on November 30, 1835.
2. Almost everyone is familiar with *The Nutcracker.*
3. On December 16, 1773, an amazing event took place in the Massachusetts Colony.

Part B.

Topic sentences will vary. One possible answer is: It's easy to prepare scrambled eggs.

4–4. WRITING A TOPIC SENTENCE (PART TWO)

Paragraphs will vary.

4–5. WRITING A CONCLUDING SENTENCE (PART ONE)

Concluding sentences will vary. Some possible answers are:

1. The ball sailed over the fence and I was a hero.
2. It's not always easy to live up to these ideals, but I do my best.
3. It was a narrow escape, and Jason was shaky for days afterwards.

4–6. WRITING A CONCLUDING SENTENCE (PART TWO)

Sentences will vary. Some possible ones are:

Topic sentence—Mornings are always the same in a dull life like mine.

Concluding sentence—Then, it's off to school and another long day.

4–7. DEVELOPING THE TOPIC (PART ONE)

Part A.

Topic sentence to be underlined: Sunday is my favorite day of the week.

Development to be double underlined: I can sleep late on Sunday morning and I don't have to go to school. We have time for a big breakfast, and Mom usually makes her special pancakes that taste so delicious. The best thing about Sunday is that our whole family does things together. Sometimes, we just hang around the house reading the Sunday paper or playing board games. Occasionally, we go on a picnic or to the movies.

Concluding sentence to be circled: It would be great if every day could be Sunday.

Part B.

Paragraphs will vary.

4–8. Developing the Topic (part two)

Paragraphs will vary.

4–9. Using Tense Consistently (part one)

Part A.

This paragraph changes tense in the last sentence.

Part B.

1. He had a mean curve, too, when he wanted to use it.
2. Then she blows out her knee, and that's it for the rest of the season.

Part C.

Paragraphs will vary.

4–10. Using Tense Consistently (part two)

Part A.

1. His name is Jeff Reid and I admire him a lot.
2. Now, we have hurricane shutters so we will be prepared for the next hurricane.

(Paragraph #2 is correct and should be checked.)

Part B.

Paragraphs will vary.

4–11. Using Pronouns Consistently

The sentence to be underlined is: You will always have a good time at a drama club production.

The revised paragraphs will vary. One possibility is:

Jackie and I enjoy ourselves immensely whenever we attend a performance by the school drama club. We like to watch kids we know in their different roles as actors. Everyone in the audience always has a good time at a drama club production.

4–12. Using Transitional Words and Phrases (part one)

Part A.

The transitional words and phrases that appear in the paragraph are: however, in fact, moreover, on the other hand. *The rest of the list will vary.*

Part B.

Paragraphs will vary. One possibility is:

There are several reasons why the Parker Hotel is considered the best hotel in town. First of all, it is the newest, and all its rooms are large and modern. Also, the staff has been trained to be polite and helpful to guests. Furthermore, there is an excellent restaurant on the lobby floor.

4–13. Using Transitional Words and Phrases (part two)

Sentences will vary.

4–14. Using Transitional Words and Phrases (part three)

Answers will vary. Some possible transitional words and phrases for filling in the blank spaces are:

1. First of all, Also, Furthermore, In fact
2. First of all, After all, Also, For example, However

4–15. Staying on the Subject (part one)

Part A.

Once I was in a swim meet together with my friend, Jim.

Part B.

Paragraphs will vary. The sentence that should be crossed out is: Thomas Jefferson's home in Virginia is called Monticello and you can still see it today just as it was when he lived there.

4–16. Staying on the Subject (part two)

Part A.

The paragraph should be copied without the sentence discussed as changing the subject.

Part B.

Sentences that do not relate to the topic and should be underlined are:

1. My favorite kind of candy is chocolate, but Billy likes caramel.
2. I found two books in his room and read them both. I like science fiction stories about spaceships and aliens.

4–17. Avoiding Irrelevant Details

The irrelevant sentences to be crossed out are:

My friend Chuck thinks we won four games, but he doesn't know what he is talking about.

Mark has brown hair and blue eyes and lives around the corner from me.

Mr. Jensen, who owns the pizza shop, installed that fence for the league.

4–18. Using Variety in Sentence Length (part one)

Paragraphs will vary.

4–19. Using Variety in Sentence Length (part two)

Paragraphs will vary.

4–20. Using Variety in Sentence Structure (part one)

1. simple
2. compound
3. complex
4. simple

4–21. Using Variety in Sentence Structure (part two)

Paragraphs will vary.

4–22. Using a Variety of Sentence Types
Paragraphs will vary.

4–23. Using the Writing Process: Prewriting
Brainstorming lists will vary.

4–24. Using the Writing Process: Writing the First Draft
First drafts will vary.

4–25. Using the Writing Process: Revising and Writing the Final Copy
Revisions and final copies will vary.

Name ______________________________ Date ______________

4–1. ORGANIZING A PARAGRAPH (PART ONE)

A paragraph is like a very short story. It has a beginning, middle, and end.

- The **beginning sentence** introduces the story and is called the **topic sentence.**
- The **middle sentences** tell the story in logical order.
- The **last sentence** brings the story to an end and is called the **concluding sentence.**

DIRECTIONS: The six sentences below can be combined into one paragraph, but they are not in the correct order. Unscramble these sentences and copy them, in the correct order, into a paragraph. The topic sentence should come first, the concluding sentence last, and the other four sentences in a logical order between them.

1. **The trip there would be uncomfortable if our car was not air-conditioned.**
2. **It is fun to spend a hot summer day at the seashore.**
3. **I spend most of the day in the water riding the waves.**
4. **When we arrive, we spread our blanket on the sand close to the ocean's edge.**
5. **We get home at the end of the day, tired, covered with sand, but happy.**
6. **The hot dogs and soft drinks we buy on the boardwalk have a special flavor.**

____

____

____

____

____

____

____

____

(Continue on the back of this sheet, if necessary.)

Name ______________________________ Date ______________

4–2. ORGANIZING A PARAGRAPH (PART TWO)

DIRECTIONS: The following six sentences are in the wrong order. Unscramble them and copy them, in the correct order, into a paragraph. The topic sentence should come first, the concluding sentence last, and the other four sentences in logical order between them.

1. **Mike was chosen for his intelligence, character, and health.**
2. **Mike O'Hara was a passenger on the first voyage from Earth to Venus.**
3. **The trip made Mike famous, and his life was never the same again.**
4. **They wanted to test the effect of space travel on adolescents.**
5. **There was a nationwide search that lasted two months.**
6. **NASA had decided to send one thirteen-year-old.**

(Continue on the back of this sheet, if necessary.)

Name ______________________________________ Date ________________

4–3. WRITING A TOPIC SENTENCE (PART ONE)

A topic sentence tells what the paragraph is about. It is usually the first sentence of a paragraph.

A. DIRECTIONS: In the following paragraphs, the topic sentence is in the middle of the paragraph. Find the topic sentence and circle it.

1. His name was Samuel Clemens. Never heard of him? That's because he is better known by his pen name—Mark Twain. He wrote many stories and books. A famous American writer was born on November 30, 1835. Some of his best-known works are *The Prince and the Pauper, The Adventures of Huckleberry Finn,* and *Tom Sawyer.* Mark Twain is considered by many people to be one of the greatest writers of all time.
2. This ballet is performed all over the world in big cities and small towns. Did you know that the music was written by Peter Ilyitch Tchaikovsky? He was born May 7, 1840 in Russia. He was a shy person who expressed his feelings with music. Although he became famous, he did not have a happy life. Almost everyone is familiar with *The Nutcracker.* However, he produced some of the most beautiful and popular music ever written, including the music for the best-known ballet of all time.
3. Workmen and merchants, dressed in Native American clothing, boarded a ship bringing tea into Boston Harbor, and dumped the tea overboard. They did not believe they should have to pay taxes imposed on them by the English King. On December 16, 1773, an amazing event took place in the Massachusetts Colony. The American colonists liked tea, but they valued their freedom more.

B. DIRECTIONS: Insert a topic sentence at the beginning of this paragraph.

____

____

First, crack four eggs and put them into a bowl. Stir until mixed. Heat butter in a skillet and add the eggs. Stir while cooking until the eggs are firm. Spoon onto a plate and enjoy.

Name ______________________________ **Date** ______________

4–4. Writing a Topic Sentence (part two)

A topic sentence should do two things:

1. It should introduce the subject.
2. It should get the reader's attention in an interesting way.

A good topic sentence can be either:

- Declarative (*Our class trip provided some unusual adventures.*)
- Exclamatory *(You won't believe what happened on our class trip!)*
- Interrogative (*Have you ever gone on a class trip that was exciting and dangerous?)*

DIRECTIONS: Choose one of the following topic sentences to use in writing a paragraph, and put a checkmark next to it.

❑ I'll never forget that day!
❑ What do you look for in a friend?
❑ I really like my math class this year.

Write a paragraph that begins with the topic sentence you have chosen. You should have *at least four* additional sentences.

____

____

____

____

____

____

____

____

____

(Continue on the back of this sheet, if necessary.)

Name ______________________ Date ____________

4–5. Writing a Concluding Sentence (part one)

The concluding (last) sentence ends a paragraph by concluding or summing up the topic, and bringing it to a satisfying end, as in the following example:

> **A paragraph is like a brief story. It has a beginning, a middle, and an end. The beginning (topic sentence) introduces the story. The middle develops the story. The last sentence brings the tale to an end. This concluding sentence tells the reader, "It's over now!"**

DIRECTIONS: Add a concluding sentence to each of the following paragraphs.

1. There I was at the plate. It was my first time at bat on my new team. I was nervous. I felt that I had to prove myself to my new teammates. I watched the pitcher carefully. He wound up and threw the ball. It looked good, so I swung. To my surprise, I connected hard.

   ____

   ____

   ____

2. My mother gave me three guidelines for living well. The first one is to follow the Golden Rule and treat other people the way I want to be treated myself. Next, she said that I must try to discover my own, unique talents and work hard to excel at them. She also told me to always be true to myself.

   ____

   ____

   ____

3. Jason had a scary experience last week. He was on his way home from school when a passing car suddenly went out of control. It careened up onto the sidewalk. Jason had to leap out of the way. The car came within inches of hitting Jason.

   ____

   ____

   ____

Name ______________________________ Date ______________

4–6. WRITING A CONCLUDING SENTENCE (PART TWO)

The **topic sentence** of a paragraph introduces the subject. The **concluding sentence** brings the paragraph to a satisfying end.

DIRECTIONS: Read this paragraph.

> **My alarm clock goes off at 6 A.M. Then I usually stay in bed until I hear my mom yelling at me to get up. I drag myself out of bed, go to the bathroom, and brush my teeth. I try to get in there before my sister because once she's in there, she never gets out. I take a shower and get dressed. Then I go into the kitchen and have my usual breakfast of cereal, toast, and milk.**

Write a topic sentence for the above paragraph.

____

____

____

____

____

____

Write a concluding sentence for the above paragraph.

____

____

____

____

____

____

Name ______________________________ Date ______________

4–7. Developing the Topic (Part One)

A paragraph begins with a topic sentence that introduces the subject. The story or idea must then be developed with sentences that provide details about the subject in a logical way. The concluding sentence then brings the paragraph topic to a satisfying conclusion.

A. DIRECTIONS: In the paragraph below, draw a single line under the topic sentence. Then draw a double line under the middle sentences that develop the subject. Finally, circle the concluding sentence.

> **Sunday is my favorite day of the week. I can sleep late on Sunday morning and I don't have to go to school. We have time for a big breakfast, and Mom usually makes her special pancakes that taste so delicious. The best thing about Sunday is that our whole family does things together. Sometimes, we just hang around the house reading the Sunday paper or playing board games. Occasionally we go on a picnic or to the movies. It would be great if every day could be Sunday.**

B. DIRECTIONS: Now, you are going to write a paragraph about your favorite day of the week and why it is special to you. Write the topic sentence first. Then develop the topic with at least four middle sentences. Write a concluding sentence to sum up your ideas. Write your paragraph on the lines below.

____

____

____

____

____

____

____

(Continue on the back of this sheet, if necessary.)

Name ______________________________ Date ______________

4–8. DEVELOPING THE TOPIC (PART TWO)

DIRECTIONS: Each of the following sentences is the topic sentence of a paragraph. Complete each paragraph by developing the topic (with at least three sentences) and then adding a concluding sentence.

There are good and bad things about being a teenager. ______________________

Yesterday, Anita got into an argument with her parents about her allowance.

Name ______________________________ Date ______________

4–9. Using Tense Consistently (Part One)

It is confusing when a writer switches tense in the middle of a paragraph for no good reason, as in this example:

> ***The Mystery of the Sand Creatures*** **is about a young girl who is spending her winter vacation with her aunt at a beach house in Florida. It is a scary story. The girl has nightmares about horrible, ugly monsters. Then these same monsters suddenly appear on her beach in the form of sand sculptures. More exciting, frightening things happened until the mystery is solved.**

A. DIRECTIONS: This paragraph is written in present tense. Where does it suddenly change tense?

____

B. DIRECTIONS: Each paragraph below suddenly switches tense in the middle. Underline the sentence where this incorrect change begins.

> **1. My friend, Matt, is the best pitcher on the team. He is just a natural! When he throws the ball, it zooms through the air at the speed of light! He had a mean curve, too, when he wanted to use it.**

> **2. Laurie was our best pitcher last year. She kept demolishing the batters that came up against her. Then she blows out her knee, and that's it for the rest of the season.**

C. DIRECTIONS: On the lines below, write an original paragraph about an experience (real or imaginary) involving a game or sport. Be sure to keep the tense consistent.

____

____

____

____

____

____

(Continue on the back of this sheet, if necessary.)

Name ______________________________ Date ______________

4–10. Using Tense Consistently (part two)

It is confusing when a writer switches tense in the middle of a paragraph for no good reason. Sometimes, however, there is a good reason to change, as in the following example:

> **Jonathan hangs out with his friend, Alonso, every day after school. They ride their bikes, listen to tapes, or do their homework together. Last February, Alonso was in bed with the flu for a whole week. Jonathan spent the afternoons alone. He missed his friend a lot that week.**

The first two sentences are in the present tense. Then it changes to the past because it describes an event that happened in the past. This is a correct change of tense.

A. DIRECTIONS: Both paragraphs below switch tense in the middle. Underline the sentence that switches tense. Then put a checkmark next to the paragraph that switches tense correctly.

> **❑ 1. I really liked the main character in the last book I read. He was a kid around my age with a lot of problems. His name is Jeff Reid and I admire him a lot.**

> **❑ 2. Last month, a hurricane passed through our town. Trees were knocked down and roofs blown off houses. It was scary to hear the wind and rain pounding against our windows. We were lucky they didn't break. Now, we have hurricane shutters so we will be prepared for the next hurricane.**

Name ______________________________ Date ______________

4–10. Using Tense Consistently (Part Two) *(continued)*

B. DIRECTIONS: Finish the paragraph below. Add at least three more sentences. Be sure you do not change tense in the middle unless there is a good reason to do so.

I like to listen to many kinds of music. ______________________________

____

____

____

____

____

____

____

____

____

____

____

Name ______________________________ Date ______________

4–11. Using Pronouns Consistently

If you begin a paragraph by referring to certain pronouns (*you, we, I,* or *one*), you must try to remain consistently within the same case and not change it, unless for a good reason. Can you find the error in the following paragraph where the pronoun changes?

> **I enjoyed reading *Sparkles in the Sky.* The main character was realistic and interesting at first, and I was able to see the world through her eyes. About halfway along, however, you could see that the story was false. It was no longer believable. That spoiled the book for me.**

In the third sentence, the pronoun suddenly changed from *I* to *you* for no good reason. This sentence should be changed as follows:

About halfway along, however, it was clear that the story was false. (**OR**)
About halfway along, however, I could see that the story was false.

DIRECTIONS: Pronouns are used inconsistently in the following paragraph. Underline the sentence (or sentences) where this occurs. Then rewrite the paragraph correctly on the lines below.

> **Jackie and I enjoy ourselves immensely whenever we attend a performance by the school drama club. We like to watch kids we know in their different roles as actors. You will always have a good time at a drama club production.**

____

____

____

____

____

____

(Continue on the back of this sheet, if necessary.)

Name ______________________________ Date ______________

4–12. Using Transitional Words and Phrases (Part One)

A. DIRECTIONS: Read the following paragraph *twice.* The first time, read it just as it is written. The second time you read it, omit the words that are underlined.

> **Mrs. Halsey seems strict and stern at first. <u>However,</u> once you have been in her class for a while, you will see that she is not like that at all. <u>In fact,</u> she is just the opposite. She is kind and understanding. <u>Moreover,</u> she is always ready to provide help. <u>On the other hand,</u> she does demand that her students always do their best.**

Note how smooth and clear this paragraph reads with the transitional words and phrases, and how choppy it seems without them.

List below the transitional words and phrases that appear in the above paragraph. Then add at least five more of your own.

________________ ________________ ________________

________________ ________________ ________________

________________ ________________ ________________

B. DIRECTIONS: Rewrite the following paragraph, adding transitional words and phrases to make it smoother and clearer.

> **There are several reasons why the Parker Hotel is considered the best hotel in town. It is the newest, and all its rooms are large and modern. The staff has been trained to be polite and helpful to guests. There is an excellent restaurant on the lobby floor.**

____

____

____

____

____

____

(Continue on the back of this sheet, if necessary.)

Name ______________________________ Date ______________

4–13. Using Transitional Words and Phrases (Part Two)

Here is a chart of common transitional words and phrases. They are grouped according to the purpose they best serve in a paragraph.

ADDITION: **again, also, and, and then, besides, finally, first, furthermore, in addition, in the first place, last, moreover, next, still, too**

COMPARISON: **also, in the same way, likewise**

CONTRAST: **although, at the same time, despite that, even though, however, in spite of, instead, nevertheless, on the other hand, still, though, yet**

EMPHASIS: **certainly, indeed, in fact, of course**

EXAMPLE: **after all, even, for example, for instance, indeed, in fact, in other words, of course, namely, that is, truly**

SUMMARY: **all in all, altogether, finally, in conclusion, in other words, on the whole, that is, therefore, to summarize**

TIME: **after a while, afterward, again, also, and then, as long as, at last, at that time, before, besides, finally, furthermore, in the first place, last, lately, meanwhile, moreover, next, now, shortly, since, so far, soon, still, then, too, until, until now, when**

DIRECTIONS: Write a sentence using an example of a transitional word or phrase from each of the seven categories above.

1. ______________________________

2. ______________________________

3. ______________________________

4. ______________________________

5. ______________________________

6. ______________________________

7. ______________________________

Name ______________________________ Date ______________

4–14. Using Transitional Words and Phrases (Part Three)

Here is a short list of common transitional words and phrases:

at that time	besides	finally	furthermore
soon	therefore	however	afterward
first of all	moreover	for example	nevertheless
also	now	of course	in fact
naturally	in spite of	still	on the other hand
after all	for instance	lately	at last
meanwhile	next		

DIRECTIONS: Fill in the blank spaces in the following paragraphs with transitional words or phrases.

1. There are many reasons why a computer is an excellent investment for a student. ______________, it is a great aid for doing homework. ______________, you can do research for your reports on the web. ______________, it really helps if your handwriting is bad. ______________, a computer can be a big help to any student.

2. I think it is a terrible idea to do away with week-long school vacations. ______________, a break from school is good for everyone, including teachers and students. ______________, the human brain needs time to assimilate the information it has received and get ready to learn more. It is good for the economy, ______________. ______________, hotels and airlines need these special weeks in order to make a profit. Some people can just keep on working forever. ______________, most of us need regular vacations.

Name ______________________________ Date ______________

4–15. Staying on the Subject (Part One)

A. DIRECTIONS: The following paragraph changes subjects in the middle. This is confusing to the reader. Underline the sentence where the subject suddenly changes from the one stated in the topic sentence.

> **Bicycling is my favorite sport. I like it because of the way it makes me feel. When I'm racing down the street, pumping the pedals, I get a rush of pleasure and forget all my troubles. It is also fun because the only person I have to compete against is myself. Once I was in a swim meet together with my friend, Jim.**

This sudden change of focus is disturbing and confusing to the reader because it takes attention away from the subject of bicycling.

B. DIRECTIONS: The following paragraph changes subjects in the middle. Cross out the sentence that does not relate to the topic. Then rewrite and complete the paragraph on the lines below. Be sure you stick to the topic.

> **The Fourth of July is an important holiday. It celebrates the birth of the United States of America. On July 4, 1776, the Continental Congress issued the Declaration of Independence, written by Thomas Jefferson. Thomas Jefferson's home in Virginia is called Monticello and you can still see it today just as it was when he lived there.**

____

____

____

____

____

____

____

(Continue on the back of this sheet, if necessary.)

Name ______________________________ Date ______________

4–16. Staying on the Subject (Part Two)

A. DIRECTIONS: Read the following paragraph. It is confusing because it changes subjects in the middle.

> **I saw the most amazing sight yesterday. I was looking out my bedroom window. Suddenly a bird flew into the big oak tree that stands near the house. I never saw such a bird before! It had a black beak and a bright orange body. My mom once had an orange dress that she liked a lot, even though everyone else thought it looked ridiculous.**

This paragraph loses its focus with the sentence beginning *My mom once had an orange dress. . . .* Cross out that sentence. Then copy the paragraph below *without that sentence* and complete it. Be sure to stick to the subject that is stated in the topic sentence. (Continue your paragraph on the back of this sheet.)

____

____

____

____

____

____

____

B. DIRECTIONS: The following paragraphs change subjects in the middle. Underline the sentences that do not relate to the topic.

> **1. I don't usually respond to dares, but yesterday was an exception. Billy Carras dared me to ring old Mrs. Trulove's doorbell and offer to sell her a box of candy. Everyone says that Ms. Trulove is mean. I don't believe that and, besides, our school's annual candy sale is for a good cause. My favorite kind of candy is chocolate, but Billy likes caramel.**
>
> **2. My brother Rob is the person I admire most in the world. I wish I could be like him because he is brave, honest, and kind. He is six years older than I am and is in the U.S. Air Force. He is stationed overseas and I miss him a lot. I found two books in his room and read them both. I like science fiction stories about spaceships and aliens.**

Name ______________________________ Date ______________

4–17. Avoiding Irrelevant Details

The topic sentence in a paragraph tells what the paragraph is about. The rest of the paragraph should develop from this topic. Sometimes, the writer includes a lot of irrelevant (unnecessary) details that shift the focus away from the subject, as in this example:

> **Last month, I got the biggest surprise of my life. I won first prize in a district essay contest. Not every school district has an essay contest, but ours does. The title of my essay was, "The Best Summer of My Life." I wrote it last August when my family spent a month at the shore. I like the shore, but my brother prefers to travel, and we argue about that. My brother is very argumentative. My prize was twenty-five dollars and a brass plaque.**

This paragraph is about winning an essay contest, but it contains a few sentences that are irrelevant. These sentences are:

Not every school district has an essay contest, but ours does.

I like the shore, but my brother prefers to travel, and we argue about that.

My brother is very argumentative.

See how much more effective the paragraph is without these sentences.

> **Last month, I got the biggest surprise of my life. I won first prize in a district essay contest. The title of my essay was "The Best Summer of My Life." I wrote it last August when my family spent a month at the shore. My prize was twenty-five dollars and a brass plaque.**

DIRECTIONS: In the following paragraph, cross out any sentences that are not relevant.

> **Nobody thought our team had a chance of winning the last game of the season. We were playing the Bulldozers who had a record of ten wins and no losses. Our team had a dismal record of three wins and seven losses. My friend Chuck thinks we won four games, but he doesn't know what he is talking about. By some miracle, we managed to tie the game in the last inning. Mark Malone came up to bat. Mark has brown hair and blue eyes and lives around the corner from me. We all held our breath. Mark swung and slammed the ball over the fence for a home run. Mr. Jensen, who owns the pizza shop, installed that fence for the league. I'll never forget that game and how we won it against all odds.**

Name ______________________________ Date ______________

4–18. USING VARIETY IN SENTENCE LENGTH (PART ONE)

There is nothing wrong with short sentences. They can be clear and snappy and easy to read. All short sentences in a paragraph, however, can make the paragraph seem awkward and choppy. Read the following paragraphs aloud to get a better feeling of the way they flow.

CHOPPY: **Personal computers are good. All kids should have their own. They are useful for homework. They are good for research. They have e-mail, too. There are many good computer games. Computers are useful. They are fun.**

BETTER: **All kids should have their own personal computers. They are useful for homework and research. They have e-mail, too. There are many good computer games. Computers are useful and fun.**

There is no variety in the first paragraph. *All* the sentences are short, which makes it choppy and boring. The second paragraph keeps some of these short sentences, but combines others. Now there are both short and long sentences. The story flows, with no choppiness.

DIRECTIONS: The sentences in the following paragraph are too short and choppy. Rewrite the paragraph. Combine and rearrange some of the sentences so that there is a variety of short and long sentences.

I admire my dad. He is the person I admire most. He is as strong as a wrestler. He can open stuck windows. He can move heavy furniture. He is gentle, too. He gives our dog, Ruff, a bath. Ruff loves his gentle touch. Dad is honest. He tells the truth. He always helps others. That's why I admire him.

____

____

____

____

____

(Continue on the back of this sheet, if necessary.)

Name ______________________________ Date ______________

4–19. Using Variety in Sentence Length (Part Two)

Long sentences are fine. However, if every sentence in a paragraph consists of lengthy, complicated sentences, the writing can be unclear and dull, as in this example.

> **This is an example of a paragraph that contains only long sentences, with no short ones as well. As you can see, all these long sentences one after the other make the paragraph difficult to read as well as boring. A sentence that goes on and on for a long time with no variety in length can be difficult for the reader to follow and comprehend. In almost all cases, a paragraph will be improved by alternating long sentences with shorter ones.**

This paragraph sounds much better when short sentences are inserted to provide variety, as in this example:

> **As you can see, this is an example of a paragraph that contains a variety of sentence lengths. Some sentences, such as the beginning sentence and this one, are quite long. Others are short. This provides a pleasant contrast for the reader. Both long and short sentences are used. This kind of paragraph reads easily.**

DIRECTIONS: Here is another paragraph that contains too many long, stretched-out sentences. Rewrite the paragraph on the back of this page. Break up some of the long sentences into short ones to achieve variety.

> **Some people in my family don't understand why I sometimes prefer to be alone. My three brothers and my parents are different from me and always like to be part of a group. I enjoy being with people, too, but I don't want to be with them all the time. Sometimes, I need to be alone because that is when I can read or listen to music in privacy, which helps me get in touch with my inner self. I wish my family could realize that I can love them a lot and still want to have private time.**

Name ______________________________ **Date** ______________

4–20. Using Variety in Sentence Structure (Part One)

A paragraph can be improved by using a variety of the following sentence structures:

- A **simple sentence** contains one independent clause. **Example:** *I went to the jazz concert with my uncle.*
- A **compound sentence** contains more than one independent clause. **Example:** *There was a lot of traffic along the way, but we arrived in time to see the opening act.*
- A **complex sentence** contains one independent clause and at least one dependent clause. **Example:** *Although our seats were far back, we were able to enjoy all the exciting performances.*

These sentences can be combined into a paragraph that contains all three types of sentences, as follows:

> **I went to the jazz concert with my uncle. There was a lot of traffic along the way, but we arrived in time to see the opening act. Although our seats were far back, we were able to enjoy all the exciting performances.**

DIRECTIONS: Here are four sentences that can be combined into a paragraph. Circle the correct word, indicating whether each is a simple, compound, or complex sentence.

1. Thomas Jefferson was a great American leader.
   (Simple, Compound, Complex)

2. He was the third president of the United States, and he also founded the University of Virginia.
   (Simple, Compound, Complex)

3. Even if he had done nothing else, he will always be remembered for writing the Declaration of Independence.
   (Simple, Compound, Complex)

4. Our country is lucky to have had a leader like Thomas Jefferson.
   (Simple, Compound, Complex)

Name ______________________________ Date ______________

4–21. USING VARIETY IN SENTENCE STRUCTURE (PART TWO)

A paragraph can be improved by using a variety of sentence structures.

- **A simple sentence has one independent clause.**
- **A compound sentence has more than one independent clause.**
- **A complex sentence has one independent clause and at least one dependent clause.**

DIRECTIONS: Write a paragraph that contains all three kinds of sentence structure: simple, compound, and complex. Choose one of the following topic sentences (and place a checkmark next to it).

- ❑ My career choice is to work with computers.
- ❑ Our team won an important game recently.
- ❑ I have a new best friend.
- ❑ My mom has an interesting job.
- ❑ I saw a good movie.
- ❑ Halloween is my favorite holiday.

Copy the topic sentence you have chosen on the lines below. Then write a paragraph developing that topic. Your paragraph should:

- Have at least four sentences.
- Include at least one simple sentence, one compound sentence, and one complex sentence.
- Include a variety of long and short sentences.

____

____

____

____

____

____

____

____

(Continue on the back of this sheet, if necessary.)

Name ______________________________ Date ______________

4–22. Using a Variety of Sentence Types

Make your paragraphs more interesting and fun to read with different types of sentences.

1. Most sentences are **declarative** sentences. They make a statement, such as: *I am going to play in the game today.*
2. Some sentences ask questions. These are **interrogative** sentences and can be especially useful at the beginning of a paragraph to create interest, as in: *Is anyone going to play in the game today?*
3. **Exclamatory** sentences make an exclamation or command, and can grab the reader's interest, as in: *You must play today!*

DIRECTIONS: Rewrite the following paragraph on the lines below. Make it more interesting by changing some of the declarative sentences to interrogative or exclamatory ones.

Every kid should be given an allowance. It is important that young people learn how to manage cash. How much they get depends on several things. Age is one consideration since older kids usually need more money. Family income is important, too. Obviously, rich parents can afford to give bigger allowances. Parents should also look at how responsible their kid is with money, but every kid deserves an allowance, no matter how small.

____

____

____

____

____

____

____

(Continue on the back of this sheet, if necessary.)

Name ______________________________ **Date** ____________

4–23. USING THE WRITING PROCESS: PREWRITING

A. DIRECTIONS: You are going to write a paragraph describing a person or thing. Here are some suggestions:

- ❑ Someone in your family
- ❑ A friend
- ❑ A TV personality or film star
- ❑ A neighbor
- ❑ A pet
- ❑ Your most treasured possession
- ❑ Other (____________________)

Check one of the above choices. If you checked "Other," write what or who it is.

B. DIRECTIONS: It will be easy to write this paragraph if you first complete this **brainstorming list**.

1. In the left-hand column, list all the words and phrases you can think of that describe this person or thing. Include *sensory words* and at least one *simile.*
2. In the right-hand column, list all the words and phrases you can think of that describe your feelings about this person or thing.

BRAINSTORMING LIST	
Description of Person or Thing	**Your Feelings**

C. DIRECTIONS: On the back of this sheet, write a topic sentence for the beginning of your paragraph and a concluding sentence for the end of your paragraph.

Name ______________________________ Date ______________

4–24. Using the Writing Process: Writing the First Draft

DIRECTIONS: Write the first draft of a paragraph describing a person or thing.

1. **Copy the topic sentence from your brainstorming list.**
2. **Develop the topic by describing what the person or thing looks like. Use the descriptive words and phrases on your brainstorming list.**
3. **Develop the topic further by describing your feelings about this person or thing. Use words and phrases from your brainstorming list.**
4. **Copy the concluding sentence from your brainstorming list.**

Write your paragraph below. This is just a **first draft**, so don't be concerned about spelling or grammar. Concentrate on getting your thoughts on paper.

____

____

____

____

____

____

____

____

____

____

____

____

____

(Continue on the back of this sheet, if necessary.)

Name ______________________________ Date ______________

4–25. Using the Writing Process: Revising and Writing the Final Copy

A. DIRECTIONS: Correct and revise the first draft of your paragraph. Make the corrections directly on your draft copy. Use proofreading marks wherever they would be helpful.

1. **Does your topic sentence state the subject? Can you make it more interesting?**
2. **Do you develop the topic in a logical order in the sentences that follow?**
3. **Does your paragraph stay on the topic? Take out anything that does not relate to the subject.**
4. **Can you add *colorful adjectives* and *sensory words* to make the description more vivid?**
5. **Does your description contain at least one *simile?* If not, add one.**
6. **Does your concluding sentence sum up the topic?**
7. **Are your sentences complete? Do subjects and verbs agree?**
8. **Is your spelling correct? If you are not sure, consult a dictionary.**

B. DIRECTIONS: When your paragraph is as good as you can make it, write the final copy below. Indent at the beginning of the paragraph.

____

____

____

____

____

____

____

____

____

(Continue on the back of this sheet, if necessary.)

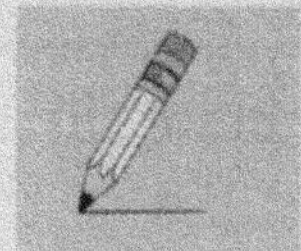

EIGHTH-GRADE LEVEL

WRITING PARAGRAPHS PRACTICE TEST

Name ______________________________ Date ______________

PRACTICE TEST: WRITING PARAGRAPHS

DIRECTIONS: Think about one thing that is important to you and why. It could be something you found, made, or had given to you. Write a paragraph of at least six sentences describing this item and why it is important to you.

Follow these four steps to write your paragraph:

- FIRST, on the page labeled PREWRITING, brainstorm ideas for your paragraph, as follows:
  a. Make a list of words and phrases that describe this item.
  b. Make a list of words and phrases that explain its importance to you.
  c. Write a topic sentence.
  d. If you wish, also write a concluding sentence.
- SECOND, on a separate sheet of paper, write the first draft of your paragraph. Be sure to use the middle portion of the paragraph to develop the topic.
- THIRD, revise and edit your first draft, using the checklist. You may wish to refer to your list of proofreading symbols.
- FOURTH, write the final copy of your paragraph on a separate sheet of paper.

CHECKLIST

- ❑ Does your topic sentence introduce the subject? Can you make it more interesting with a question or exclamation?
- ❑ Are your sentences arranged logically?
- ❑ Does your concluding sentence sum up the topic?
- ❑ Do you stay on the subject throughout the paragraph? Are there any irrelevant details that should be cut?
- ❑ Are there any run-on sentences or sentence fragments? If so, correct them.
- ❑ Do all your subjects and verbs agree?
- ❑ Have you used punctuation marks and capitals correctly?
- ❑ Are all words spelled correctly? Use a dictionary if necessary.

Name ______________________________ Date ______________

PRACTICE TEST: WRITING PARAGRAPHS *(continued)*

Prewriting

DIRECTIONS: Brainstorm ideas for your paragraph on the lines below. You may do this in any way that works for you. One good idea is to write a list of words and phrases that describe the item, and then write a list of words and phrases that explain its importance.

BRAINSTORMING LIST

Write your topic sentence here. ______________________________

____

Write your concluding sentence here. ______________________________

____

Name ______________________________ Date ______________

PRACTICE TEST: WRITING PARAGRAPHS *(continued)*

Student Samples

DIRECTIONS: Rate the paragraphs with a score from 1 (lowest) to 6 (highest). Use the information on the scoring guide to help you.

PARAGRAPH A

I just moved to Florida. The house is big and it is in the suburbs I have a big room with a hot tub a movie screen and much much more and that is all I have to say.

Score ______________

PARAGRAPH B

I just started to move to a new house in Ohio. At my new house, my bedroom will be big and cozy. It will have lots of room and a big closet. I will hang posters on the walls of many different things. There will be cars, airplanes, and famous athletes like Michael "Air" Jordan. There will be a king sized waterbed for me, a kingsize kid. My carpet will be dark blue so it's harder to tell if it's dirty. There is going to be a lamp on my bed so I can read at night without having to get out of bed. Mom and dad said when we get settled in, I can invite a friend for the weekend.

Score ______________

Scoring Guide

SCORE	Unsatisfactory—1	Insufficient—2
Content	Attempts to respond to prompt, but provides little or no clear information; may only paraphrase the prompt	Presents fragmented information OR may be very repetitive OR may be very undeveloped
Organization	Has no clear organization OR consists of a single statement	Is very disorganized; ideas are weakly connected OR the response is too brief to detect organization
Sentence Structure	Little or no control over sentence boundaries and sentence structure; word choice may be incorrect in much or all of the response	Little control over sentence boundaries and sentence structure; word choice may often be correct
Grammar, Usage, and Mechanics	Many errors in grammar or usage—such as tense inconsistency, lack of subject–verb agreement—spelling, and punctuation severely interfere with understanding	Errors in grammar or usage—such as tense inconsistency, lack of subject–verb agreement—spelling, and punctuation interfere with understanding in much of the response

SCORE	Uneven—3	Sufficient—4
Content	Presents some clear information, but is list-like, undeveloped, or repetitive OR offers no more than a well-written beginning	Develops information with some details
Organization	Is unevenly organized; the paragraph may be disjointed	The paragraph is organized with ideas that are generally related but has few or no transitions
Sentence Structure	Exhibits uneven control over sentence boundaries and sentence structure; may have some incorrect word choices	Exhibits control over sentence boundaries and sentence structure, but sentences and word choice may be simple and unvaried
Grammar, Usage, and Mechanics	Errors in grammar or usage—such as tense inconsistency, lack of subject–verb agreement—spelling, and punctuation sometimes interfere with understanding	Errors in grammar or usage—such as tense inconsistency, lack of subject–verb agreement—spelling, and punctuation do not interfere with understanding

PRACTICE TEST: WRITING PARAGRAPHS *(continued)*

Scoring Guide

SCORE	Skillful—5	Excellent—6
Content	Develops and shapes information with details in parts of the paragraph	Develops and shapes information with well-chosen details across the paragraph
Organization	Is clearly organized, but may lack some transitions and/or have lapses in continuity	Is well organized with strong transitions
Sentence Structure	Exhibits some variety in sentence structure and some good word choices	Sustains variety in sentence structure and exhibits good word choice
Grammar, Usage, and Mechanics	Errors in grammar, spelling, and punctuation do not interfere with understanding	Errors in grammar, spelling, and punctuation are few and do not interfere with understanding

SECTION 5

ESSAY-WRITING TECHNIQUES

Standardized Testing Information

Essay writing is the heart and basic structure of standardized writing tests. In almost all cases, students are evaluated on their abilities to state a theme and develop it in a clear and logical fashion, leading toward a satisfactory conclusion. Three types of essays are required: **expository/informational, narrative/imaginative,** and **persuasive.** Some tests require students to write samples of each of these; other tests ask for only one.

Most standardized tests encourage the students to use the following steps in the writing process: **prewriting** (outlining, brainstorming, clustering), writing a **first draft**, making **revisions**, and writing a **final copy.** Pennsylvania, for example, assigns two 40-minute sessions over two days for the writing test. During Session 1, the student is instructed to "think about what you want to say, make notes, and write a draft of your paper." During Session 2, the student is directed to "read the prompt, read your draft, make any changes in your draft you feel are necessary, and when you are satisfied with what you have written, copy it onto the FINAL COPY pages of the assessment folder."

Other state and national standardized tests follow a similar procedure. Students are given one or more topics on which to write (sometimes called "prompts" or "strands") and are expected to produce a final copy that meets grade standards for achievement. Scorers are given scoring guides listing the traits upon which the samples are evaluated. Among the traits listed are:

- clearness of beginning, middle, and end
- logical progression of writing
- a response that stays on topic
- use of details to support that topic
- use of a variety of words and sentence patterns with correct spelling and usage of most high-frequency, grade-appropriate language
- correct capitalization and punctuation at grade level

It is encouraging to note that many school districts are now mandating regularly scheduled writing assignments, sometimes on a daily basis, in their classrooms. A person learns to write by writing. However, an aspiring violinist may practice assiduously and often, but will never become an accomplished musician without guidance and instruction in the techniques and methods of playing the violin. In the same way, the student-writer needs instruction and guidance in order to communicate clearly and effectively. This section on writing essays, and the ones on writing letters and stories (which are sometimes also included in standardized writing tests), offer a wealth of suggestions and activities to augment the teacher's own writing instruction. Most of the activities in these sections will have multiple parts in order to include practice in all the steps of the writing process.

Teacher Preparation and Lessons

The activities in Section 5 provide students with instruction and practice in the techniques of essay writing. They begin with prewriting activities, such as brainstorming, clustering, and outlining, that will help them formulate, develop, and organize their ideas. These are followed by lessons and activities in writing an introductory/topic paragraph; developing the topic in a logical, coherent, and focused manner; and writing a concluding paragraph.

You can introduce the unit by proposing that anyone who can write a paragraph can also write an essay. Review the structure of a paragraph: topic sentence, developing the topic, and concluding sentence. Point out that the structure of an essay is the same, except for the scope and length. Instead of a topic sentence, there is a topic paragraph (also called an introductory paragraph). Instead of developing the topic with a few sentences, it is done with one or more paragraphs. In an essay, the concluding sentence is developed into a concluding paragraph.

A good analogy to use when trying to get this concept across is that of states and a nation. Elicit from the students that the components of a state are cities, but that the components of a nation like the U.S. are states. Point out that the cities that make up a state are analogous to the sentences in a paragraph, and the states themselves are analogous to the paragraphs, uniting into the final, whole product (the nation or the essay).

Selected answers are given on page 195. The PRACTICE TEST assesses students' ability to apply their knowledge of language and writing skills in sample essays.

ACTIVITIES 5-1 through 5-6 focus on organizing thoughts logically through **brainstorming, clustering,** and **outlining**. Discuss the advantages of making lists before going shopping or having a party. Elicit that the advantages include saving time, not forgetting something you need, and being more efficient and organized. Discuss why this sort of preparation can also be advantageous when writing an essay and what kinds of prewriting activities can be helpful (for example, lists, research, outlines, discussion, interviews). Distribute **Activity 5-1 Brainstorming (Part One)**. Read and discuss the description of brainstorming. Then read and discuss the directions for preparing a brainstorming list. When students have completed their brainstorming lists, have them shared aloud with the class or exchanged and passed around. Distribute **Activity 5-2 Brainstorming (Part Two)**. Read and discuss the directions for preparing the brainstorming lists. When students have completed their lists, have them shared aloud or exchanged and passed around.

Distribute **Activity 5-3 Clustering (Part One)**. Read and discuss the description of clustering and the example. Read and, if necessary, clarify the directions. When students have completed the clustering activity, have them share their clusters aloud or exchange and pass them around. Distribute **Activity 5-4 Clustering (Part Two)**. Review the definition of clustering and discuss the suggestions set forth. Read and, if necessary, clarify the directions. When students have completed the clustering activity, have them share their clusters.

Create a simple essay outline on the board, such as the one shown here, with the input of the class.

COOKING AND SERVING A MEAL

I. Getting ready
   A. Decide number of diners
   B. Set the table
II. Cooking the meal
   A. Choose recipes
   B. Choose cooking utensils
   C. Set out all ingredients
   D. Follow directions on recipes
III. Serving the meal
   A. Use serving platters
   B. Decide the order in which to serve

Point out that sentences are written for each item in the outline and combined into paragraphs when developing the essay.

Distribute **Activity 5-5 Outlining (Part One).** Read and discuss the directions. When students have completed their outlines, have them read aloud and discussed. Distribute **Activity 5-6 Outlining (Part Two).** Read and discuss the directions. When students have completed their outlines, have them read their outlines aloud and discuss them.

ACTIVITIES 5-7 through 5-14 deal with **writing the introductory paragraph**. Review the purpose of the topic sentence in a paragraph. Point out that in an essay, the topic is stated in the first (introductory) paragraph. Read the following paragraph to the class:

> *There seems to be a lack of heroes today. We read about many brave and courageous men and women of the past. These people were willing to stand up for their principles and even give their lives, if necessary.*

Identify this as the introductory paragraph (topic paragraph) of an essay. Elicit that the subject of the essay is "today's lack of heroes," and that the purpose of this paragraph is to state the topic.

Distribute **Activity 5-7 Stating the Topic (Part One).** Read and discuss the purpose of the introductory paragraph. Then read the directions and clarify, if necessary. When students have completed their paragraphs, have samples read aloud and discussed. Distribute **Activity 5-8 Stating the Topic (Part Two).** Read and discuss the purpose of the introductory paragraph. Then read the directions and clarify, if necessary. When students have completed their paragraphs, have samples read aloud and discussed.

Review that the purpose of the introductory/topic paragraph is to state the topic. Point out that there are ways of doing this to create greater interest on the part of the reader. Read the following paragraph aloud to the class:

> *Have you ever had a really, really scary experience? I did. It happened last August when I was involved in a serious automobile accident.*

Elicit from the students that this introductory paragraph is made more exciting and provokes the reader's interest with the use of a **question.** Distribute **Activity 5-9 Introductory Paragraph with a Question (Part One).** Read and discuss the directions. When students have completed both introductory paragraphs, have samples read aloud and discussed. Repeat the procedure with **Activity 5-10 Introductory Paragraph with a Question (Part Two)**.

Tell student that a second way to attract the reader's attention is to write a **surprising statement** in the paragraph. Distribute **Activity 5-11 Introductory Paragraph with a Surprising Statement**. Read aloud the sample paragraph. Elicit how it gets the reader's attention by using a surprising statement. Read and discuss the directions. When these paragraphs have been completed, have samples read aloud and discussed.

Tell students that a third way to attract attention is to include an **anecdote,** or story, in the introductory paragraph of an essay. Distribute **Activity 5-12 Introductory Paragraph with an Anecdote**. Read aloud the sample paragraph and discuss the manner in which it uses an anecdote to spark the reader's interest. Read and discuss the directions. When students have completed their paragraphs, have samples read aloud and discussed.

Distribute **Activity 5-13 Introductory Paragraph: What Not to Do (Part One)**. Read and discuss the two examples of things not to do in an introductory paragraph. Then read and discuss the directions. When students are finished, have samples of revised paragraphs read aloud and discussed. Distribute **Activity 5-14 Introductory Paragraph: What Not to Do (Part Two)**. Read and discuss the list and examples of things not to do in an introductory paragraph. Then read and discuss the directions. When students are finished, have samples read aloud and discussed.

ACTIVITIES 5-15 through 5-20 focus on **developing the topic**. Distribute **Activity 5-15 Developing the Topic Using Examples (Part One)**. Read the sample paragraphs in Part A. Discuss the manner in which the subject is developed by using examples. Then read the directions for Part B. When paragraphs have been completed, have several samples read aloud and discussed. Distribute **Activity 5-16 Developing the Topic Using Examples (Part Two)**. Read and discuss the directions. Emphasize that students use examples. When students have completed these two paragraphs, have several samples read aloud and discussed.

Distribute **Activity 5-17 Avoiding Irrelevancies (Part One)**. Read aloud both paragraphs in Part A. Discuss which paragraph is better and why. Have students underline the irrelevancies in the weak paragraph. Share and discuss the results. Then read aloud the directions for Part B. When these have been completed, have students share and discuss their results. Distribute **Activity 5-18 Avoiding Irrelevancies (Part Two)**. Read and discuss the directions. When both paragraphs have been completed, collect the papers. Read several samples aloud and discuss the results, with emphasis on avoiding irrelevancies.

Ask the students to describe the goal of a basketball game. Elicit the fact that the ball needs to go into the basket. Ask what happens when a player looks away from the basket while throwing and smiles at someone in the stands. Point out that an athlete needs to focus—to constantly keep the aim of the game in mind. State that the same is true of an essay. It is important to stay on the subject. Distribute **Activity 5-19 Staying on the Subject (Part One)**. Read aloud the essay excerpt. Have students write answers to the questions, and then discuss where the paragraph goes astray and gets off the subject. Read and discuss the directions. When the activity is completed, have students exchange papers with a partner and discuss whether or not the essay stays on the subject. Distribute **Activity 5-20 Staying on the Subject (Part Two)**. Read the directions for Part A. Have students answer the question, and discuss how use of a brainstorming list can help a writer stay on the subject. Read and discuss the directions for Part B. When students are finished, collect the papers and read several samples aloud for discussing how well each writer has stayed on the subject.

ACTIVITIES 5-21 and 5-22 teach how to write a **concluding paragraph**. Review the purposes of the introductory paragraph and developing the topic. Elicit that the purposes of a concluding paragraph are: (1) to restate the topic; (2) to summarize the points in the body of the essay; and (3) to bring the essay to a satisfying conclusion. Write these three points on the chalkboard. Distribute **Activity 5-21 Concluding Paragraph (Part One)**. Read the example aloud and discuss how the concluding paragraph includes the three points. Then read the directions. When students have completed their concluding paragraph, have several samples read aloud and discussed. Distribute **Activity 5-22 Concluding Paragraph (Part Two)**. Read the review of the purposes of a concluding paragraph and the example of an incorrect concluding paragraph. Discuss why this paragraph does not work. Then read the directions. When students are finished, read several samples aloud and discuss their effectiveness.

ACTIVITIES 5-23 and 5-24 deal with **avoiding confusion** when writing and revising an essay. Distribute **Activity 5-23 Avoiding Confusion**. Read and discuss the types of errors that can confuse the reader. Point out that the reader depends on the writer's organization, focus, and correct use of punctuation to be able to understand the essay. Read and discuss the examples and ask students to contribute additional examples of missteps that can occur in essay writing. Then read and discuss the directions. When students are finished, have sample revised paragraphs read aloud and discussed.

Write on the chalkboard:

Is the essay well organized, with a clear beginning, middle, and end?
Does the introductory paragraph state the topic? Is there a more interesting way to begin this essay?
Do the middle paragraphs develop the topic logically?
Does the concluding paragraph restate the topic, sum up, and bring the essay to an end?

Tell the students that these are some of the questions they should ask themselves when evaluating and revising an essay. Ask students to contribute additional questions to this list. Others that might be added are: *Are active verbs, sensory language, similes, and metaphors used to make the writing more vivid? Are commas used correctly to make the meaning clear? Are all sentences complete without run-ons or fragments? Do subjects and verbs agree? Is the topic supported with good examples?* Distribute **Activity 5-24 Self-Evaluation, Revision, Use of Proofreading Symbols**. Read and discuss the suggestions for self-evaluation and revision. Read about the use of proofreading symbols. Distribute the list of proofreading symbols on page 360 for students to keep on hand whenever they are revising their work.

ACTIVITIES 5-25 through 5-28 focus on **writing three- and five-paragraph essays.** Distribute **Activity 5-25 Writing a Simple Three-Paragraph Essay (Part One)**. Read and discuss the description of a three-paragraph essay. Read and discuss the directions and the example for an introductory paragraph. When students have finished their introductory paragraphs, have samples read aloud and discussed. Follow the same procedure for the middle paragraph and concluding paragraph. Distribute **Activity 5-26 Writing a Simple Three-Paragraph Essay (Part Two)**. Read and discuss the directions for choosing a topic. Read and discuss the directions for preparing a brainstorming list. When students have completed the lists, read the directions for writing a first draft. When these have been completed, read and discuss the directions for revising and writing a final copy. After students are finished, have samples read aloud and discussed. (*This activity may take more than one class session.*)

Distribute **Activity 5-27 Writing a Five-Paragraph Essay: Brainstorming and First Draft**. Read and discuss the description of a five-paragraph essay. Read the directions, and be sure students understand the purpose of the brainstorming list and how to complete it. When this has been finished, have several samples of the brainstorming list read aloud and give students an opportunity to change or add to their own lists. Read and discuss the directions for completing the activity. Distribute **Activity 5-28 Writing a Five-Paragraph Essay: Revising and Writing a Final Copy.** Read and discuss the directions and list of guidelines for revising. Review the use of proofreading symbols. When the final copies have been completed, collect the papers and read several samples aloud for discussion.

Practice Test: Essay-Writing Techniques

The sample student essays A and B on page 228 are rated 2 and 6, respectively.

Essay A offers some supporting ideas with specific added information, but the development is uneven and disorganized. Errors in sentence structure and punctuation interfere with understanding in much of the response. This essay scored a 2.

Essay B focuses on the topic with ample supporting ideas and examples, and has a logical structure. The three paragraphs convey a sense of wholeness and completeness. The essay is well organized and demonstrates a mature command of language. Errors in grammar, spelling, and punctuation are few and do not interfere with understanding. This essay scored a 6.

ANSWER KEY

5–1 through 5–16.

Answers will vary.

5–17. Avoiding Irrelevancies (part one)

Part A.

The first paragraph should be marked. The following irrelevant sentences should be crossed out:

Years ago, people used . . .
My friend, Jon, . . .

Part B.

The following sentences with irrelevant details should be crossed out:

Paragraph 1: We had a cat once.
Her name was Muffin . . .

Paragraph 2: Mr. Grosso, who lies on my block . . .
I have scary dreams sometimes . . .

5–18. Avoiding Irrelevancies (part two)

Students should rewrite each paragraph without the following sentences:

Paragraph 1: Two of my cousins . . .
My dad works . . .

Paragraph 2: Last Saturday . . .
A bee got into the house . . .

5–19. Staying on the Subject (part one)

Part A.

1. My Billion-Dollar Gift List
2. My brother, Alex

Part B.

Paragraphs will vary.

5–20. Staying on the Subject (part two)

Part A.

My dad's Civil War books; lunchroom

Part B.

Paragraphs will vary.

5–21 through 5–28.

Answers will vary.

Name ______________________________ Date ______________

5–1. Brainstorming (Part One)

Brainstorming is a way to set down and organize your thoughts and ideas before you begin to write an essay or story. A good cook sets out all the ingredients, utensils, and recipe information before beginning to prepare a meal. Without organization, the meal, as well as the cook, could end up limp and unappetizing. In the same way, a writer needs to get together everything he or she needs for the essay. If you have a detailed brainstorming list before you begin a writing project, you will be ready to turn out a clear and well-organized essay.

DIRECTIONS: Prepare a brainstorming list for an essay on the subject "Awesome Characters in Books I Have Read," as follows: In the first column, list the names of the book characters you have chosen. (Choose at least three names.) In the second column, next to each name, write as many words and phrases as you can that describe that character's appearance, personality, and nature. In the third column, jot down words and phrases that can be used to describe that person's actions in the story.

Name	Description	Actions

(Use the back of this sheet if you need more space for your brainstorming list.)

Name ______________________ **Date** ____________

5–2. BRAINSTORMING (PART TWO)

A. DIRECTIONS: Prepare a brainstorming list for an essay on the subject "Important Dates in My Life." In the first column, list three important dates in your life. In the second column, list the event that occurred on that date. In the third column, list words and phrases that could be used to describe the event and your feelings about it.

Date	Event	Description

B. DIRECTIONS: Prepare a brainstorming list for an essay on the subject "Wild Animals." In the first column, list the names of at least three animals. In the second column, list words and phrases that describe this animal's appearance (what it looks like). In the third column, list words and phrases that describe this animal's environment and actions.

Name of Animal	Appearance	Environment & Actions

Name ______________________ Date ______________

5–3. Clustering (Part One)

Clustering is an effective way to get ready to write an essay or story. Just follow these easy steps, and you, too, can be a "clusterer."

1. Draw a large circle on a piece of paper. Write the subject of the essay or story in the middle of the circle in BIG letters.
2. Using somewhat smaller print, jot down the main points about this subject in different parts of the circle around the subject.
3. Near each main point, write descriptive words and phrases in smaller letters.

Here is an example of clustering for an essay called "Sports Equipment."

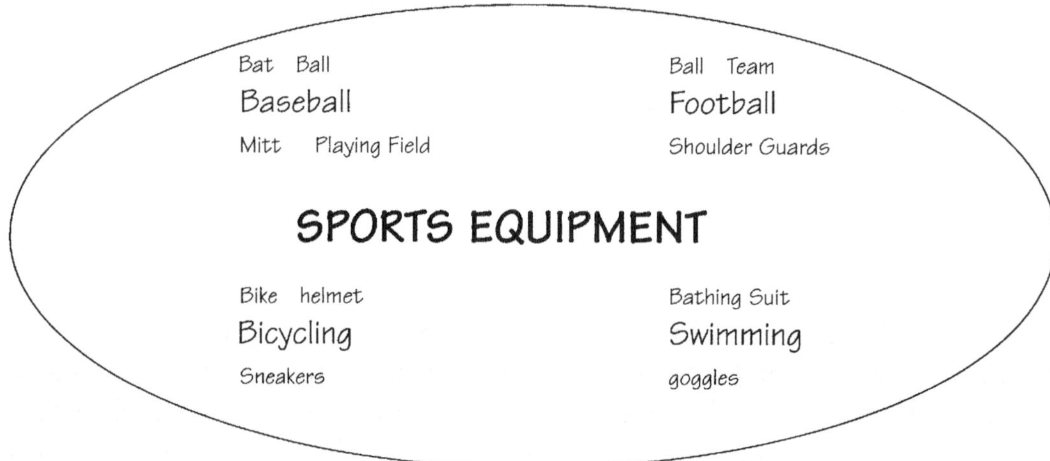

DIRECTIONS: On another sheet of paper, prepare a cluster for an essay called "My Social Studies Class." Use different-sized lettering or different-colored pens for the subject, the main points, and descriptions.

Name ______________________________ Date ______________

5–4. Clustering (Part Two)

Setting down thoughts and arranging them in clusters makes essay writing easy. Here are some useful hints for clustering.

1. Put down all ideas that occur to you. You don't have to use every word and phrase that appears in your cluster in the essay—just the best ones. The bigger your cluster, the more you will have from which to choose.
2. Set the subject in the center of the circle. Write the main points around the subject. Then put down as many descriptive words as you can think of that relate to each main point.
3. Use different-sized lettering (or different-colored pens) for subject, main points, and descriptive words.

DIRECTIONS: In the circle below, prepare a cluster for an essay called "My Teachers."

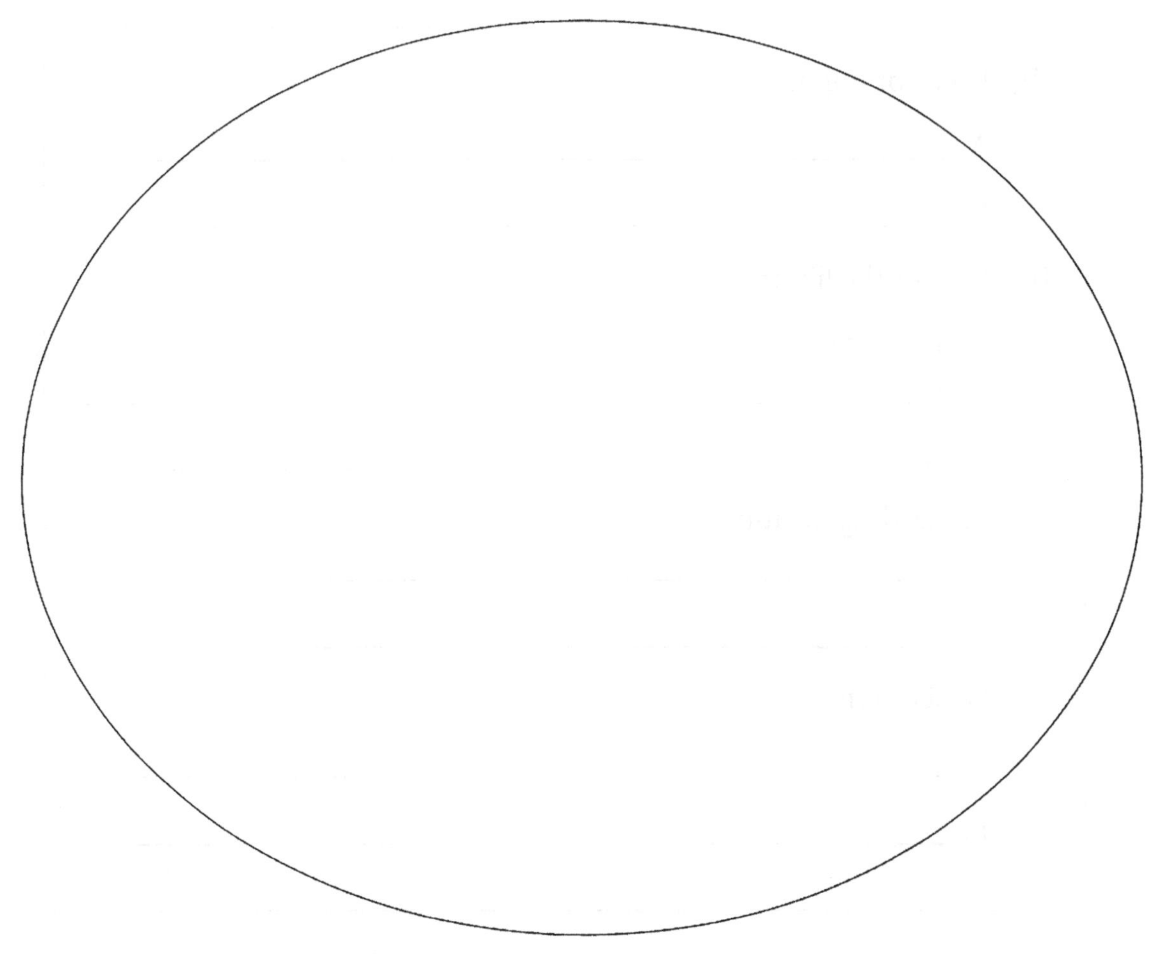

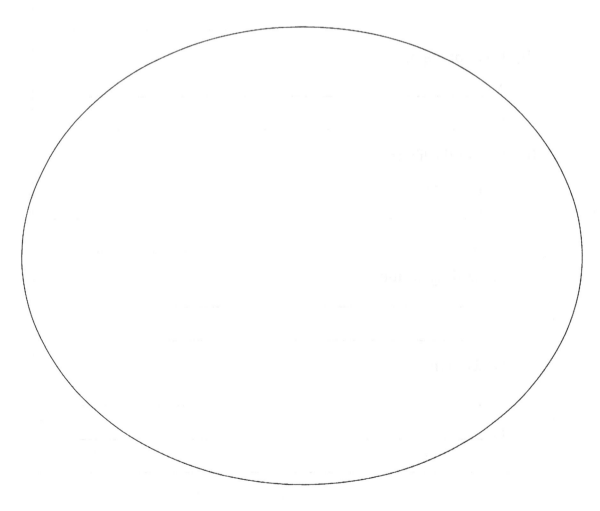

Name ______________________________ Date ______________

5–5. Outlining (Part One)

An outline is like a skeleton. When it is put together, all you have to do is "flesh it out" and, like magic, you will have a complete essay. Nothing could be easier! First, write the subject at the top. Then use Roman numerals (I, II, III, IV, V, and so on) for the main points. Use capital letters for the descriptive words. If you need to add further details for any of the descriptive words, use Arabic numerals (1, 2, 3, and so on). Although not everyone needs an outline in order to write an essay, it can be a helpful step between brainstorming or clustering and the final product.

DIRECTIONS: Complete the following outline for an essay called "Using the Library."

Using the Library

I. Topic paragraph

   A. ______________________________

   B. ______________________________

II. Kinds of libraries

   A. ______________________________

   B. ______________________________

III. Uses of the library

   A. Research

      1. ______________________________

      2. ______________________________

   B. Reading for fun

      1. ______________________________

      2. ______________________________

IV. Conclusion

   A. ______________________________

   B. ______________________________

Name ______________________________ Date ______________

5–6. Outlining (part two)

DIRECTIONS: Write an outline for the following essay.

Forms of Transportation

Name ______________________ Date ____________

5–7. Stating the Topic (Part One)

DIRECTIONS: The purpose of an introductory paragraph of an essay is to tell the reader what the essay is about in an interesting way. One or more sentences in this paragraph should clearly state the topic. Write an introductory paragraph that clearly states the topic for each essay below.

How to Stay Healthy

____

____

____

____

____

____

____

____

____

Making Friends

____

____

____

____

____

____

____

____

____

Name ________________________________ Date ______________

5–8. Stating the Topic (part two)

DIRECTIONS: The introductory paragraph of an essay must state the topic so that the reader knows immediately what subject he or she is going to read about. Write an introductory paragraph that clearly states the topic for each essay below.

The View from My Bedroom Window

____

____

____

____

____

____

____

____

____

Embarrassing Experiences

____

____

____

____

____

____

____

____

____

Name ______________________________ **Date** ______________

5–9. INTRODUCTORY PARAGRAPH WITH A QUESTION (PART ONE)

DIRECTIONS: How can you make your introductory paragraph more interesting to the reader? One way of getting attention is to do what this paragraph does: Begin with a question. For each essay below, write an introductory paragraph that begins with a question. Your introductory paragraph should contain two or three sentences.

Common Fears of Teenagers

____

____

____

____

____

____

____

____

Magazines for Teens

____

____

____

____

____

____

____

____

Name ______________________________ Date ______________

5–10. Introductory Paragraph with a Question (Part Two)

DIRECTIONS: Your introductory paragraph won't be boring if you begin it with a question. Write an introductory paragraph with a question for each essay below. Be sure your introductory paragraph also states the topic, as that is its main purpose. (Remember, you are not writing the complete essay, just the introductory paragraph, which should contain two or three sentences.)

Movies I Like

____

____

____

____

____

____

____

____

Shopping at the Mall

____

____

____

____

____

____

____

____

Name ________________________________ **Date** ______________

5–11. Introductory Paragraph with a Surprising Statement

You can do it! One way of getting the reader's interest is by starting your introductory paragraph with a surprising statement, such as the one at the beginning of this paragraph. Here is another example of an introductory paragraph with a surprising statement.

> **It is later than you think! Many people spend their days in useless activities that get them nowhere. Here are some examples of common time-wasting activities.**

DIRECTIONS: Write an introductory paragraph with a surprising statement for each topic below.

Career Choices

____

____

____

____

____

____

My Favorite Computer Games

____

____

____

____

____

____

Name ______________________________ Date ______________

5–12. Introductory Paragraph with an Anecdote

Telling an interesting anecdote (little story) in the introductory paragraph can arouse the reader's interest. Here is an example:

> **I saw an unusual sight on my way to school today. Two little kids, about eight or nine years of age, were helping an elderly woman pick up items that had fallen from her shopping bag onto the sidewalk. Surely, it would be a better world if we all helped our neighbors like this.**

DIRECTIONS: Write an introductory paragraph with an interesting anecdote for an essay on each topic below. Be sure each paragraph states the topic clearly.

My Dream Vacation

____

____

____

____

____

____

Cars I Would Love to Drive

____

____

____

____

____

____

Name ______________________________ **Date** ______________

5–13. Introductory Paragraph: What Not to Do (Part One)

Here are a few things you should NOT do in an introductory paragraph.

1. **Never apologize!** This suggests to the reader that you don't know what you are talking about. Why should he or she want to read on? Avoid phrases like these: *It's only my opinion* . . . and *I'm not sure about this, but* . . . .
2. **Do not make an announcement!** It is unnecessary and boring to announce your intentions about what you are planning to say in the essay. Avoid the following phrases: *In this essay I will* . . . and *The purpose of this essay is* . . . .

DIRECTIONS: Rewrite each introductory paragraph below by taking out the apology or announcement and replacing it with something more effective.

In this essay, I will try to describe my feelings when I first met my wonderful dog, Mutty. It was the happiest moment of my life.

____

____

____

____

I am not an expert on history. In my opinion, however, the greatest president of the United States was Theodore Roosevelt. There are many reasons why he was so exceptional.

____

____

____

____

Name ______________________________ Date ______________

5–14. Introductory Paragraph: What Not to Do (Part Two)

Here are two more things you should NOT do in an introductory paragraph.

3. **Do not begin with a definition from the dictionary or encyclopedia.** This type of beginning will turn the reader off, as in these examples: *According to Webster's dictionary* . . . and *My online Encarta encyclopedia says* . . . .
4. **Do not begin with a lot of details.** Your introductory paragraph should get right to the point and state the topic quickly. Details such as those in the following example should be saved for later. They don't belong in an introductory paragraph.

> **My Aunt Rosie loves all animals. Her favorites are dogs and horses. She lives on a big farm way out in the country. It takes us five hours to drive there in our blue minivan. I love animals, especially horses, almost as much as she does. That's why Aunt Rosie's farm is my favorite place in the world.**

All the details here obscure the topic of the essay, which is "My Favorite Place."

A. DIRECTIONS: On the lines below, rewrite the above introductory paragraph. Take out the unnecessary details and state the topic sooner.

____

____

____

B. DIRECTIONS: On the lines below, revise the following paragraph, taking out the dictionary definition.

> **Webster's dictionary defines football as "any or several games played with an inflated leather ball by two teams in a field with goals at either end." Football means a lot more to me than that. I live for football. It is my favorite sport.**

____

____

____

Name ______________________________ Date ______________

5–15. DEVELOPING THE TOPIC USING EXAMPLES (PART ONE)

When you have completed your introductory paragraph, the next step is to develop the topic. One way of doing this easily and effectively is to illustrate the topic by using examples. Below is the introductory paragraph for an essay called "Career Choices." It is followed by a second paragraph that develops the topic by using examples.

> **Have you decided upon your life's work? Like most teenagers, I have not yet made this choice. There are several careers that I am considering.**
>
> **My first choice is to become an astronaut. Nothing could be more thrilling than to explore the universe. That may not be a realistic goal, however, so I am considering a few other options. Archaeology seems like an exciting profession. I can see myself traveling to exotic locations to search for ancient civilizations. My last choice is to become a lawyer like my mother. That would please my parents.**

DIRECTIONS: Write two paragraphs of an essay on the same topic: "Career Choices". You can use the introductory paragraph in the example above, or, even better, make up one of your own. Follow this with one or two paragraphs that develop the topic. Use examples like those above to organize your essay. (Remember, you don't have to write a complete essay here—just a topic paragraph and one or two more paragraphs to develop the topic.)

____

____

____

____

____

____

____

____

____

(Use the back of this sheet to continue your writing.)

Name ______________________________ Date ______________

5–16. Developing the Topic Using Examples (Part Two)

DIRECTIONS: It is easy to develop the topic of an essay by using examples. Below you will find two introductory paragraphs. Write a second paragraph for each essay that develops the topic.

The Best Times of the Day

Some days are so boring that they seem to go on forever! Even the worst days, however, usually have some periods of fun and enjoyment. There are three times of the day that I like a lot.

____

____

____

____

____

Weird Music

Do you like music? So do I! However, there are some kinds of music and some performers that seem pretty weird to me.

____

____

____

____

____

____

Name ______________________________ Date ______________

5–17. Avoiding Irrelevancies (Part One)

A. DIRECTIONS: An irrelevancy is something that has nothing to do with the topic. When an irrelevancy creeps into an essay, the reader becomes distracted and confused about the subject. Read the two paragraphs below. One of them is better because everything in it has something to do with the topic. The other paragraph contains irrelevancies that have nothing to do with the topic. Place a checkmark next to the paragraph with the irrelevant details and cross out the irrelevant sentence(s).

❑ Computers are important in today's world. Years ago, people used to write everything by hand. School assignments, e-mail, research, and games are only some of the ways computers are used. Soon, it will be necessary for every house to have a computer. My friend, Jon, has two computers in his house. This is definitely the computer age.

❑ Computers are important in today's world. School assignments, e-mail, research, and games are only some of the ways computers are used. Soon, it will be necessary for every house to have a computer. This is definitely the computer age.

B. DIRECTIONS: In the following paragraphs, cross out any sentences that are not relevant.

The difference between me and other pet owners is that I am devoted to my turtles. You would like them, too, if you knew their interesting personalities and habits. We had a cat once. Her name was Muffin and she had a disgusting habit of bringing dead mice into the house. I call my turtle Princess because she seems royal to me.

A Christmas Carol by Charles Dickens is one of the most famous stories ever written. It was published on December 17, 1843. It is about Ebenezer Scrooge. He is miserly, greedy, and mean. Mr. Grosso, who lives on my block, is sometimes mean to kids when they walk on his lawn. Scrooge learns to be a better person after dreaming about a terrifying adventure with three ghosts. I have scary dreams sometimes, especially if I'm worried about a test the next day. One of the lovable characters in A Christmas Carol is Tiny Tim Cratchit, a poor, lame boy who is always cheerful and sees the good in everyone.

Name ______________________________ Date ______________

5–18. Avoiding Irrelevancies (Part Two)

DIRECTIONS: Each of the following paragraphs contains irrelevancies that have nothing to do with the topic. Rewrite each paragraph correctly on the lines below.

Theodore Roosevelt, the 26th president of the United States, was born on October 27, 1858. Two of my cousins have birthdays in October. T.R., as he was called, was a forceful and active person with many strong opinions. He worked to pass laws to limit the power of large corporations and provide better conditions for workers. My dad works for a large corporation in the city. Roosevelt had a deep interest in ecology and land conservation. Under his guidance, millions of acres of forest were made national forest land.

____

____

____

____

(Use the back of this sheet if you need more space to write.)

April is an important month for sports fans. It marks the beginning of the baseball season. Baseball is often called America's national game. Everyone plays it—little kids, teenagers, men, women, professionals, and amateurs. Last Saturday, I wanted to watch a game on TV, but we had to visit my grandparents. All over America, baseball diamonds become as busy as beehives in April. A bee got into our house once and buzzed all around.

____

____

____

____

(Use the back of this sheet if you need more space to write.)

Name ________________________________ Date ______________

5–19. Staying on the Subject (Part One)

A. DIRECTIONS: Have you ever been on a trip where the driver took a wrong turn and ended up on a road that went somewhere else? It is confusing to a reader when that happens in an essay—when the writer suddenly veers off onto a path that goes in another direction from the topic. Here is part of an essay called "My Billion-Dollar Gift List."

> **Wouldn't it be fun to have a billion dollars to spend on gifts for your friends and family? Here are some things I would do with that billion dollars.**
>
> **My first purchase would be a new house for our family. The one we have is okay, but it is somewhat crowded. The house I buy would be big enough for me to have a room of my own instead of sharing one with my brother. My brother, Alex, can be a real pain. It is probably not his fault because he is only six, but he does a lot of annoying things. He takes clothes out of my closet to try on. He uses my comb. Once, he went into my computer and it was out of order for three days.**

1. What is the topic of this essay? ______________________________
2. Write the first three words of the sentence where the writer gets lost and fails to stay on the subject. ______________________________

B. DIRECTIONS: Write the first two paragraphs of an essay on the same subject, "My Billion-Dollar Gift List." Write an introductory paragraph that states the topic in an interesting way. Then develop the topic by using examples. Be sure to stay on the subject.

____

____

____

____

____

____

(Use the back of this sheet to continue your writing.)

Name ______________________________ Date ______________

5–20. STAYING ON THE SUBJECT (PART TWO)

A. DIRECTIONS: It is important to stay on the subject when writing. If you first prepare a brainstorming list, cluster, or outline, this will help you stay focused on the topic. For example, here is a brainstorming list for an essay called "My Favorite Class."

BRAINSTORMING LIST FOR "MY FAVORITE CLASS"		
Subject & Classroom	**People**	**Activities**
Social studies Bright, sunny room Pictures of famous people My dad's Civil War books	Mr. Abrahams, teacher Brett, my best friend The class clown Shawn, my second best friend	History games Discussions Lunchroom Computer research

List the items that do not belong on this list. ______________________________

____

B. DIRECTIONS: Write the first two paragraphs of an essay on the same subject, "My Favorite Class." First, prepare a brainstorming list on a separate sheet of paper. Then write the first two paragraphs of the essay below. Introduce the topic in the first paragraph. Develop the topic with examples in the second paragraph. Use your brainstorming list to help you stay on the subject.

____

____

____

____

____

____

____

____

(Use the back of this sheet to continue your writing.)

Name ______________________________ Date ______________

5–21. Concluding Paragraph (part one)

A good film or book usually has a strong and satisfying ending. The same can be said of a good essay. The final paragraph of an essay is called the concluding paragraph. It must let the reader know that the essay has come to an end. The concluding paragraph:

- Restates the topic that is in the introductory paragraph
- Summarizes the points (examples) in the body of the essay
- Brings the essay to a satisfying conclusion

Here is an example of a concluding paragraph. It appears at the end of an essay called "A Dangerous Vehicle."

> **Snowmobiles can be fun. They are useful in many situations. If they are not operated by a trained driver who is familiar with the rules and regulations, however, they can be dangerous and even deadly.**

DIRECTIONS: Write a concluding paragraph for the following essay.

> **Do you feel proud when you see our country's flag? Francis Scott Key was so moved by the sight of the Stars and Stripes still flying after a terrible battle that he wrote "The Star-Spangled Banner." Old Glory is important to me, too.**
>
> **The flag is a symbol of our country. It expresses the hopes and ideals of the people who founded the United States of America in 1776. When we salute the flag, we are saluting our democracy and those who fought and died to preserve it. It represents the liberty and freedom that we are guaranteed by the Constitution.**

____

____

____

____

____

____

(Use the back of this sheet if you need more space to write.)

Name ______________________________ Date ____________

5–22. Concluding Paragraph (part two)

The concluding paragraph of an essay should restate the topic, summarize the points in the body of the essay, and bring it to an end. The concluding paragraph should NOT:

- Include new information that has not been mentioned earlier.
- Mention something that has nothing to do with the topic.
- Leave the reader unsure whether or not the essay is concluded.

For example, the following concluding paragraph would be incorrect for the essay about the flag that appears in Activity 5-21:

> **Other songs, such as "America the Beautiful," have also been written about the United States. Everyone knows the words to "America." Most of us take pride in the flag and the ideals it represents such as the Declaration of Independence.**

This concluding paragraph is NOT effective because:

- The topic is the American flag, *not* patriotic songs. Therefore, the first two sentences have nothing to do with this subject.
- The Declaration of Independence is not mentioned anywhere else in the essay. Therefore, it does not belong in the concluding paragraph.
- There is nothing in this paragraph to indicate the essay has ended.

DIRECTIONS: Rewrite this concluding paragraph correctly.

____

____

____

____

____

____

____

____

(Use the back of this sheet if you need more space to write.)

Name ______________________________ Date ______________

5–23. Avoiding Confusion

A reader will not understand an essay that is not clear. Some common ways of causing confusion in an essay are:

- lack of organization and logical sequence
- not staying on the topic (lack of focus)
- irrelevancies (details that have nothing to do with the topic)
- misuse of punctuation marks, mostly commas

  WRONG: *Jane Smith my aunt and her daughter* (How many people are here?)

  RIGHT: *Jane Smith (my aunt) and her daughter* (2 people)

- sentence fragments and run-on sentences

  WRONG: *Went to the park yesterday.* (fragment—no subject)

  RIGHT: *I went to the park yesterday.*

  WRONG: *Joe went to the park I wanted to go, too.* (run-on)

  RIGHT: *Joe went to the park. I wanted to go, too.*

DIRECTIONS: The following paragraph contains errors that could confuse a reader. Rewrite the paragraph correctly on the lines below.

> **Do you know what a spectator sport is? The word <u>spectator</u> means someone who watches a spectator sport is one that people watch. You may play baseball soccer football or basketball yourself but when you attend a professional game. You become a spectator. My brother Alan does not like football. Sometimes it's fun to play yourself. At other times being a spectator is quite satisfying.**

____

____

____

____

____

____

(Use the back of this sheet if you need more space to write.)

Name ______________________ Date ____________

5–24. Self-Evaluation, Revision, Use of Proofreading Symbols

A. It is important to know what to look for when you evaluate and revise your own work. Keep this handy checklist available whenever you write an essay or other type of writing.

- ❑ Is the essay well organized, with a clear beginning, middle, and end?
- ❑ Does the introductory paragraph clearly state the topic? Could this be stated in a more interesting way?
- ❑ Do the middle paragraphs develop the topic logically?
- ❑ Does the concluding paragraph restate the topic, sum up, and bring the essay to an end?
- ❑ Are active verbs, sensory language, similes, and metaphors used to make the writing more vivid?
- ❑ Are commas used correctly to make the meaning clear?
- ❑ Are all sentences complete without run-ons or fragments?
- ❑ Do subjects and verbs agree?
- ❑ Is the topic supported with good examples?
- ❑ Is spelling correct? (If unsure, consult a dictionary.)
- ❑ Are transitional words used to smoothly move the writing?

B. Many people find the use of proofreading symbols helpful when evaluating and revising their work. Your teacher will give you a list of proofreading symbols. Keep these symbols handy so you can use them whenever you revise your work.

Name ________________________________ **Date** ______________

5–25. WRITING A SIMPLE THREE-PARAGRAPH ESSAY (PART ONE)

Do you know how to write a paragraph? If your answer is yes, then it will be easy for you to write an essay. An essay is organized like a paragraph, with a beginning, middle, and conclusion. Anyone who can write a paragraph can expand it into a simple, three-paragraph essay. It's as easy as A, B, C.

In a paragraph, the topic is introduced in the first sentence, as in: *The village of Mapleton has a fascinating history.* In an essay, this is expanded into an **introductory paragraph**, as in: *Did you know that there was once a witch trial in Mapleton? That is only one of the unusual things about this town. It has a long and fascinating history.*

A. DIRECTIONS: Write a beginning paragraph for an essay about your town (or any other town or city you prefer). Use the back of this sheet for your paragraph.

The **middle paragraph** of a three-paragraph essay develops the subject with description, detail, or list of reasons, as in: *In the early 18th century, Lizzy Hickam was accused of witchcraft and brought to trial. Fortunately for her, she was found not guilty. In 1864, Confederate soldiers occupied the village for three days until they were driven out by Union troops. During the 20th century, Mapleton had the distinction of having the most robberies for a town of its size.*

B. DIRECTIONS: Write a middle paragraph for an essay about your town. Use the back of this sheet to write your paragraph.

The **final paragraph** concludes and sums up the topic, as in: *Mapleton seems like a quiet, pleasant, friendly village. This just proves that one can never judge the history of a place from appearances.*

C. DIRECTIONS: Write a concluding paragraph to sum up the topic. Use the back of this sheet for your paragraph.

Name ______________________________ Date ______________

5–26. WRITING A SIMPLE THREE-PARAGRAPH ESSAY (PART TWO)

A. DIRECTIONS: Choose one of the following topics for a three-paragraph essay. Place a checkmark in the box.

- ❑ The Best Day of My Life
- ❑ The Worst Day of My Life
- ❑ Music I Like
- ❑ My Favorite TV Shows

B. DIRECTIONS: Complete the following brainstorming list about your topic. In the first column, list examples. In the second column, list words to describe that example. In the third column, list words and phrases that express why you like it.

Examples	Description	Things I Like About It

C. DIRECTIONS: On a separate sheet of paper, write a first draft of your three-paragraph essay. Write your name at the top of the paper. Write the title of the essay underneath your name. Be sure to introduce the topic in the first paragraph, develop the topic in the second paragraph, and conclude the essay in the last paragraph. Use the words and phrases from your brainstorming list as a guide.

Name ______________________________ Date ______________

5–26. Writing a Simple Three-Paragraph Essay (Part Two) *(continued)*

D. DIRECTIONS: Revise your first draft. Use proofreading symbols if they are useful. Use the following questions as a guide:

1. **Is the essay well organized with a clear beginning, middle, and end?**
2. **Does the introductory paragraph clearly state the topic? Can you say it in a more interesting way?**
3. **Does the middle paragraph develop the topic? Does it need any transitional words to make it move more smoothly?**
4. **Does the concluding paragraph restate the topic and bring it to an end?**
5. **Can you add active verbs, sensory words, or similes to make it more vivid?**
6. **Are all sentences complete without run-ons or fragments?**
7. **Do subjects and verbs agree?**
8. **Are all words spelled correctly? When in doubt, consult the dictionary.**

When your essay is as good as you can make it, write your final copy on a separate sheet of paper. Write your name and date at the top, and the title beneath that. Be sure to indent at the beginning of each new paragraph.

Name ______________________________ Date ______________

5–27. Writing a Five-Paragraph Essay: Brainstorming and First Draft

A five-paragraph essay gives the writer more opportunity to develop the topic. Like the three-paragraph essay, it has an introductory paragraph at the beginning and a concluding paragraph at the end. The middle part, however, consists of three paragraphs instead of one. If the writer is offering three points or examples to develop the topic, he or she has a full paragraph to do so instead of only a sentence or two. In this activity, you will write a five-paragraph essay on the topic "Three Interesting Characters I Have Met in Books."

A. DIRECTIONS: First, prepare a brainstorming list. In the first column, list the names of the three characters you have chosen. In the second column, next to each name, write the name of the book (and author, if you know it) in which that character appears. In the third column, write words and phrases that describe that character. In the fourth column, write words or phrases describing why you have chosen that character. Underneath the brainstorming list, write a first sentence for your introductory paragraph. Spark the reader's interest by using a question or a surprising statement.

Name	Book/Author	Description	Why Chosen

First sentence of your introductory paragraph: ______________________________

____

____

B. DIRECTIONS: On a separate sheet of paper, write a first draft of your five-paragraph essay. Write your name at the top of the paper. Write the title under your name. Be sure to introduce the topic in an interesting way in the first paragraph, develop the topic with three middle paragraphs, one about each character, and conclude the essay in the last paragraph. Use words and phrases from your brainstorming list as a guide.

Name ______________________________ Date ______________

5–28. Writing a Five-Paragraph Essay: Revising and Writing a Final Copy

DIRECTIONS: Revise the first draft of your essay about "Three Interesting Characters I Have Met in Books." Put the corrections on the draft. Use proofreading symbols if you find them useful. Use the following questions as a guide:

1. **Is the essay well organized with a clear beginning, middle, and end?**
2. **Does the introductory paragraph state the topic? Can you say it in a more interesting way?**
3. **Do the three middle paragraphs develop the topic? Do you name and describe one character in each paragraph? Are there any interesting details you can add?**
4. **Does the concluding paragraph restate the topic and bring it to an end?**
5. **Do you use transitional words to move smoothly between ideas?**
6. **Can you add active verbs, sensory words, or similes to make the writing more vivid?**
7. **Do subjects and verbs agree?**
8. **Are there any run-on sentences? Fragments?**
9. **Have you used commas, where necessary, to make the meaning clear?**
10. **Are all words spelled correctly? When in doubt, consult the dictionary.**

When your essay is as good as you can make it, write your final copy on a separate sheet of paper. Put your name and date at the top, and the title below that. Be sure to indent at the beginning of each paragraph.

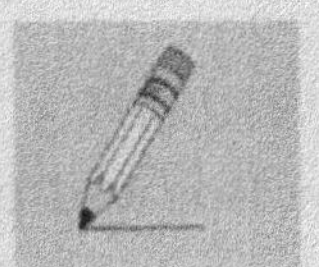

EIGHTH-GRADE LEVEL

ESSAY-WRITING TECHNIQUES PRACTICE TEST

Name ______________________________ Date ______________

PRACTICE TEST: ESSAY-WRITING TECHNIQUES

DIRECTIONS: Write an essay of three or more paragraphs about your favorite season. List and describe at least three reasons why you like this season best.

Follow these four steps to write your essay:

- FIRST, on the page labeled PREWRITING, brainstorm essay ideas and examples that support the topic. Include words and phrases that you can use.
- SECOND, write the first draft of your essay on a separate sheet of paper. Write your name and date at the top, and the title of the essay. Use your notes from the brainstorming page.
- THIRD, revise and edit your first draft. Refer to your list of proofreading symbols if you wish to make use of these. Use the checklist as a guide, and check off each item when it is revised to your satisfaction.
- FOURTH, write your final copy on a separate sheet of paper with your name and date at the top.

CHECKLIST

- ❑ Does your introductory paragraph state the topic clearly? Could you say it in a more interesting way by using a surprising statement, a question, or an anecdote?
- ❑ Does your middle paragraph or paragraphs develop the topic in a clear and logical way?
- ❑ Do you stay on the subject and use only examples and details that are related to the topic?
- ❑ Do all your subjects and verbs agree?
- ❑ Can you add active verbs or sensory words to make your writing more vivid?
- ❑ Are you certain there are no run-on sentences or fragments?
- ❑ Do you vary sentence length, using short and long sentences?
- ❑ Are all words spelled correctly?

Name ______________________________ Date ______________

Practice Test: Essay-Writing Techniques *(continued)*

Prewriting

DIRECTIONS: Use the brainstorming chart below to organize your essay by outlining the ideas that support your choice of a favorite season. Outline or list words and phrases that describe the season and provide details for these ideas. Arrange the brainstorming chart in any way that will be helpful to you when writing the essay.

Below the brainstorming chart, write a first sentence for your introductory paragraph that will spark a reader's interest.

BRAINSTORMING CHART FOR "MY FAVORITE SEASON"

First sentence of your introductory paragraph: ______________________

____

____

Name ______________________________ Date ______________

PRACTICE TEST: ESSAY-WRITING TECHNIQUES *(continued)*

Student Samples

DIRECTIONS: Read the sample student essays below. Rate each paragraph with a score from 1 (lowest) to 6 (highest). Use the information on the scoring guide to help you.

ESSAY A: My Favorite Season

I think my favorite time of the year is summer because you can do a lot more things than Just Sit home, in my case I like to work on my car. Its cool cause when summer break rolls around that's all I like to do, Oh and we also go on vacation to Florida, South Carolina, New York, Virginia. You also don't have to worry about school anymore because your get 2½ months off. You can stay up late, go to a party, or you can have a party. And usually when summer is here I take my car down to a quarter mile racetrak and have it timed.

Score ____________

ESSAY B: My Favorite Season

My favorite season is spring. After a long and cold winter, nothing feels better than to step outside and feel that first warm breeze. The sky will be that spring blue with big and puffy white clouds and everything starts to come alive. Suddenly, there are birds. Spring birds like the goldfinch turn a bright yellow from their winter maize. Animals come out from hibernation and are busily scurrying around. The trees start to look olive again and everything turns green., All the wildflowers come out and make everything colorful.

I start to get spring fever and am really hard to keep indoors. I don't feel like school any more and I anticipate summer. My favorite spring activity is horseback riding. That's the best time of year for riding, not too cold and not too hot. The horses don't even seem to mind the exercise after being cooped up all winter. Bicycle riding and hiking are great then, too.

My favorite spring event is spring break. I love to get out and it gives me hope that I can make it to summer without going crazy!

Score ____________

Scoring Guide

SCORE	Unsatisfactory—1	Insufficient—2
Content	Attempts to respond to prompt, but provides few details to persuade the reader; may only paraphrase prompt	Presents very few details OR may be very repetitive OR may be very undeveloped
Organization	Has no clear organization OR consists of a single statement; no attempt is made to introduce the topic	Is very disorganized; ideas are weakly connected OR the response is too brief to detect organization
Sentence Structure	Far too many fragments and/or run-ons; word choice may be incorrect in much or all of the response	Too many fragments and/or run ons; word choice may often be incorrect in much of the response
Grammar, Usage, and Mechanics	Many errors in grammar or usage—such as tense inconsistency, lack of subject–verb agreement—spelling, and punctuation severely interfere with understanding	Errors in grammar or usage—such as tense inconsistency, lack of subject–verb agreement—spelling, and punctuation interfere with understanding in much of the response

SCORE	Uneven—3	Sufficient—4
Content	Presents a few clear details, but is list-like, undeveloped, or repetitive OR offers no more than a well-written beginning	Develops information with some details; some attempt is made to persuade the reader
Organization	Is unevenly organized; the paragraph may be disjointed; no attempt to back up the topic	Is organized with ideas that are generally related but has few or no transitions
Sentence Structure	Frequent run-ons and/or fragments; may have some incorrect word choices	A few run-ons and/or sentence fragments; sentences and word choice may be simple and unvaried
Grammar, Usage, and Mechanics	Errors in grammar or usage—such as verb inconsistency, lack of subject–verb agreement—spelling, and punctuation sometimes interfere with understanding	Errors in grammar or usage—such as tense inconsistency, lack of subject–verb agreement—spelling, and punctuation do not interfere with understanding

SCORE	Skillful—5	Excellent—6
Content	Develops and shapes information with clear, well-chosen details	Develops and shapes information with well-chosen persuasive details across the paragraph
Organization	Is clearly organized with introductory and closing paragraphs; may lack some transitions	Is well organized with clear introductory and closing paragraphs; has strong transitions; makes clear persuasive statement
Sentence Structure	Exhibits some variety in sentence structure and some good word choices	Sustains variety in sentence structure and exhibits good word choice
Grammar, Usage, and Mechanics	Errors in grammar, spelling, and punctuation do not interfere with understanding	Errors in grammar, spelling, and punctuation are few and do not interfere with understanding

SECTION 6

WRITING INFORMATIVE ESSAYS

Standardized Testing Information

Students in grade 8 will be required to write samples of one or more of the following essays on their state or national writing tests: informative/expository, narrative/imaginative, and/or persuasive. Section 6 deals with informative/expository essays.

According to the National Assessment of Educational Progress (NAEP), a sample of informative writing "communicates information to the reader to share knowledge or to convey messages, instructions, and ideas." The topics that students are given in these tests require them "to write on specified subjects in a variety of formats, such as reports, reviews, and letters." The NAEP also recommends that "students should write on a variety of tasks and for many different audiences . . ." and "from a variety of stimulus materials" such as "photographs, cartoons, or poems, . . . newspaper articles, charts. . . ." These are called prompts. The NAEP also suggests that "students should generate, draft, revise, and edit ideas and forms of expression in their writing." This suggests mastery of the writing process that is used throughout this resource.

The NAEP offers guidelines or rubrics for scoring its writing tests, as does each state. The rubric at the end of this section is based on the NAEP guidelines for scoring informative/expository writing. NOTE: Information on the NAEP can be found at www.NAGB.org or at www.nces.ed.gov/nationsreportcard.

Here is an example of the official scoring guide for the Idaho writing assessment for eighth grade. It is based on a scale of 1 to 5.

5 (ADVANCED)—A 5 paper demonstrates advanced control of the conventions of written language as well as unique qualities in style and content. A 5 paper is clear, organized, easy to understand, and characterized by a unique perspective or a mature approach to the topic. Its length is appropriate for the writer to demonstrate skills and conventions to fulfill the prompt's purpose. A score of 5 indicates that a student's writing for that particular day and prompt is clearly advanced beyond grade level. A 5 paper will exhibit *most* of the traits listed below:

Audience/Purpose/Content/Organization

- Unique introduction which captivates reader
- Satisfying conclusion
- Writer establishes a purpose and maintains a clear focus
- Advanced or creative approaches to prompt
- Effective topic sentences with supporting and/or sensory details and/or examples

- Mature paragraph organization which enhances the central idea or story line
- Logical development: no stray sentences or paragraphs; every part adds to whole
- Thoughtful transitions: alignment, phrases, clauses, parallelism
- Strong sense of audience awareness
- Higher-level thinking: application, analysis, and/or evaluation

Tone/Mood/Voice/Style

- Powerful and engaging; holds reader's attention
- Clear understanding and use of above-grade-level vocabulary
- Powerful verbs and precise nouns and modifiers
- Reader feels strong interaction with writer and senses person behind words
- Writer speaks directly to reader with an individualistic style
- Confident; reader senses strong commitment to topic
- Advanced use of such literary devices as personification, similes, metaphors, alliteration, allusion, irony, hyperboles, oxymorons, and understatements

Mechanics/Usage/Sentence Structure

- Mechanically correct; may manipulate mechanics to enhance style or voice
- Strong command of standard written English with few or no surface errors
- Varied sentence types and structures which include complex sentences

3 (SATISFACTORY)—A 3 paper demonstrates a basic understanding of the organization and development of expository writing ideas. A 3 indicates that the writer has satisfactory control of the conventions of written language at grade level. Its length is appropriate for the writer to demonstrate satisfactory skills and conventions to fulfill the prompt's purpose. A score of 3 indicates that the student's writing for that particular day and prompt is satisfactory at grade level. A 3 paper will exhibit most of the traits listed below:

Audience/Purpose/Content/Organization

- Evident introduction
- Conclusion may not effectively tie up all loose ends
- Sense of purpose
- Thinking skills are appropriate to subject, audience, and purpose
- Minor shifts in topic
- Paragraphs work together to support whole
- Limited supporting details
- Redundant sentence patterns; similar beginnings
- Some effective transitions help to unify essay
- Awareness of audience

Time/Mood/Voice/Style

- Seemingly sincere, but not fully engaged or involved in writing
- Appropriate vocabulary; may be mechanical or quite general
- Variety of verb choices
- Generally consistent point of view, verb tense, and voice; occasional drifting
- Moments of enlightenment—reader longs to learn more
- Attempts to use colorful language; may include jargon or cliches
- Does not overuse "I"

Mechanics/Usage/Sentence Structure

- Most surface errors do not detract from meaning and/or readability
- Some short, unvaried sentences
- Correct end punctuation; some correct internal punctuation
- Correctly uses and spells such priority words as the following: *their, they're, to, two, too, your, you're, its, it's, then, than, which, witch,* and *a lot*
- Infrequent nonstandard sentence structure
- Evident paragraphing

This is just one example of a state rubric for expository writing. Whichever rubrics are used, however, a plethora of guided practice, as in the activities that follow, will thoroughly prepare students for any standardized writing test.

Teacher Preparation and Lessons

The activities in this section are designed to provide a variety of interesting experiences in **informative/expository** writing with guidelines and supportive instructions that student-writers can use to hone their writing skills. Students are encouraged to use the steps of the writing process. Some of the topics, including that used for the PRACTICE TEST, are adapted from actual prompts from various state and national standardized writing tests.

Each activity has three parts.

- **Part One** consists of **prewriting activities** such as **brainstorming, outlining,** or **clustering.** These can be done individually, with class participation, or by some combination of these two procedures.
- **Part Two** is the **writing of a first draft.** Students should be encouraged to write freely at this point without worrying about grammar, spelling, or punctuation. The aim is to overcome the blocks that so many student-writers face by making this part of the process less threatening.
- **Part Three** offers directions for **revising and writing a final copy.** The revision and editing process can be done by the individual student-writer alone, in association with the teacher, or with class participation by having students exchange papers and make

suggestions for revision. The last method can be valuable for both the writer and the "editor" since it is easier for anyone (student or adult) to recognize the flaws in someone else's writing and then transfer this knowledge to one's own work. Teachers are urged to use this occasionally in their lessons on revision.

The informative/expository activities in this section range from simple three-paragraph essays to more detailed ones of five or more paragraphs.

Practice Test: Writing Informative Essays

The sample student essays A and B on page 261 are rated 3 and 5, respectively.

Essay A contains two supporting ideas ("snow") and ("Christmas") with only minimal development. An organizational pattern has been attempted, but the response is sparse and the paper lacks a sense of wholeness or completeness. Readability is limited by errors in sentence structure and inaccurate sentence boundaries. Knowledge of the conventions of punctuation is demonstrated, but not consistent. With some exceptions, commonly used words are spelled correctly. This essay scored a 3.

Essay B supports the topic with adequate supporting ideas and examples. Even though the essay is not five paragraphs, there is a logical progression of ideas with a sense of completeness. Word choice is adequate and precise. Adequate sentence boundaries make for clear communication. The conventions of punctuation, capitalization, and spelling are generally followed. This essay scored a 5.

Name ______________________________ Date ______________

6–1. Writing About the School Cafeteria (Prewriting)

DIRECTIONS: This will be a simple, three-paragraph essay called "How to Improve Our School Cafeteria." It will be even easier to write if you first prepare this **brainstorming list**.

BRAINSTORMING LIST

A. List three things about your school cafeteria that could be improved.

1. ______________________________
2. ______________________________
3. ______________________________

B. List the reasons why you think each of these improvements is necessary. (You don't need complete sentences here—words and phrases are good enough.)

1. ______________________________
2. ______________________________
3. ______________________________

C. List ways in which each of these things could be improved. (Words and phrases are good enough here.)

1. ______________________________
2. ______________________________
3. ______________________________

D. Write an opening sentence for your introductory paragraph. Make it as interesting as you can by using a surprising statement or a question.

____

____

____

____

Name ______________________________ **Date** ______________

6–2. Writing About the School Cafeteria (First Draft)

DIRECTIONS: Write the first draft of a three-paragraph essay called "How to Improve Our School Cafeteria." It will be easy to do if you keep your brainstorming list handy and follow this easy guide.

First Paragraph: Use the opening sentence from the brainstorming list and introduce the topic in your introductory paragraph. Write the first paragraph (*at least three sentences*) here or on another sheet of paper.

____

____

____

____

Second Paragraph: Develop the topic in your middle paragraph. Use the three examples from your brainstorming list. Describe why each change is necessary and ways in which improvements can be made. Write the second paragraph (*at least five sentences*) here or on the other sheet of paper.

____

____

____

____

____

____

____

Concluding Paragraph: In the third and last paragraph, restate and sum up your topic. It is satisfying to the reader if you refer to something in the introductory paragraph and bring it to a conclusion. Write your concluding paragraph (*at least two sentences*) here or on the other sheet of paper.

____

____

____

Name ______________________________ Date ______________

6–3. Writing About the School Cafeteria (Final Copy)

A. DIRECTIONS: Correct and revise your first draft of "How to Improve Our School Cafeteria." Follow and check off the guidelines below.

- ❑ **Are your sentences complete? Correct any run-on sentences or fragments.**
- ❑ **Do subjects and verbs agree?**
- ❑ **Does your first paragraph introduce the topic? Is there any way you can make it more interesting to the reader?**
- ❑ **Does the second paragraph develop the topic? Have you chosen the most interesting words and phrases from your brainstorming list?**
- ❑ **Can you make your writing more vivid with active verbs and sensory language?**
- ❑ **Can you add one simile to spark interest?**
- ❑ **Does the final paragraph restate and sum up the topic?**
- ❑ **Use a dictionary to check the spelling.**

B. DIRECTIONS: Begin the final copy of your essay below and continue on the back of this sheet. Write the title on the first line and indent at the beginning of each paragraph.

Name ______________________________ Date ______________

6–4. Writing About a Memorable Class Trip (Prewriting)

DIRECTIONS: You are going to write a simple five-paragraph essay called "A Memorable Class Trip." First, prepare a **brainstorming list** as follows:

1. In the first column, write a list of words and phrases that describe general details about the trip, such as date, year, class, teacher, purpose, and so on.
2. In the second column, write a list of words and phrases that describe the journey, such as things about the bus, students, driver, teacher, chaperones, length of trip, route, interesting sights, funny things that happened on the way.
3. In the third column, write a list of words and phrases that describe the place you visited and what you saw and did there.

BRAINSTORMING LIST		
When, Why, Where	**The Journey**	**Place Visited**

Name ______________________________ Date ______________

6–5. Writing About a Memorable Class Trip (First Draft)

DIRECTIONS: Write the first draft of a five-paragraph essay called "A Memorable Class Trip." It will be easy to do if you keep your brainstorming list handy and follow these suggestions.

- **In the first paragraph (*two or three sentences*), introduce the topic in an exciting way that will get the reader's attention.**
- **In the second paragraph (*at least three sentences*), describe how this trip came about, the purpose of the trip, and the activities leading up to it.**
- **In the third paragraph (*at least three sentences*), describe the actual journey itself: manner of transportation (bus, car, etc.), length of trip, actions of the students and others, and so on.**
- **In the fourth paragraph (*at least three sentences*), describe the place you visited and what you did there. Use colorful adjectives, sensory words, and active verbs to make the writing more interesting.**
- **In the concluding paragraph (*two to three sentences*), restate and sum up the topic.**

Begin your essay on the lines below and continue on the back of this sheet. This is a first draft, so just concentrate on getting your thoughts down on paper and don't be too concerned about spelling or grammar at this point. Write the title on the first line and indent at the beginning of each paragraph.

Name ______________________________ Date ______________

6–6. Writing About a Memorable Class Trip (Final Copy)

A. DIRECTIONS: Correct and revise the first draft of your essay "A Memorable Class Trip." Follow and check off the guidelines below.

- ❑ **Are your sentences complete? Correct any run-on sentences or fragments.**
- ❑ **Do subjects and verbs agree?**
- ❑ **Does your first paragraph introduce the topic? Can you make it more interesting with a question, a surprising statement, or an anecdote?**
- ❑ **Do the three middle paragraphs develop the topic in a clear and logical way? Have you chosen the best words and phrases from your brainstorming list?**
- ❑ **Can you add active verbs and sensory language to make your writing more exciting? Include at least one simile.**
- ❑ **Do you vary sentence length, using short and long sentences?**
- ❑ **Does the final paragraph clearly sum up the topic?**
- ❑ **Do you indent at the beginning of each paragraph?**
- ❑ **Use a dictionary to check spelling.**

B. DIRECTIONS: Begin the final copy of your essay below and continue on the back of this sheet. Write the title on the first line and indent at the beginning of each paragraph.

Name ______________________________ Date ______________

6–7. WRITING ABOUT YOUR NEW ROOM (PREWRITING)

DIRECTIONS: Imagine that you are moving into a different home and you can put anything you would like in one room (a bedroom, a family room, or another particular room). Write a five-paragraph essay describing what would be in the room. You might describe the furniture, the decorations, the arrangement, or what it would feel like to be in the room. First, prepare an **outline** below, which has been framed out for you. All you have to do is fill in the blanks.

OUTLINE FOR "MY NEW ROOM"

I. Introductory Paragraph
   A. State topic
   B. Get reader's interest

II. Paragraph #2—Furniture (List furniture as A, B, C, and write descriptive words after each listing as 1, 2.)
   A. Bed
      1. ______________________________
      2. ______________________________
   B. ______________________________
      1. ______________________________
      2. ______________________________
   C. ______________________________
      1. ______________________________
      2. ______________________________

III. Paragraph #3—Other items (computer, TV, stereo, etc. List each item as A, B, C, and write descriptive words after each as 1, 2.)
   A. ______________________________
      1. ______________________________
      2. ______________________________

Name ______________________________ Date ______________

6–7. Writing About Your New Room (PREWRITING) *(continued)*

B. ______________________________

1. ______________________________

2. ______________________________

C. ______________________________

1. ______________________________

2. ______________________________

IV. Paragraph #4—Your feelings about the room

A. ______________________________

B. ______________________________

V. Paragraph #5—Conclusion (List what you will include in this paragraph.)

A ______________________________

B. ______________________________

Name ______________________________ Date ______________

6–8. Writing About Your New Room (first draft)

DIRECTIONS: Write the first draft of a five-paragraph essay about your new room. It will be easy to do if you keep your outline handy and follow these suggestions.

- **In the first paragraph (*two to three sentences*), get the reader's interest with an exciting beginning.**
- **In the second paragraph (*at least three sentences*), describe the furniture in the room. Use colorful adjectives.**
- **In the third paragraph (*at least three sentences*), describe the other items you listed on your outline.**
- **In the fourth paragraph (*at least two sentences*), describe how you would feel in this room. Use strong, active verbs. Include a simile.**
- **In the fifth paragraph (*two to three sentences*), restate and sum up the topic.**

Begin your essay below and continue on the back of this sheet. This is a first draft, so just concentrate on getting your thoughts down on paper and don't be too concerned about spelling or grammar. Write the title on the top line and indent at the beginning of each paragraph.

____

____

____

____

____

____

____

____

____

____

____

Name ______________________________ Date ______________

6–9. Writing About Your New Room (final copy)

A. DIRECTIONS: Correct and revise the first draft of your essay "My New Room." Follow and check off the guidelines below.

- ❑ **Are your sentences complete? Correct any run-on sentences or fragments.**
- ❑ **Do subjects and verbs agree?**
- ❑ **Does your first paragraph introduce the topic? Can you make it more exciting?**
- ❑ **Do the three middle paragraphs develop the topic in a clear and logical way?**
- ❑ **Do you stay on the topic? Take out any irrelevancies.**
- ❑ **Add active verbs and sensory language to make your writing more interesting.**
- ❑ **Do you include at least one simile or metaphor?**
- ❑ **Does the final paragraph sum up the topic?**
- ❑ **Do you indent at the beginning of each paragraph?**
- ❑ **Use a dictionary to check spelling.**

B. DIRECTIONS: Begin the final copy of your essay below and continue on the back of this sheet. Write the title on the first line and indent at the beginning of each paragraph.

Name ______________________________ Date ______________

6–10. Writing About Winning the Lottery (Prewriting)

DIRECTIONS: Congratulations! You have just won a million dollars in the lottery! Think about the things you would do with the money. Write an essay telling what you would do with the money. It will be easy if you first prepare a **brainstorming list,** as follows:

1. In the first column, list three things you would do with the money.
2. In the second column, next to each item, write words and phrases you will be able to use in your essay to describe the reasons why you will do this.
3. In the third column, write words and phrases to describe how you will do this and what the results will be.

BRAINSTORMING LIST		
Uses for the Money	**Reasons**	**Methods and Results**

Name ______________________________ Date ______________

6–11. Writing About Winning the Lottery (First Draft)

DIRECTIONS: Write the first draft of a five-paragraph essay called "Winning the Lottery." It will be easy to do if you keep your brainstorming list in front of you and follow these suggestions.

- **In the first paragraph (*two to three sentences*), introduce the topic in a snappy, exciting way. (Example: *Did you ever dream of winning the lottery? In my case, the dream came true. It is unbelievable that I am a millionaire!*)**
- **In the second paragraph (*at least three sentences*), describe the first thing you will do with the money. Use the words and phrases in your brainstorming list to describe details of why and how you will do this.**
- **In the third paragraph (*at least three sentences*), describe the second thing you will do with the money.**
- **In the fourth paragraph (*at least three sentences*), describe one more thing you will do. Use colorful adjectives and active verbs to provide interesting details.**
- **In the concluding paragraph (*two to three sentences*), restate and sum up the topic.**

Begin your essay on the lines below and continue on the back of this sheet. This is a first draft, so just concentrate on getting your thoughts down. Don't be too concerned at this point about spelling or grammar. Write the title on the top line and indent at the beginning of each paragraph.

Name ______________________________ Date ______________

6–12. Writing About Winning the Lottery (Final Copy)

A. DIRECTIONS: Correct and revise the first draft of your essay, "Winning the Lottery." Follow and check off the guidelines below.

- ❑ Are your sentences complete? Correct any run-on sentences or fragments.
- ❑ Do subjects and verbs agree?
- ❑ Can you introduce the topic in a more exciting way in the first paragraph?
- ❑ Do the three middle paragraphs develop the topic clearly?
- ❑ Do you stay on the topic? Take out any irrelevancies.
- ❑ Add at least one simile or metaphor to make your writing more interesting.
- ❑ Add active verbs and sensory language.
- ❑ Does the final paragraph sum up the topic?
- ❑ Do you vary the sentence length between short and long sentences?
- ❑ Do you indent at the beginning of each sentence?
- ❑ Use a dictionary to check your spelling.

B. DIRECTIONS: Begin the final copy of your essay below and continue on the back of this sheet. Write the title on the first line and indent at the beginning of each paragraph.

____

____

____

____

____

____

____

____

Name ______________________________ Date ______________

6–13. Writing About Becoming a Chef (prewriting)

DIRECTIONS: Everyone admires the famous chefs we read about and see on TV. Now you can follow their examples. You have been asked to prepare dinner for your family tonight. Think about the foods you will make, and how you will prepare and serve them. Then write an essay called "The Night I Became a Chef." Use the **brainstorming list** below to write your menu, together with words and phrases you can use in your essay.

1. In the first column, list three or four foods that you will prepare.
2. In the second column, next to each item, write words and phrases to describe how you will prepare it.
3. In the third column, write words and phrases that describe how each item will be served.

BRAINSTORMING LIST		
Food	**Preparation**	**Serving**

Name ______________________________ Date ______________

6–14. Writing About Becoming a Chef (first draft)

DIRECTIONS: Write the first draft of a five-paragraph essay called "The Night I Became a Chef." Keep your brainstorming list handy and follow these suggestions.

- **In the first paragraph (*two to three sentences*), introduce the topic in an interesting way. Humor is often a fun way to begin, as in this example: *Why would anyone ask me to cook dinner? I'm all thumbs in the kitchen. Nevertheless, this is what I've been asked to do, and here's how I'll go about it.***
- **In the second paragraph (*three to five sentences*), describe one of the foods you will make. Tell how you will prepare it and how it will be served. Choose mouth-watering words from your brainstorming list to make it seem appetizing.**
- **In the third paragraph (*three to five sentences*), describe another food you will prepare. Follow the suggestions for the previous paragraph.**
- **In the fourth paragraph (*three to five sentences*), follow the same procedure for one or two more items on your menu.**
- **In the concluding paragraph (*two to three sentences*), restate and sum up the topic.**

Begin your essay on the lines below and continue on the back of this sheet. This is a first draft, so just concentrate on getting your thoughts down on paper. Don't be concerned about spelling or grammar at this point. Write the title on the top line and indent at the beginning of each paragraph.

Name ______________________________ Date ______________

6–15. Writing About Becoming a Chef (final copy)

A. DIRECTIONS: Correct and revise the first draft of your essay, "The Night I Became a Chef." Follow and check off the guidelines below.

- ❑ Are your sentences complete? Correct any run-on sentences or fragments.
- ❑ Do all subjects and verbs agree?
- ❑ Is your introduction exciting enough to spark the reader's interest? If not, change it.
- ❑ Do you develop the topic in each of the three middle paragraphs?
- ❑ Do you stay on the subject? Take out any irrelevancies.
- ❑ Can you add sensory words and similes to make your descriptions of food more stimulating?
- ❑ Does the final paragraph restate and sum up the topic?
- ❑ Do you vary sentence length between short and long sentences?
- ❑ Do you indent at the beginning of each sentence?
- ❑ Use a dictionary to check spelling.

B. DIRECTIONS: Begin the final copy of your essay below and continue on the back of this sheet. Write the title on the first line and indent at the beginning of each paragraph.

____

____

____

____

____

____

____

____

____

Name ______________________________ Date ______________

6–16. Writing About Dangerous Situations (Prewriting)

DIRECTIONS: Do your parents and teachers sometimes warn you not to do something because it might be dangerous? Think about what types of situations could be dangerous. Then write a four- or five-paragraph essay called "Dangerous Situations." The essay will contain four paragraphs if you are describing two kinds of dangerous situations, or five paragraphs if you are discussing three dangerous situations. First, follow the directions for preparing a **brainstorming list** below.

BRAINSTORMING LIST

1. Name one type of dangerous situation: ______________________

   In the box below, write words and phrases to describe it.

2. Name another dangerous situation: ______________________

   In the box below, write words and phrases to describe it.

3. Name one more dangerous situation: ______________________

   In the box below, write words and phrases to describe it.

Name ______________________________ **Date** ______________

6–17. WRITING ABOUT DANGEROUS SITUATIONS (FIRST DRAFT)

DIRECTIONS: Write the first draft of a four- or five-paragraph essay about "Dangerous Situations." Keep your brainstorming list handy, and follow these suggestions.

- **In the first paragraph (*two to three sentences*), introduce the topic in an interesting way. A good way to begin might be to briefly describe a shocking, dangerous situation.**
- **In the middle paragraphs (*at least three sentences each*), use lots of active verbs and colorful adjectives to emphasize the danger. Use at least one simile or metaphor. (There will either be two or three middle paragraphs, depending on the number of situations you describe.)**
- **In the concluding paragraph (*two to three sentences*), restate and sum up the topic.**

Begin your essay below and continue on the back of this sheet. This is a first draft, so just concentrate on getting your thoughts down on paper. Don't be too concerned at this point about spelling or grammar. Write the title on the top line and indent at the beginning of each paragraph.

Name ______________________________ Date ______________

6–18. Writing About Dangerous Situations (Final Copy)

A. DIRECTIONS: Correct and revise the first draft of your essay, "Dangerous Situations." Follow and check off the guidelines below.

- ❑ **Are all your sentences complete? Correct any run-ons or fragments.**
- ❑ **Do subjects and verbs agree? Do pronouns agree with their antecedents?**
- ❑ **Is your introductory paragraph interesting? Can you make it more exciting?**
- ❑ **Do the middle paragraphs develop the topic? Do you fully describe and discuss one dangerous situation in each paragraph?**
- ❑ **Do you stay on the topic? Take out any irrelevancies.**
- ❑ **Do you use active verbs, colorful adjectives, and sensory language? Can you add more of these? Add one simile or metaphor.**
- ❑ **Do you vary sentence length, using short and long sentences?**
- ❑ **Does the final paragraph restate and sum up the topic?**
- ❑ **Do you indent at the beginning of each paragraph?**
- ❑ **Use a dictionary to check your spelling.**

B. DIRECTIONS: Begin the final copy of your essay below and continue on the back of this sheet. Write the title on the first line and indent at the beginning of each paragraph.

Name ______________________________ Date ______________

6–19. Describing a New TV Series (prewriting)

A. DIRECTIONS: Wouldn't it be fun to create and design a TV series? A public television network is seeking ideas for a new series of shows that would be educational for teenagers. The series will include five one-hour episodes. Some titles under consideration are:

- ❑ *"Great Cities of the World"*
- ❑ *"Nature Walks"*
- ❑ *"Women in History"*
- ❑ *"Sports Legends"*

Choose one of these titles for your project by checking the box next to your selection.

B. DIRECTIONS: You are now going to suggest subjects for three episodes in your chosen series. First, prepare a **brainstorming list** below.

1. In the first column, write the name of the subject you want to use for that episode.
2. In the second column, write words and phrases to describe that subject.
3. In the third column, write words and phrases to describe why that subject is important and interesting.

BRAINSTORMING LIST		
Subject	**Description**	**Reasons to Include**

Name ______________________________ Date ______________

6–20. Describing a New TV Series (first draft)

DIRECTIONS: Write the first draft of a five-paragraph essay about the TV series you have chosen to create and design. Keep your brainstorming list handy and follow these suggestions.

- **In the first paragraph (*two to four sentences*), introduce the topic in a way that will get the reader's attention, such as *Why should adults be the ones who decide what we will watch on TV? After all, who knows what will interest adolescents better than teenagers themselves? Here are my suggestions for a TV series called* "Women in History."**
- **In the second paragraph (*four to seven sentences*), name the subject of the first episode. Give many interesting details about it, and tell why it should be included in the series. Use action verbs, colorful adjectives, and sensory language to make the writing vivid.**
- **In the third paragraph (*four to seven sentences*), follow the same procedure with the second subject.**
- **In the fourth paragraph (*four to seven sentences*), follow the same procedure with the third subject.**
- **In the concluding paragraph (*four to seven sentences*), restate and sum up the topic.**

Begin your essay below and continue on the back of this sheet. This is a first draft, so just concentrate on getting your thoughts down on paper. Don't be concerned about spelling and grammar at this point. Write the title on the first line and indent at the beginning of each paragraph.

____

____

____

____

____

____

____

____

Name ________________________________ Date ______________

6–21. Describing a New TV Series (final copy)

A. DIRECTIONS: Correct and revise the first draft of your essay proposing an educational TV series for teenagers. Follow and check off the guidelines below.

- ❑ Are all your sentences complete? Correct any run-ons or fragments.
- ❑ Do you use commas correctly? Do you need to insert commas anywhere?
- ❑ Do subjects and verbs agree?
- ❑ Can you make the introductory paragraph more interesting?
- ❑ Do you describe one subject in detail in each of the three middle paragraphs?
- ❑ Do you stay on the topic? Take out any irrelevancies.
- ❑ Add active verbs, colorful adjectives, and sensory words to make the writing more vivid.
- ❑ Does the concluding paragraph restate and sum up the topic?
- ❑ Use a dictionary to check your spelling.

B. DIRECTIONS: Begin the final copy of your essay below and continue on the back of this sheet. Write the title of the series on the first line and indent at the beginning of paragraphs.

____

____

____

____

____

____

____

____

____

____

____

Name ______________________________ Date ______________

6–22. Describing Your Dream Vacation (Prewriting)

DIRECTIONS: What is your "dream" vacation? How would you most like to spend a vacation? Would it be traveling to a distant, exotic land? Swimming and snorkeling at a seaside resort? Visiting a special theme park? Perhaps your idea of a perfect vacation is just hanging out in the neighborhood with your friends. Think about your choice for an ideal vacation and write it here:

____

Before writing an essay giving all the details of your dream vacation, first prepare a **brainstorming list** below.

1. The destination for your dream vacation: ______________________

2. In the box below, write words and phrases to describe the place and who will be there.

3. In the box below, write words and phrases to describe what you will do there.

4. In the box below, write words and phrases to describe the reasons you prefer this vacation.

5. Write an eye-catching opening sentence, such as *Call me crazy, but I am a Civil War buff, and for many years, I've longed to visit the major battlefields of that conflict.* Write your opening sentence on the back of this sheet.

Name ______________________________ Date ______________

6–23. DESCRIBING YOUR DREAM VACATION (FIRST DRAFT)

DIRECTIONS: Write a five-paragraph essay called "My Dream Vacation." Keep your brainstorming list in front of you and follow these suggestions.

- **In the first paragraph (*two to four sentences*), use the eye-catching opening sentence in your brainstorming list, and then complete the introduction of the topic.**
- **In the second paragraph (*three to seven sentences*), use words and phrases from your brainstorming list to describe the place and who will be there. Be sure to include active verbs, colorful adjectives, sensory words, and at least one simile or metaphor.**
- **In the third paragraph (*three to seven sentences*), follow the same procedure to describe what you will do there.**
- **In the fourth paragraph (*three to seven sentences*), follow the same procedure to describe the reasons why you prefer this vacation.**
- **In the concluding paragraph (*two to four sentences*), restate and sum up the topic.**

Begin your essay below and continue on the back of this sheet. This is a first draft, so just concentrate on getting your thoughts on paper at this point. Write the title on the top line and indent at the beginning of each paragraph.

Name ______________________________ Date ______________

6–24. Describing Your Dream Vacation (final copy)

A. DIRECTIONS: Correct and revise the first draft of your essay "My Dream Vacation." Follow and check off the guidelines below.

- ❑ Are sentences complete? Correct any fragments or run-ons.
- ❑ Do subjects and verbs agree? Do pronouns agree with antecedents?
- ❑ Do you introduce the topic in the first paragraph? Can you make it more exciting so the reader will want to continue?
- ❑ Does the second paragraph describe the place and who will be there? Can you add more vivid language, such as active verbs, sensory words, and colorful adjectives?
- ❑ Does the third paragraph describe what you will do there? Can you make your verbs show more action? Do you use at least one simile?
- ❑ Does the fourth paragraph describe your reasons for wanting this vacation? Can you be more convincing?
- ❑ Do you stay focused on the topic? Take out any irrelevancies.
- ❑ Does the concluding paragraph restate and sum up the topic?
- ❑ Check spelling with a dictionary.

B. DIRECTIONS: Begin the final copy of your essay below and continue on the back of this sheet. Write the title on the first line and indent at the beginning of each paragraph.

____

____

____

____

____

____

____

____

____

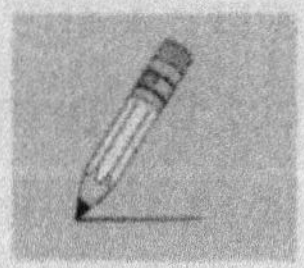

Eighth-Grade Level

Writing Informative Essays Practice Test

Name ______________________________ Date ______________

PRACTICE TEST: WRITING INFORMATIVE ESSAYS

DIRECTIONS: You and a friend have been talking about how classes at school are very different. Both of you like some classes but dislike others. Some things you talked about were the difficulty of the work, the instruction, other students, and your overall impression of the classrooms. Write a five-paragraph informative essay *comparing two classes* and explaining what you like or dislike about each class.

Follow these four steps to write your essay:

- FIRST, on the page labeled PREWRITING, brainstorm essay ideas and examples that support the topic. Include words and phrases you can use.
- SECOND, write the first draft of your essay on a separate sheet of paper. Write your name and date at the top, and the title of the essay. Use your notes from the brainstorming page.
- THIRD, revise and edit your first draft. Refer to your list of proofreading symbols if you wish to make use of these. Use the checklist as a guide, and check off each item when it is revised to your satisfaction.
- FOURTH, write your final copy on a separate sheet of paper with your name and date at the top.

CHECKLIST

- ❑ **Does your introductory paragraph state the topic clearly? Could you say it in a more interesting way by using a surprising statement, a question, or an anecdote?**
- ❑ **Do your three middle paragraphs develop the topic in a clear and logical way?**
- ❑ **Do you stay on the subject and avoid irrelevancies? Do you use only examples and details that are related to the topic?**
- ❑ **Do all your subjects and verbs agree? Do pronouns agree with antecedents?**
- ❑ **Can you add active verbs, sensory words, or colorful adjectives to make your writing more vivid?**
- ❑ **Are you certain there are no run-on sentences or fragments?**
- ❑ **Do you vary sentence length, using short and long sentences?**
- ❑ **Are all words spelled correctly?**

Name ______________________________ Date ______________

PRACTICE TEST: WRITING INFORMATIVE ESSAYS *(continued)*

Prewriting

DIRECTIONS: Use the framework below to brainstorm your ideas about comparing two classes. In the box labeled "Class #1," write the name of that class, followed by words and phrases you can use to describe your likes and dislikes about that class. Do the same in the box labeled "Class #2."

Class #1: ______________________________	
Likes	**Dislikes**

Class #2: ______________________________	
Likes	**Dislikes**

Name ______________________________ Date ______________

PRACTICE TEST: WRITING INFORMATIVE ESSAYS *(continued)*

Student Samples

ESSAY A: My Favorite Season of the Year

My favorite season of the year is witer. I like witer because I like the snow it's fun to throw show ball at cars and to go sliding the best thing I like about winter is chrismas. Chrismas is my favorite hoiladay. I like to see the houses and trees with lights on them and that is why my favorite season is winter.

Score ____________

ESSAY B: My Favorite Season of the Year

The season that I like best definitely has to be winter. While some people look at winter as being cold, dead, boring, and just an all around pain, I choose to look at it from a different perspective.

Winter is such a special time because nature takes on a whole new look. When the first snow comes, you look outside and see a "fairy land" type setting. Also, the activities that go along with winter make this season very special. Christmas, Hanukkah, and the New Year, are all special holidays that make winter just perfect.

I most look forward to that special feeling when my house is all decorated for the holiday and the snow is gently falling down. There is a certain spirit that could not be the same with any other season. Winter is a memorable time that I will always cherish.

Score ____________

Scoring Guide

SCORE	Unsatisfactory—1	Insufficient—2
Content	Attempts to respond to prompt, but provides little or no clear information; may only paraphrase the prompt	Presents fragmented information OR may be very repetitive OR may be very undeveloped
Organization	Has no clear organization OR consists of a single statement; has no clear beginning, middle, or end	Is very disorganized; ideas are weakly connected OR the response is too brief to detect organization
Sentence Structure	Little or no control over sentence boundaries and sentence structure; word choice may be incorrect in much or all of the response	Little control over sentence boundaries and sentence structure; word choice may often be incorrect
Grammar, Usage, and Mechanics	Many errors in grammar or usage—such as tense inconsistency, lack of subject–verb agreement—spelling, and punctuation severely interfere with understanding	Errors in grammar or usage—such as tense inconsistency, lack of subject–verb agreement—spelling, and punctuation interfere with understanding in much of the response

SCORE	Uneven—3	Sufficient—4
Content	Presents some clear information, but is list-like, undeveloped, or repetitive OR offers no more than a well-written beginning	Develops information with some details
Organization	Is unevenly organized; the essay may be disjointed	The essay is organized with ideas that are generally related but has few or no transitions
Sentence Structure	Exhibits uneven control over sentence boundaries and sentence structure; may have some incorrect word choices	Exhibits control over sentence boundaries and sentence structure, but sentences and word choice may be simple and unvaried
Grammar, Usage, and Mechanics	Errors in grammar or usage—such as tense inconsistency, lack of subject–verb agreement—spelling, and punctuation sometimes interfere with understanding	Errors in grammar or usage—such as tense inconsistency, lack of subject–verb agreement—spelling, and punctuation do not interfere with understanding

SCORE	Skillful—5	Excellent—6
Content	Develops and shapes information with details in parts of the essay	Develops and shapes information with well-chosen details across the essay
Organization	Is clearly organized; but may lack some transitions and/or have lapses in continuity	Is well organized with strong transitions; has clear beginning, middle, and end
Sentence Structure	Exhibits some variety in sentence structure and some good word choices	Sustains variety in sentence structure and exhibits good word choice
Grammar, Usage, and Mechanics	Errors in grammar, spelling, and punctuation do not interfere with understanding	Errors in grammar, spelling, and punctuation are few and do not interfere with understanding

SECTION 7

WRITING PERSUASIVE ESSAYS

Standardized Testing Information

Students in grade 8 are often asked to write persuasive essays on state or national assessment tests. Eighth graders usually enjoy this type of writing since it gives them an opportunity to express their opinions, which are often strongly held. The National Assessment of Educational Progress (NAEP) defines a persuasive essay as one that "seeks to influence the reader to take action or bring about change. It may contain factual information such as reasons, examples, or comparisons; however, its main purpose is to persuade."

The NAEP guidelines go on to say, "In all persuasive writing, authors must choose the approach they will use. They may, for instance, use emotional or logical appeals or an accommodating or demanding tone. Regardless of the situation or approach, persuasive writers must be concerned with having a particular desired effect upon their readers, beyond merely adding to knowledge of the topic."

Most state guidelines for scoring persuasive essays are similar to the NAEP guidelines. The scoring rubric at the end of this section is adapted from the NAEP rubric for scoring persuasive essays. NOTE: Information on the NAEP can be found at www.NAGB.org or at www.nces.ed.gov/nationsreportcard.

A good example of a state rubric is the following eighth-grade scoring guide used in Illinois. Illinois rates writing samples as "exceeds standards," "meets standards," "below standards," or "academic warning" on the basis of five writing features. These are:

- **focus** (the clarity with which a paper presents and maintains a clear main idea, point of view, theme, or unifying event)
- **support/elaboration** (the degree to which the main point is explained by specific details and reasons)
- **organization** (the clarity of the logical flow of ideas and the explicitness of the text structure or plan)
- **conventions** (the use of standard written English)
- **integration** (the global judgment of how effectively the paper as a whole uses the basic features to address the assignment)

Meets Standards

Writers at the "meets standards" level write basically developed papers in which all features are developed but not equally well developed throughout the paper. The paper is purposeful and supported with specificity using multiple strategies. The lines of reasoning show both coherence and cohesion throughout. The writers show command of appropriate conventions with few errors in proportion to the amount written and the writing conditions.

Writing features at the "meets standards" level for persuasive samples are as follows:

- **Focus:** The writing clearly states a subject/position with a general opening or with major points previewed. The writing maintains a logical position throughout the paper and, if previewed, develops only previewed points. The closing must be present and consistent with the opening.
- **Support/Elaboration:** Writing at this level contains adequate support for most points. An imbalance of specificity, depth, and accuracy or credibility may exist. Word choice enhances the specificity.
- **Organization:** The writing structure is evident. Both coherence and cohesion are demonstrated with the use of appropriate transition or other devices to connect. A minor digression may exist, but most points are logically presented and organized in appropriate paragraphs.
- **Conventions:** Evaluation of conventions takes into consideration the draft status of the writing assessment. (NOTE: The Illinois State Assessment Test does not provide time for revisions and rewriting.) Writing demonstrates mastery of sentence construction with few run-on sentences, subject/verb disagreements, or fragments according to the amount of writing present. Most pronouns are used correctly. Writing shows a mastery of common grade-appropriate punctuation/capitalization with few minor or major errors in proportion to amount of writing.
- **Integration:** The writing demonstrates a basically formed paper that ranges from a simple and clear presentation of the features to their adequate but unequal development.

Below Standards

Writers at the "below standards" level for persuasive writing demonstrate difficulty addressing the topic and write partially developed papers in which all features are present but may not be sufficiently formed. The paper may develop just general support and/or use only a single strategy. The lines of reasoning may show coherence *or* cohesion instead of both. The writers may have limited command of appropriate conventions with many errors in proportion to the amount written and the writing conditions.

Writing features at the "below standards" level for persuasive writing are as follows:

- **Focus:** The writing may identify a subject/position by at least a brief, general opening statement or one that is established somewhere in the paper. A partial focus may occur if the writing develops more or fewer points than are summarized in the introduction or conclusion. It may have minor drifts in logic or lack sufficiency to demonstrate a developed focus. It may lack a closing.
- **Support/Elaboration:** The writing may have some major points developed by specific or general details but may lack depth. It lacks sufficiency to demonstrate developed support.
- **Organization:** The structure is noticeable with some appropriate paragraphing but may have a major digression. Inappropriate or intrusive transitions between and within paragraphs may disrupt the progression of ideas. The writing may lack sufficiency to demonstrate developed organization.
- **Conventions:** Writing demonstrates problems in the mastery of sentence construction with run-on sentences, subject/verb disagreements, or fragments according to

the amount of writing present. Pronouns may be used incorrectly. Writing shows a problem with grade-appropriate spelling and punctuation/capitalization. There may be many major errors in proportion to the amount of writing.

- **Integration:** The writing is partially developed with only some features sufficiently formed. Inference is usually required.

This scoring guide is typical of those in many states. The classroom teacher should keep these goals in mind when leading students through the exercises in this section. The teacher may also find it helpful to occasionally present and discuss selected guidelines from this rubric or those supplied by the NAEP.

Teacher Preparation and Lessons

The activities in this section are designed to provide a variety of interesting experiences in **persuasive** writing with guidelines and supportive instructions that will help students improve their skills. Students are encouraged to use the steps of the writing process.

Each activity has three parts.

- **Part One** consists of **prewriting activities** such as **brainstorming, outlining,** or **clustering.** These can be done individually, with class participation, or by some combination of these two procedures.
- **Part Two** is the writing of a **first draft**. Students should be encouraged to write freely at this point without too much concern about grammar, spelling, or punctuation, thus helping overcome the blocks that many student-writers face by making this part of the process less threatening.
- **Part Three** offers directions for **revising and writing a final copy.** The revision/editing process can be done by the individual student-writer alone, in association with the teacher, or with class participation by having students exchange papers and make suggestions for revisions. It will be helpful to review the proofreading symbols on page 360 and encourage their use as part of the revision process.

It is important that students fully understand the nature and purpose of a persuasive essay and what is expected of them. The directions for each activity offer insight into the purpose of persuasive essays and methods of organization, and it is suggested that these be read aloud and discussed.

The persuasive essays in this section range from simple three-paragraph essays to more detailed ones of five paragraphs. The sample student essays and their scores are taken from actual examples of student writing on standardized tests. They are not meant to be responses to the prompts on this practice test.

Practice Test: Writing Persuasive Essays

The sample student essays on page 296 received ratings of 6 and 3, respectively.

Essay A takes a clear position, the importance of the telephone, and develops it consistently with well-chosen reasons and examples. It is well organized with clear transitions, exhibits a variety in sentence structure, and good word choice. There are few errors in convention except for lack of paragraphing, and this does not interfere with comprehension. This essay scored a 6.

Essay B takes a position, that the light bulb is good for society, but there is no unifying theme beyond that simple observation, which remains undeveloped, and only vague, repetitious ideas are offered as examples. There is some control over sentence boundaries, spelling, and grammar conventions, but not enough to overcome the lack of theme development. This essay scored a 3.

Name ______________________________ Date ______________

7–1. Writing an Editorial (Prewriting)

DIRECTIONS: Congratulations! You have just been appointed editor of your junior high school newspaper, and you are preparing to write your first editorial. (An editorial is an article that expresses the writer's opinion.)

You want to use your first editorial to persuade students to become more involved in school activities. You want to convince them that it is *their* school and that there are many things they can do to make their junior high experience more rewarding and exciting. Think about the many ways they can participate and why they should do so. Then prepare a **brainstorming list** that will help you focus on the subject and write your editorial.

BRAINSTORMING LIST

1. On the lines below, jot down reasons why students should be more active in school. (You don't need sentences here—words and phrases are sufficient.)

   ______________________ ______________________

   ______________________ ______________________

   ______________________ ______________________

2. List all the activities you can think of that are available for student participation.

   ______________________ ______________________

   ______________________ ______________________

   ______________________ ______________________

   ______________________ ______________________

3. Make a list of words and phrases that you can use to make your argument strong and vivid. (Examples: *fun, new friends, thrilling, popular*)

   ______________________ ______________________

   ______________________ ______________________

   ______________________ ______________________

   ______________________ ______________________

4. On the back of this sheet, write an attention-grabbing first sentence for your editorial, such as *Could it be your own fault that you are not having fun in school?*

Name ______________________________ **Date** ______________

7–2. Writing an Editorial (first draft)

A. DIRECTIONS: Write the first draft of a three-paragraph editorial persuading students to participate in school activities. In a newspaper, a title is called a *headline.* Write an appropriate headline for your editorial on the line below. (Example: *A Wake-up Call to Students*)

____

Keep your brainstorming list handy and follow these guidelines:

- **In the first paragraph (*two to three sentences*), state the topic in an interesting way. Begin with a question, a shocking statement, or an anecdote.**
- **In the second paragraph (*at least five sentences*), list the many activities available for students and tell why they will benefit from participating. Use strong, active verbs, colorful adjectives, and sensory language to make your arguments more persuasive.**
- **In the third paragraph (*two to three sentences*), restate and sum up your topic convincingly.**

B. DIRECTIONS: Begin your editorial below and continue on the back of this sheet. This is a first draft, so don't be concerned about grammar, spelling, and punctuation at this point. Concentrate on getting your thoughts down on paper. Remember to indent at the beginning of each paragraph.

____

____

____

____

____

____

____

____

____

Name ______________________________ Date ______________

7–3. Writing an Editorial (final copy)

A. DIRECTIONS: Correct and revise the first draft of your editorial persuading students to become involved in school activities. Use proofreading symbols if you find them helpful. Use the guidelines below and check off each item as you complete it.

- ❑ Are your sentences complete? Correct any run-ons or fragments.
- ❑ Do subjects and verbs agree? Do you use transitional phrases appropriately?
- ❑ Can you make the introductory paragraph more appealing?
- ❑ Does the middle paragraph develop the topic logically? Is it convincing?
- ❑ Do you stay on the topic? Take out any irrelevancies.
- ❑ Do you use active verbs, colorful adjectives, and sensory language? Can you add more of these?
- ❑ Does the final paragraph sum up the topic? Can you make it more convincing?
- ❑ Use a dictionary to check your spelling.

B. DIRECTIONS: Begin the final copy of your editoral below and continue on the back of this sheet. Write the headline on the first line and indent at the beginning of each paragraph.

Name ______________________________ **Date** ______________

7–4. Entering a Contest (prewriting)

DIRECTIONS: A community organization in your town is running a contest for student essays on the topic "Making This a Better Country." Your class has been assigned to write essays on this subject. Think about ways in which you believe this country could be improved. Use the **brainstorming list** below to organize your thoughts in preparation for producing a five-paragraph essay.

BRAINSTORMING LIST

1. Think of three suggestions for making this a better country. List each of these ideas on the lines below.
2. In the box below each item, write as many words and phrases you can think of that describe this idea and its benefits to the country. Include at least one simile.
3. On the back of this sheet, write an interesting or provoking opening sentence for your introductory paragraph. (Example: *I love my country with all my heart, but even the best country in the world is not perfect.*)

Suggestion #1: ______________________________

Suggestion #2: ______________________________

Suggestion #3: ______________________________

Name ____ Date ________________

7–5. Entering a Contest (first draft)

Are you ready to write the first draft of a five-paragraph essay on "Making This a Better Country"? It will be easy to do if you keep your brainstorming list in front of you and organize your essay as follows:

- **In the introductory paragraph (*two to four sentences*), state the topic in a way that will spark the reader's interest. Begin with a question, a provocative statement, or an anecdote.**
- **In the second paragraph (*four to seven sentences*), state your first suggestion. Develop it with descriptive details and persuasive reasons why it will benefit the country. Make the writing vivid with active verbs, sensory words, and colorful adjectives. Include a simile or metaphor if appropriate.**
- **In the third and fourth paragraphs (*four to seven sentences each*), do the same with your second and third suggestions.**
- **In the concluding paragraph (*two to four sentences*), restate and sum up the topic convincingly.**

DIRECTIONS: Begin your five-paragraph essay below and continue on the back of this sheet. This is a first draft, so don't be concerned about grammar, spelling, and punctuation at this point. Concentrate on getting your thoughts down on paper. Remember to indent at the beginning of each paragraph.

Name ______________________________ Date ______________

7–6. ENTERING A CONTEST (FINAL COPY)

A. DIRECTIONS: Exchange copies of the first draft of your essay about "Making This a Better Country" with another student and share suggestions for improvement. Then revise and correct your own paper. Use proofreading symbols if you find them helpful. Use the guidelines below and check off each item as you complete it.

- ❑ Are your sentences complete? Correct any run-ons or fragments.
- ❑ Do subjects and verbs agree?
- ❑ Can you add or change anything to make the introductory paragraph more appealing?
- ❑ Do the three middle paragraphs develop the topic logically? Do you introduce and detail one suggestion in each paragraph?
- ❑ Are your arguments persuasive? Can you change or add anything to make them more convincing?
- ❑ Do you use active verbs, sensory words, and colorful adjectives? Does your essay contain at least one strong simile?
- ❑ Do you stay on the topic at all times? Take out any irrelevancies.
- ❑ Does the final paragraph sum up the topic? Can it be more convincing?
- ❑ Do you vary sentence length, using short and long sentences?
- ❑ Use a dictionary to check your spelling.

B. DIRECTIONS: Begin the final copy of your essay below and continue on the back of this sheet. Write a title on the first line and indent at the beginning of each paragraph.

Name ______________________________ Date ____________

7–7. SHOULD THE LUNCH PROGRAM BE CHANGED? (PREWRITING)

DIRECTIONS: The Board of Education is considering changing the food service in the school cafeteria to a "fast-food lunch program." Are you in favor of this change, or would you prefer to keep the present lunch program? Choose one of these options, and write an article for the school newspaper persuading the readers that your position is better.

- ❑ Fast-food program
- ❑ Present program

Get ready to write a five-paragraph persuasive essay on this topic by first organizing your ideas within a **cluster,** as follows:

1. Write the subject of the essay (FAST-FOOD PROGRAM or PRESENT PROGRAM) in big letters in the center of the circle below.
2. Using smaller print, jot down three main points you wish to make to support your opinion.
3. Near each main point, write words and phrases that describe details about that point in even smaller letters.

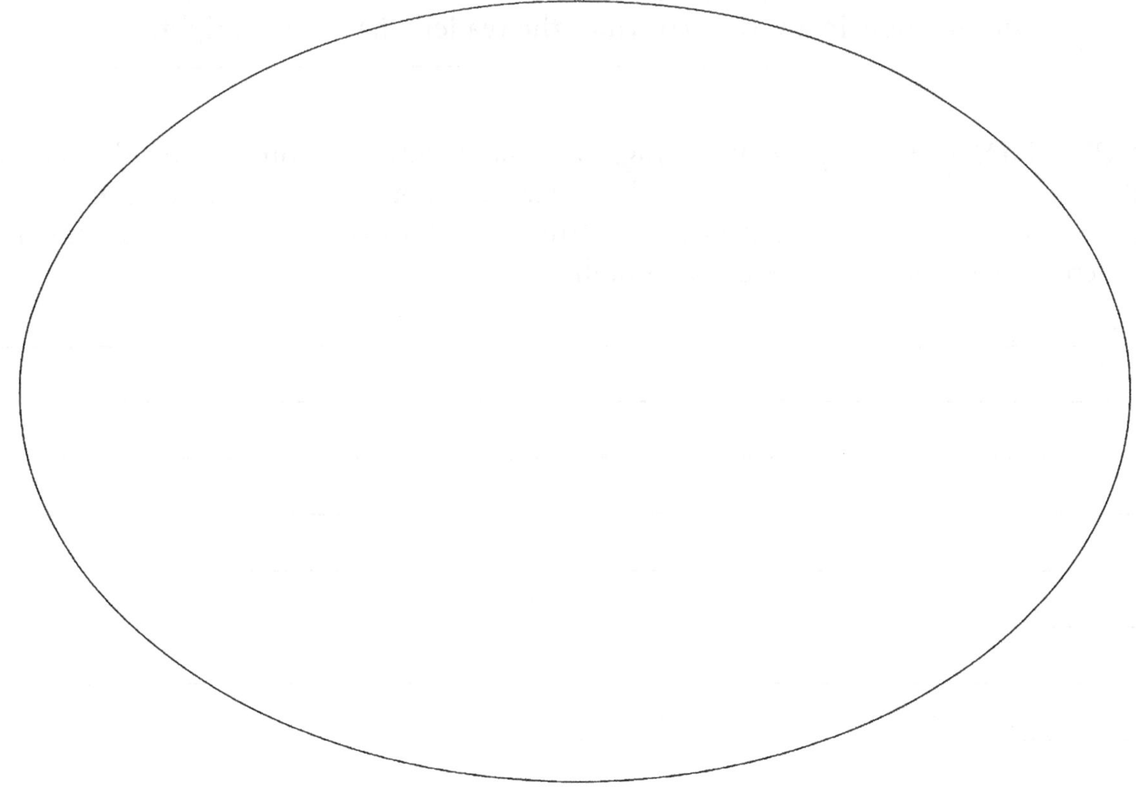

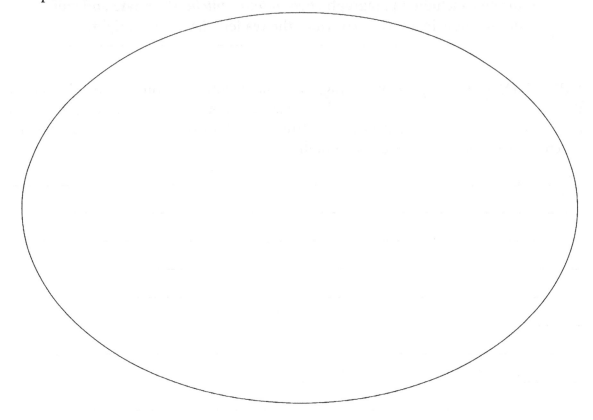

Name ______________________________ Date ______________

7–8. Should the Lunch Program Be Changed? (First Draft)

Get ready to write the first draft of a five-paragraph essay on the issue of keeping the present food service in the school cafeteria or changing it to a fast-food program. Use your cluster as a guide, and organize your essay as follows:

- **In the introductory paragraph (*two to four sentences*), state the topic in an interesting or provocative way. (Example: *Do you gag every time you are faced with the food in our cafeteria? It doesn't have to be that way!*)**
- **In the second paragraph (*four to seven sentences*), state the first main point of your argument. Develop it with details and convincing reasons. Use active verbs, vivid adjectives, and sensory language to enhance your writing.**
- **In the third paragraph (*four to seven sentences*), do the same with your second main point. Use a simile or metaphor to bring your ideas to life.**
- **In the fourth paragraph (*four to seven sentences*), do the same with your third main point.**
- **In the concluding paragraph (*two to four sentences*), restate and sum up the topic in a way to convince the readers that you are right.**

DIRECTIONS: Begin your five-paragraph essay below and continue on the back of this sheet. This is a first draft, so don't be concerned about grammar, spelling, and punctuation at this point. Concentrate on getting your thoughts on paper. Remember to indent at the beginning of each paragraph.

Name ______________________________ Date ______________

7–9. Should the Lunch Program Be Changed? (Final Copy)

A. DIRECTIONS: Correct and revise the first draft of your essay about changing (or keeping) the food program in your school cafeteria. Use proofreading symbols if you find them helpful. Use the guidelines below and check off each item as you complete it.

- ❑ **Are your sentences complete? Correct any run-ons or fragments.**
- ❑ **Do subjects and verbs agree? Do pronouns agree with antecedents?**
- ❑ **Do you use transitional words and phrases where needed?**
- ❑ **Can you make the introductory paragraph more interesting?**
- ❑ **Does each middle paragraph state and develop one main point? Can you strengthen your arguments in any way?**
- ❑ **Do you stay on the topic? Remove any irrelevancies.**
- ❑ **Do you use active verbs, colorful adjectives, sensory language, and at least one simile?**
- ❑ **Does the final paragraph restate and sum up the topic?**
- ❑ **Use a dictionary to check your spelling.**

B. DIRECTIONS: Begin the final copy of your essay below and continue on the back of this sheet. Indent at the beginning of each paragraph.

Name ______________________________ Date ______________

7–10. Country Living vs. City Living (Prewriting)

DIRECTIONS: Your best friend is moving from the city to the country. He and his parents say that country living is better. Do you agree, or do you think it is better to live in a city? You will write a five-paragraph persuasive essay. Choose one of the titles below and place a check next to the one you have chosen.

- ❑ Country Living Is Better
- ❑ City Living Is Better

Think of three reasons to support your choice. Organize these thoughts in a **brainstorming list** below. In the box following each point, write as many words and phrases as you can to detail and support this point. Include active verbs, sensory words, and vivid adjectives.

BRAINSTORMING LIST

First main point: ______________________________

Second main point: ______________________________

Third main point: ______________________________

Now, on the back of this sheet, write an interesting or provocative opening sentence for your introductory paragraph.

Name ______________________________ **Date** ______________

7–11. Country Living vs. City Living (first draft)

It's time to write the first draft of a five-paragraph essay on whether country living or city living is better. Keep your brainstorming list handy and organize your essay as follows:

- **In the introductory paragraph (*two to four sentences*), write a beginning that will spark reader interest, such as *I always considered myself a city person, but now I am beginning to believe that country living is better. I find myself strangely attracted to wide open spaces, clean air, and friendly neighbors.***
- **In the second paragraph (*four to seven sentences*), state your first main point. It is usually best to introduce your strongest point first. Make the writing vivid with active verbs, sensory words, and colorful adjectives. Use a simile, if possible. Be convincing!**
- **In the third paragraph (*four to seven sentences*), follow the same procedure with your second main point. Stay on the topic!**
- **In the fourth paragraph (*four to seven sentences*), follow the same procedure with your third main point.**
- **In the concluding paragraph (*two to four sentences*), restate and sum up the topic. Make your conclusion convincing to the reader.**

DIRECTIONS: Begin your five-paragraph essay below and continue on the back of this sheet. This is just a first draft, so don't be concerned about grammar, spelling, and punctuation at this point. Concentrate on getting your thoughts down on paper. Remember to indent at the beginning of each paragraph.

Name ______________________________ Date ______________

7–12. Country Living vs. City Living (Final Copy)

A. DIRECTIONS: Correct and revise the first draft of your essay. Try to make it as perfect as you can. Use proofreading symbols if these are helpful. Use the guidelines below and check off each item as you complete it.

- ❑ **Are your sentences complete? Correct any run-ons or fragments.**
- ❑ **Do subjects and verbs agree? Do pronouns agree with antecedents?**
- ❑ **Can you make the introductory paragraph more exciting?**
- ❑ **Do you introduce one main point in each of the three middle paragraphs?**
- ❑ **Can you add more details to make your argument convincing?**
- ❑ **Can you add more active verbs, colorful adjectives, and sensory language?**
- ❑ **Do you use at least one simile effectively?**
- ❑ **Do you stay on the topic? Take out any irrelevancies.**
- ❑ **Does the final paragraph restate and sum up the topic convincingly?**
- ❑ **Use a dictionary to check your spelling.**

B. DIRECTIONS: Begin the final copy of your essay below and continue on the back of this sheet. Write a title on the first line and indent at the beginning of each paragraph.

Name ______________________________ Date ____________

7–13. Does Watching TV Affect Students' Grades? (Prewriting)

DIRECTIONS: *Watching TV affects students' grades adversely.* Do you agree or disagree with this statement? Express your opinion in a five-paragraph persuasive essay. First, organize your thoughts by completing the **brainstorming list** below.

BRAINSTORMING LIST

1. Choose one of the following titles for your essay.
   - ❑ Watching TV Affects Students' Grades Adversely
   - ❑ Watching TV Does Not Affect Students' Grades Adversely
2. Think of three main points that you can use to support your opinion and list each one below. In the box below each item, write a list of words and phrases you can use to develop this point in your essay. Be sure to include active verbs, colorful adjectives, and sensory language.

   Point #1: ______________________________

   Point #2: ______________________________

   Point #3: ______________________________
3. On the back of this sheet, write an interesting or provocative opening sentence for your introductory paragraph.

Name ______________________________ Date ______________

7–14. Does Watching TV Affect Students' Grades? (First Draft)

Get ready to write a five-paragraph essay expressing your opinion whether or not watching TV affects students' grades. Use the notes on your brainstorming list and the following suggestions as guidelines.

- **In the first paragraph (*two to four sentences*), state the topic. Get the reader's attention with a question, a provocative statement, or an anecdote, such as *Don't believe everything you hear! It is not true that watching TV has a bad effect on grades. In my case, just the opposite is true.***
- **In the second paragraph (*four to seven sentences*), state your first main point and support it with details and examples. Use the active verbs, sensory words, and colorful adjectives from your brainstorming list. Try to include a simile.**
- **In the third and fourth paragraphs (*four to seven sentences each*), follow the same procedure with your second and third main points.**
- **In the concluding paragraph (*two to four sentences*), restate and sum up your opinion in a convincing way.**

DIRECTIONS: Begin your five-paragraph essay below and continue on the back of this sheet. This is a first draft, so don't be concerned about spelling, grammar, or punctuation at this point. Concentrate on getting your thoughts on paper. Write the title on the first line and indent at the beginning of each paragraph.

Name ______________________________ Date ______________

7–15. Does Watching TV Affect Students' Grades? (Final Copy)

A. DIRECTIONS: Exchange copies of the first draft of your essay with another student and share suggestions for improvement. Then revise and correct your own paper. Use proofreading symbols if you find them helpful. Use the following guidelines and check off each item as you complete it.

- ❑ Are your sentences complete? Correct any run-ons or fragments.
- ❑ Do subjects and verbs agree?
- ❑ Can you make the introductory paragraph more exciting?
- ❑ Do the three middle paragraphs develop the topic clearly and logically? Do you introduce one main point in each paragraph and develop it?
- ❑ Can you add or change anything to make your arguments more convincing?
- ❑ Is your language as vivid, sensory, and colorful as you can make it?
- ❑ Add one interesting simile.
- ❑ Do you stay on topic? Take out any irrelevancies.
- ❑ Can you restate your argument more persuasively in the concluding paragraph?

B. DIRECTIONS: Begin the final copy of your essay below and continue on the back of the sheet. Put the title on the first line and indent at the beginning of each paragraph.

Name ________________________________ Date ______________

7–16. Convincing Others to Help Their Country (Prewriting)

DIRECTIONS: President John F. Kennedy said, "Ask not what your country can do for you. Ask what you can do for your country." Think about ways in which you could help your country or community. Then write an essay persuading teenagers that they can make a contribution to their country or community. First, complete the **brainstorming list** below.

BRAINSTORMING LIST

1. List one thing teenagers can do to help their country or community.

   ____

   In the box below, write words and phrases you will be able to use to describe this, to explain how to do it and why it should be done.

2. List a second way that teenagers can help their country or community.

   ____

   In the box below, write words and phrases you will be able to use to describe this, to explain how to do it and why it should be done.

3. List a third way that teenagers can help their country or community.

   ____

   In the box below, write words and phrases you will be able to use to describe this, to explain how to do it and why it should be done.

Name ______________________________ Date ______________

7–17. Convincing Others to Help Their Country (first draft)

Are you ready to write a five-paragraph essay persuading teenagers to do things for their country or community? Organize the essay by using your brainstorming list as a guide and following these suggestions:

- **In the first paragraph (*two to four sentences*), state the topic. You might wish to refer to President Kennedy's words or even quote them: *John F. Kennedy said, "Ask not what your country can do for you. Ask what you can do for your country." Even teenagers have talents and skills they can contribute for the benefit of all. What are some of the things you can do?***
- **In the second paragraph (*four to seven sentences*), describe the first activity on your brainstorming list, giving many details about how to do it and why. Be persuasive and convincing!**
- **In the third and fourth paragraphs (*four to seven sentences each*), follow the same procedure for the second and third activities.**
- **In the concluding paragraph (*two to four sentences*), restate and sum up the topic in a way that will convince teenagers that their contributions are important.**

DIRECTIONS: Begin your five-paragraph essay below and continue on the back of this sheet. This is a first draft, so concentrate on getting your thoughts down on paper and don't be too concerned about spelling, punctuation, and grammar at this point. Remember to indent at the beginning of paragraphs.

Name ______________________________ Date ______________

7–18. Convincing Others to Help Their Country (final draft)

A. DIRECTIONS: Revise and correct your essay about what teenagers can do for their country or their community. Use the following guidelines, and check off each item as you complete it.

- ❑ **Are your sentences complete? Correct any run-ons or fragments.**
- ❑ **Do subjects and verbs agree?**
- ❑ **Do pronouns agree with their antecedents?**
- ❑ **Do you introduce the topic in the first paragraph, and then develop it by discussing one main point in each of the three middle paragraphs?**
- ❑ **Do you stay on the topic? Remove any irrelevancies.**
- ❑ **Can you make your writing stronger with active verbs, colorful adjectives, and sensory language?**
- ❑ **Do you restate and sum up the topic in the concluding paragraph? Can you change or add anything to be more convincing?**
- ❑ **Do you vary sentence length, using short and long sentences?**

B. DIRECTIONS: Begin your final copy below and continue on the back of this sheet. Remember to indent at the beginning of each paragraph.

Name ______________________________ Date ____________

7–19. A Park vs. a Shopping Center (Prewriting)

DIRECTIONS: There is a beautiful park not far from your home. The town is considering a proposal to sell the property to a developer who wants to build a shopping center there. Many people in your community are upset at the prospect of losing this park. What do you think? Is this a good proposal? Why or why not? You are going to write an essay that expresses your opinion. First, complete the **brainstorming list** below.

BRAINSTORMING LIST

1. Choose one of the following titles. Check the one you have chosen.

   ❑ Preserve Our Beautiful Park
   ❑ We Need a Neighborhood Shopping Center

2. Think of three main points to support your opinion. List these points below. In the box below each, write words and phrases you can use to develop that point.

Main Point #1: ______________________________

Main Point #2: ______________________________

Main Point #3: ______________________________

Name ______________________________ **Date** ______________

7–20. A Park vs. a Shopping Center (First Draft)

Get ready to write a five-paragraph essay with one of these titles: "Preserve Our Beautiful Park" or "We Need a Neighborhood Shopping Center." Use your brainstorming list as a guide, and follow these suggestions:

- **In the first paragraph (*two to four sentences*), state the topic in a way that will get the reader's attention, with a question, provocative statement, or anecdote, such as *Do you want to live in a world without parks and trees? That could happen if greedy developers get their way.***
- **In the second paragraph (*four to seven sentences*), state your first point in a convincing way. Use active verbs, colorful adjectives, and sensory words to make your writing more vivid.**
- **In the third and fourth paragraphs (*four to seven sentences each*), follow the same procedure with the second and third points. Develop them convincingly with exciting details.**
- **In the concluding paragraph (*two to four sentences*), restate and sum up the topic in a way that will persuade your readers that your point of view is better.**

DIRECTIONS: Begin your five-paragraph essay below and continue on the back of this sheet. This is a first draft, so concentrate on getting your thoughts down without too much concern about spelling, punctuation, and grammar. Write the title on the first line and indent at the beginning of each paragraph.

____

____

____

____

____

____

____

____

____

Name ______________________________ Date ______________

7–21. A Park vs. a Shopping Center (final copy)

A. DIRECTIONS: Revise and correct your essay expressing your opinion on whether to build a shopping center or preserve a park. Use the following guidelines, and check off each item as you complete it.

- ❑ Do you introduce the topic clearly and in an interesting way?
- ❑ Do you state one main point in each of the middle paragraphs and provide details to support your opinion?
- ❑ Do you stay on the topic at all times? Take out any irrelevancies.
- ❑ Make your writing stronger by adding active verbs, colorful adjectives, and sensory language.
- ❑ Include at least one simile or metaphor in your essay.
- ❑ Do you restate and sum up the topic in the last paragraph? Can you make the conclusion more convincing?
- ❑ Are your sentences complete? Correct any run-ons or fragments.
- ❑ Do subjects and verbs agree? Do pronouns agree with their antecedents?
- ❑ Check spelling with a dictionary.

B. DIRECTIONS: Begin your final copy below and continue on the back of this sheet. Write the title on the first line and indent at the beginning of each paragraph.

Name ______________________________ **Date** ______________

7–22. Writing About School Violence (prewriting)

DIRECTIONS: People around the country are concerned about increased violence in schools. You are going to write a five-paragraph essay telling how you think this problem can be solved. First, organize your thoughts by completing the **brainstorming list** below.

BRAINSTORMING LIST

1. In the box below, write words and phrases that will help you describe what **communities and local school districts** can do to help this problem.

2. In the box below, write words and phrases that will help you describe what **school administrators** can do to help this problem.

3. In the box below, write words and phrases that will help you describe what **students themselves** can do to help this problem.

4. On the back of this sheet, write an attention-getting opening sentence (question, provocative statement, or anecdote) for your introductory paragraph.

Name ____ Date ________________

7–23. Writing About School Violence (first draft)

Get ready to write a five-paragraph essay about solutions to the problem of school violence. Keep your brainstorming list handy and follow these suggestions:

- **In the first paragraph (*two to four sentences*), introduce the topic in an interesting way with a question, provocative statement, or anecdote.**
- **In the second paragraph (*four to seven sentences*), discuss ways that the community or school district can help with this problem. Use words and phrases from your brainstorming list.**
- **In the third paragraph (*four to seven sentences*), discuss ways that the school administration can help with this problem. Use words and phrases from your brainstorming list.**
- **In the fourth paragraph (*four to seven sentences*), discuss how individual students can help solve this problem. Offer specific details and use words and phrases from your brainstorming list.**
- **In the concluding paragraph (*two to four sentences*), restate and sum up the topic. Emphasize its importance to your school and to the entire country.**

DIRECTIONS: Begin the first draft of your essay below and continue on the back of this sheet. This is a first draft, so don't be too concerned about spelling, punctuation, or grammar at this point. Remember to indent at the beginning of each paragraph.

Name ______________________________________ Date ______________

7–24. WRITING ABOUT SCHOOL VIOLENCE (FINAL COPY)

A. DIRECTIONS: Revise and correct the first draft of your essay about the problem of school violence. Follow the guidelines below, and check off each item as you complete it.

- ❑ **Are your sentences complete? Correct any run-ons or fragments.**
- ❑ **Do subjects and verbs agree? Do pronouns agree with their antecedents?**
- ❑ **Does the introductory paragraph state the topic in an exciting way?**
- ❑ **Do you introduce one main point in each of the three middle paragraphs?**
- ❑ **Can you add more details to make your argument more convincing?**
- ❑ **Can you add more active verbs, colorful adjectives, and sensory language?**
- ❑ **Do you stay on the topic? Take out any irrelevancies.**
- ❑ **Does the final paragraph restate and sum up the topic convincingly?**
- ❑ **Use a dictionary to check your spelling.**

B. DIRECTIONS: Begin the final copy of your essay below and continue on the back of this sheet. Remember to indent at the beginning of each paragraph.

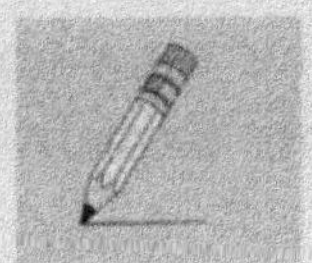

Eighth-Grade Level

Writing Persuasive Essays Practice Test

Name ______________________________ Date ______________

Practice Test: Writing Persuasive Essays

DIRECTIONS: Your Board of Education is exploring the idea of school uniforms. Some people think that students will be able to concentrate more if they aren't thinking about how they look or what they are wearing. Others think it will be easier on family budgets if students wear uniforms.

Write a five-paragraph persuasive essay about whether you agree or disagree that students should wear school uniforms. Explain how uniforms could affect students and why you think as you do.

Follow these four steps to write your essay:

- FIRST, on the page labeled PREWRITING, brainstorm essay ideas and examples that support the topic. Include words and phrases you can use.
- SECOND, write the first draft of your essay on a separate sheet of paper. Write your name and date at the top, and the title of the essay. Use your notes from the prewriting page.
- THIRD, revise and edit your first draft. Refer to your list of proofreading symbols if you wish to make use of these. Use the checklist as a guide, and check off each item when it is revised to your satisfaction.
- FOURTH, write your final copy on a separate sheet of paper with your name and date at the top.

CHECKLIST

- ❑ **Does your introductory paragraph state the topic clearly? Can you make it more interesting by using a surprising statement, a question, or an anecdote?**
- ❑ **Do your three middle paragraphs develop the topic in a clear and logical way? Can you be more convincing?**
- ❑ **Do you stay on the topic and avoid irrelevancies? Do you use only examples and details that are related to the topic?**
- ❑ **Do all your subjects and verbs agree?**
- ❑ **Do pronouns agree with their antecedents?**
- ❑ **Can you make your writing more vivid with active verbs or colorful adjectives?**
- ❑ **Are your sentences complete? Correct any run-ons or fragments.**
- ❑ **Do you vary sentence length, using short and long sentences?**
- ❑ **Have you indented at the beginning of each paragraph?**
- ❑ **Are all words spelled correctly?**

Name ______________________ Date ____________

Practice Test: Writing Persuasive Essays *(continued)*

Prewriting

Think about three main points you will use in your argument about school uniforms. List these points in the box below. You can arrange them as an outline, a brainstorming list, or a cluster. For each point, add words and phrases that will give supporting details.

Name ______________________________ Date ______________

PRACTICE TEST: WRITING PERSUASIVE ESSAYS *(continued)*

Student Samples

ESSAY A

I think an invention that has affected our lives is the telephone. It has changed the way our society works. When Alexander Bell invented the "silly contraption that would be of no use," he couldn't have possible known the difference it would make in people's lives. People used to use the telephone for only emergency phone calls and still others refused to use it at all. Now, though, in the twenty-first century, telephones are one of the most important tools in our everyday lives. We use it to make business calls, make appointments, and chat with friends we see regurlarly. How would you feel if you had to write a letter everyday just to make casual small talk? It was amazing how people eighty years ago would write an eight page letter instead of using that same hand to dial a telephone number? I know I certainly would rather hear my friends voices instead of waiting three weeks for a simple letter to be delivered. It has changed our society and our way of thinking. If the telephone had not been invented, we probably wouldn't have such things as the Internet or even television. Alexander Bell proved with his invention that a simple black contraption could change the way of a whole society. No matter what form it takes, cellular, cordless, or dial, the telephone has still affected our lives in countless ways.

Score ____________

ESSAY B

One invention this is good for our society is the light bulb. It gives us light when it is dark and if we did not have it we would not be able to see at night. Without light it would be total darkness all over the world. I think it is a good invention and has really come a long way. We use it in so many ways like in our, houses, flashlights, street lights, and many more things. Now we do not need to use candle power anymore, With the light bulb it brought many new inventions. Ever since the light bulb was invented we havent had any bad things happen besides a power out, but that is all. The light bulb is a good invention. It has worked out very well.

Score ____________

Scoring Guide

SCORE	Unsatisfactory—1	Insufficient—2
Content	Attempts to respond to prompt, but provides few details; may only paraphrase prompt	Presents fragmented information OR may be very repetitive OR may be very undeveloped
Organization	Has no clear organization OR consists of a single statement	Is very disorganized; ideas are weakly connected OR the response is too brief to detect organization
Sentence Structure	Little or no control over sentence boundaries and sentence structure; word choice may be incorrect in much or all of the response	Little control over sentence boundaries and sentence structure; word choice may often be incorrect
Grammar, Usage, and Mechanics	Many errors in grammar or usage—such as tense inconsistency, lack of subject–verb agreement—spelling, and punctuation severely interfere with understanding	Errors in grammar or usage—such as inconsistency, lack of subject–verb agreement—spelling, and punctuation interfere with understanding in much of the response

SCORE	Uneven—3	Sufficient—4
Content	Presents some clear information, but is list-like, undeveloped, or repetitive OR offers no more than a well-written beginning	Develops information with some details
Organization	Is unevenly organized; the essay may be disjointed	The essay is organized with ideas that are generally related but has few or no transitions
Sentence Structure	Exhibits uneven control over sentence boundaries and sentence structure; may have some incorrect word choices	Exhibits control over sentence boundaries and sentence structure, but sentences and word choice may be simple and unvaried
Grammar, Usage, and Mechanics	Errors in grammar or usage—such as tense inconsistency, lack of subject–verb agreement—spelling, and punctuation sometimes interfere with understanding	Errors in grammar or usage—such as tense inconsistency, lack of subject–verb agreement—spelling, and punctuation do not interfere with understanding

SCORE	Skillful—5	Excellent—6
Content	Develops and shapes information with details in parts of the essay	Develops and shapes information with well-chosen details across the essay
Organization	Is clearly organized; but may lack some transitions and/or have lapses in continuity	Is well organized with strong transitions
Sentence Structure	Exhibits some variety in sentence structure and some good word choices	Sustains variety in sentence structure and exhibits good word choice
Grammar, Usage, and Mechanics	Errors in grammar, spelling, and punctuation do not interfere with understanding	Errors in grammar, spelling, and punctuation are few and do not interfere with understanding

Section 8

NARRATIVE WRITING

Standardized Testing Information

Students generally find narrative writing the easiest type to do and the most fun because this type of writing allows for flexibility in structure and content as well as the use of imagination and personal experience. More assessment tests use narrative prompts than those of any other kind. These include personal narratives (true stories about something that has happened to or been observed by the writer) and stories (fictional narratives where the details arise from the imagination of the writer). Both personal narratives and imaginative stories use similar narrative techniques and are grouped together in this section.

The National Assessment of Educational Progress (NAEP) defines narrative writing as "the production of stories or personal essays." The NAEP guidelines go on to say that narrative writing "encourages writers to use their creativity and powers of observation to develop stories that can capture a reader's imagination." Information on the NAEP can be found at www.NAGB.org or at www.nces.ed.gov/nationsreportcard.

Narrative writing, therefore, is of two types:

The **personal narrative, or narrative essay,** is usually written from the writer's point of view. Generally, the subject is something that has actually happened and events are related in chronological order. The people and places are real as is any dialogue that is used.

An **imaginative narrative** is also generally narrated in chronological order, but is fictional in nature, and has fictional characters and fictional dialogue.

Here are examples of prompts that have been used in eighth-grade assessment tests. The first prompt is clearly for a **personal** narrative. The second is a **story** prompt.

> **Example #1**—We all have memories connected to our experiences. Think about an experience you feel you'll always remember. Try to picture the time, the place, and the people involved. Try to remember everything you can about this experience. Write about the experiences you remember. Be sure to include enough details so that your reader can share your experience. Show why this memory stands out for you.

> **Example #2**—Imagine this situation! A noise outside awakens you one night. You look out the window and see a spaceship. The door of the spaceship opens, and out walks a space creature. What does the creature look like? What do you do? Write a story about what happens next.

State guidelines for narrative writing are similar to those presented by the NAEP. Florida, for example, offers the following grade-level expectations for writing at the eighth-grade level.

- Knows and experiments with possible prewriting strategies for different writing tasks.
- Uses a prewriting strategy suitable for the task (for example, brainstorming, using a graphic organizer, listing ideas).

- Focuses on central ideas or topics (for example, excludes loosely related, extraneous, or repetitious information).
- Uses devices to develop relationships among ideas (for example, transitional devices).
- Uses supporting ideas, details, and facts from a variety of sources to develop and elaborate topic.
- Demonstrates a commitment to and an involvement with the subject that engages the reader.
- Demonstrates a command of language (including but not limited to precise word choice and appropriate figurative language).
- Uses an effective organizational pattern and substantial support to achieve a sense of completeness or wholeness (for example, considering audience, sequencing events, choosing effective words, using specific details to clarify meaning).
- Proofreads writing to correct convention errors in mechanics, usage, and punctuation, using dictionaries, handbooks, and other resources, including teacher or peers, as appropriate.
- Analyzes and revises draft to further develop a piece of writing by adding or deleting details and explanations; clarifying difficult passages; and rearranging words, sentences, and paragraphs to improve meaning.
- Uses resources such as dictionary and thesaurus to confirm spelling.
- Uses conventions of punctuation (including but not limited to end punctuation, commas, colons, semicolons, quotation marks, apostrophes).
- Uses conventions of capitalization (including but not limited to the names of organizations, nationalities, races, languages, religions).

Florida also mandates the following scoring rubrics for eighth-grade writing assessments, using a scale of 6 to 1, with 6 being the highest score and 1 being the lowest:

- **6:** The writing focuses on the topic, is logically organized, and includes ample development of supporting ideas or examples. It demonstrates a mature command of language, including precision in word choice. Sentences vary in structure. Punctuation, capitalization, and spelling are generally correct.
- **5:** The writing focuses on the topic with adequate development of supporting ideas or examples. It has an organizational pattern, though lapses may occur. Word choice is adequate. Sentences vary in structure. Punctuation, capitalization, and spelling are generally correct.
- **4:** The writing focuses on the topic, though it may contain extraneous information. An organizational pattern is evident, but lapses may occur. Some supporting ideas contain specifics and details, but others are not developed. Word choice is adequate. Sentences vary somewhat in structure, though many are simple. Punctuation, capitalization, and spelling are usually correct.
- **3:** The writing generally focuses on the topic, though it may contain extraneous information. An organizational pattern has been attempted, but lapses may occur. Some of the supporting ideas or examples may not be developed. Word choice is adequate. Sentences vary somewhat in structure, though many are simple. Punctuation and capitalization are sometimes incorrect, but most commonly used words are spelled correctly.

- **2:** The writing may be slightly related to the topic or offer little relevant information and few supporting ideas or examples. There is little evidence of an organizational pattern. Word choice may be limited or immature. Sentences may be limited to simple constructions. Frequent errors may occur in punctuation, capitalization, and spelling.
- **1:** The writing may only minimally address the topic because there is little or no development of supporting ideas or examples. No organizational pattern is evident. Ideas are provided through lists, and word choice is limited or immature. Unrelated information may be included. Frequent errors in punctuation, capitalization, and spelling may impede communication.

These guidelines and rubrics are typical, and the classroom teacher should keep them in mind when leading students through the exercises in this section. The teacher may also find it helpful to occasionally present and discuss with the students selected guidelines from this rubric or those used by NAEP.

Teacher Preparation and Lessons

The activities in this section are designed to provide a variety of interesting experiences in narrative writing with guidelines and supportive instructions that will lead the students through the writing process and enhance their skills while also stimulating interest in this kind of writing.

Each activity has three parts.

- **Part One** consists of **prewriting** activities such as **brainstorming**, **clustering**, or **outlining**. These can be done individually, in small groups, with whole class participation, or by some combination of these three procedures. In addition to jotting down ideas and making lists of words and phrases to be used in the essay, students should also be advised and guided to use this step of the writing process to provide an organizational framework for their writing.
- **Part Two** is the **writing of a first draft**. Students should be encouraged to write freely at this point without too much concern about grammar, spelling, and punctuation, thus helping overcome the blocks that many student-writers face, by making this part of the process less threatening. This is especially important in narrative writing where a free flow of imagination and creativity is called for.
- **Part Three** offers directions for **revising and writing a final copy**. The revision and editing process can be done by the individual student-writer alone, in association with the teacher, or with class participation by having students exchange papers and make suggestions for revision. Each revision activity includes a checklist for students to refer to during the editing process. It will be helpful to review the proofreading symbols on page 360. Students should have copies of these at hand and be encouraged to use them as part of the revision process.

This unit on narrative writing should be introduced in a positive, upbeat, exciting manner that will make it clear this is the sort of activity that the students will truly enjoy. The teacher can say something like, "What kind of 'composition' do you put together every day? Probably you compose at least one personal narrative—a true story about something that has happened to you or to someone you know. You usually tell these stories orally to your friends, family, and teachers. With a little practice, you can easily acquire the skill to write down these personal narratives in a way that will be interesting to other people."

Before beginning activities that involve the writing of imaginative stories, it is helpful if the teacher and/or students first read aloud one or more exciting passages from a work of fiction to prepare the students for their own flights of imagination.

The directions for each activity will help students understand the purposes and methods of narrative writing. It is suggested that these be read aloud and discussed.

The narrative essays in this section range from simple three-paragraph essays to detailed ones of five paragraphs.

Practice Test: Narrative Writing

The student samples on page 331 received ratings of 3 and 6, respectively.

Story A attempts to tell a story, but it is more like a brief outline for a story, and remains underdeveloped. Some interesting descriptions are attempted, but are not developed. The writer exhibits poor control over sentence boundaries and sentence structure. At some points, errors in grammar and punctuation interfere with understanding. This essay scored a 3.

Story B tells a clear story that is well developed and shaped with well-chosen details across the response, even including a humorous reference to "Armani suit." It is well organized with strong transitions. It sustains variety in sentence structure and shows good word choice, exhibiting a good control over language and form. The few errors in grammar and punctuation do not interfere with enjoyment and understanding. This essay scored a 6.

Name ______________________________ Date ______________

8–1. A Memorable Experience (prewriting)

DIRECTIONS: The first time we do anything can be memorable. We may forget about the many times it happens later, but the *first* such event usually stays in our minds. Think of any first-time experience you would enjoy telling about. Here are some possible topics:

The First Time I Ate Sushi

The First Time I Rode on a Roller Coaster

The First Time I Rode a Two-Wheeler

Choose one of these, or any other first-time experience of your own. Write the title here.

____

Your story will be easier to write if you first prepare a **brainstorming list.**

BRAINSTORMING LIST

1. On the lines below and on the back of this sheet, list as many facts as you can recall about the experience, including where it happened, when it happened, how old you were at the time, who else was there, what happened step by step, what everyone did, and how you felt about it. (You don't need complete sentences here—words and phrases are enough.)

____

____

____

____

____

____

2. In the box below, write vivid words and phrases that you will be able to use to make the reader see this experience as clearly as you remember it. Include active verbs, colorful adjectives, sensory words, and at least one simile or metaphor.

Name ______________________________ Date ______________

8–2. A Memorable Experience (first draft)

Are you ready to write the first draft of your narrative about a "first-time experience"? Use your brainstorming list and follow these guidelines:

- **In the first paragraph (*two to four sentences*), introduce the topic in an interesting way, such as *Today, I ride my bike all over town. It doesn't seem any harder than putting one foot in front of the other when walking, but I didn't always feel that way about my bike. In fact, the first time I saw it, I cried and ran away when my dad wanted me to get on.***
- **In the second paragraph (*three to six sentences*), describe where this event occurred, your age at the time, and who else was present. Use the colorful adjectives, active verbs, and sensory language in your brainstorming list.**
- **In the third paragraph (*three to six sentences*), tell step by step exactly what happened. Use vivid language to help the reader see the event the way you can in your mind.**
- **In the fourth paragraph (*three to six sentences*), use interesting details to describe the final outcome. Describe how you felt about it.**
- **In the concluding paragraph (*two to four sentences*), restate the topic and sum up the experience in a way that will satisfy the reader.**

DIRECTIONS: Begin your essay below and continue on the back of this sheet. This is a first draft, so concentrate on getting your thoughts on paper and don't be too concerned about spelling, punctuation, or grammar at this point. Write the title on the first line and indent at the beginning of each paragraph.

Name ______________________________ Date ______________

8–3. A Memorable Experience (Final Copy)

A. DIRECTIONS: Correct and revise the first draft of your essay about a first-time experience. Use proofreading symbols if you find these helpful. Read the following guidelines carefully, and check off each item as you complete it.

- ❑ **Does the introductory paragraph state the topic? Can you make it more attention-getting with a question or a surprising statement?**
- ❑ **Do the middle paragraphs develop the topic with supporting details? Are details clearly stated and organized?**
- ❑ **Can you add more vivid language, such as active verbs, colorful adjectives, and sensory language to bring the action to life for the reader?**
- ❑ **Add at least one simile or metaphor.**
- ❑ **Do you stay focused on the topic? Remove any irrelevancies.**
- ❑ **Does the final paragraph sum up the topic in an interesting way?**
- ❑ **Are your sentences complete? Correct any run-ons or fragments.**
- ❑ **Do subjects and verbs agree? Do pronouns agree with their antecedents?**
- ❑ **Use a dictionary to check your spelling.**

B. DIRECTIONS: Begin the final copy of your essay below and continue on the back of this sheet. Write the title on the first line and indent at the beginning of each paragraph.

____

____

____

____

____

____

____

____

____

____

Name ______________________________ Date ______________

8–4. Unfair Treatment (prewriting)

DIRECTIONS: Have you ever heard the saying "Life is not fair"? That can be true sometimes. Think about an experience you have had where you felt you were being treated unfairly, or remember a time when you observed someone else being treated unfairly. Write a five-paragraph essay telling about this incident. First, however, organize your thoughts by preparing a **brainstorming list**.

BRAINSTORMING LIST

1. Briefly note when and where the incident occurred and who was present. (You don't need sentences here—just words and/or phrases.)

   When: ______________________________

   Where: ______________________________

   Who: ______________________________

2. Briefly describe what occurred. (You don't need sentences—just words and phrases.)

   ____

   ____

   ____

   ____

3. In this box, write words and phrases you can use to make your essay come to life for the reader, such as active verbs, colorful adjectives, sensory words, and at least one simile or metaphor.

4. Choose a title for your essay and write it below. (*Example:* "It Wasn't Fair!")

   ____

Name ______________________________ Date ______________

8–5. UNFAIR TREATMENT (FIRST DRAFT)

Get ready to write the first draft of your narrative about an unfair experience. Follow the form and organization you prepared on your brainstorming list. Here are some suggested guidelines to make your writing easier.

- **In the first paragraph (*two to four sentences*), introduce the topic in an interesting way. (Example: *Have you ever been horribly disappointed in someone? That's how I felt when my favorite teacher turned out to be unfair.*)**
- **In the second paragraph (*four to seven sentences*), tell when and where this occurred. Tell who was there. Use vivid language to describe time, background, and people.**
- **In the third paragraph (*four to seven sentences*), tell step by step exactly what happened. Use active verbs and a simile or metaphor to bring the action to life.**
- **In the fourth paragraph (*three to six sentences*), describe the result of this incident and how it made you feel.**
- **In the fifth paragraph (*two to four sentences*), sum up the topic in a way that will satisfy the reader.**

DIRECTIONS: Begin your essay below and continue on the back of this sheet. This is a first draft, so don't be too concerned about spelling, grammar, or punctuation at this point. Concentrate on getting your thoughts on paper. Write the title on the first line and indent at the beginning of each paragraph.

Name ______________________________ Date ______________

8–6. Unfair Treatment (final copy)

A. DIRECTIONS: Correct and revise the first draft of your essay about an unfair experience. Refer to your list of proofreading symbols if you find these helpful. Read the guidelines below carefully and check off each item as you complete it.

- ❏ **Does the introductory paragraph state the topic in an interesting way?**
- ❏ **Do the middle paragraphs tell what happened in a logical progression?**
- ❏ **Do you stay focused on the topic? Remove any irrelevancies.**
- ❏ **Can you add more vivid language such as active verbs, colorful adjectives, sensory words, similes, or metaphors to make your writing come to life?**
- ❏ **Does the final paragraph sum up the topic in a way that satisfies the reader?**
- ❏ **Are your sentences complete? Correct any run-ons or fragments.**
- ❏ **Do subjects and verbs agree? Do pronouns agree with their antecedents?**
- ❏ **Do you vary sentence length, using both short and long sentences?**
- ❏ **Use a dictionary to check spelling.**

B. DIRECTIONS: Begin the final copy of your essay below and continue on the back of this sheet. Write the title on the first line and indent at the beginning of each paragraph.

Name ______________________________ Date ______________

8–7. A Scary Experience (prewriting)

DIRECTIONS: Everyone has had some scary experiences in their lives. Can you remember a time you were really scared? Perhaps it was a night you were alone in the house and heard strange noises. Or, it might have been a time when you were involved in an automobile accident. Perhaps you were facing surgery at the hospital. Think about a time when you were scared and write about it in a way that will make your readers share the experience with you. First, organize your thoughts and memories by preparing a **brainstorming list.**

BRAINSTORMING LIST

1. What was the scary experience you are going to write about? (Be brief here!)

   ____

2. Write words and phrases describing where and when it happened.

3. Briefly, state step by step what happened.

   ____

   ____

   ____

   ____

   ____

4. Write words and phrases you can use to describe details of your scary experience. Use active verbs, colorful adjectives, and sensory language.

5. On the back of this sheet, write a list of words and phrases that describe your feelings at the time. Use at least one scary simile or metaphor.

Name ______________________________ **Date** ______________

8–8. A SCARY EXPERIENCE (FIRST DRAFT)

Get ready to write a first draft of a five-paragraph essay entitled "A Scary Experience." Follow the organization you prepared on your brainstorming list. Here is a suggested guide you can follow to make your task easier.

- **In the first paragraph (*two to four sentences*), introduce the topic in an enticing way. (Example: *There was a time when I thought I was surely going to die. It was the scariest experience of my life.*)**
- **In the second paragraph (*four to seven sentences*), tell when and where the scary experience occurred. Describe the time and setting in detail.**
- **In the third paragraph (*four to seven sentences*), tell what happened step by step. Use transitional words where needed. Make the details as scary as you can with active verbs, colorful adjectives, and sensory words. Use at least one simile or metaphor to describe your feelings.**
- **In the fourth paragraph (*four to seven sentences*), describe how the incident ended and tell if there were any lasting effects.**
- **In the fifth paragraph (*two to four sentences*), restate and sum up the topic in a satisfying way.**

DIRECTIONS: Begin your essay below and continue on the back of this sheet. This is a first draft, so concentrate on getting your thoughts on paper without too much concern for spelling, punctuation, and grammar at this point. Write a title on the first line and indent at the beginning of each paragraph.

____

____

____

____

____

____

____

____

____

____

Name ______________________________ Date ____________

8–9. A Scary Experience (final copy)

A. DIRECTIONS: Correct and revise the first draft of your essay about a scary experience. Refer to your list of proofreading symbols if necessary. Read the guidelines below carefully and check off each item as you complete it.

- ❑ Does the introductory paragraph state the topic in an interesting way?
- ❑ Do the three middle paragraphs tell what happened in a logical progression?
- ❑ Do you stay focused on the topic? Take out any irrelevancies.
- ❑ Can you add more active verbs, colorful adjectives, or sensory words that will convey to the reader how scary this experience was? Use at least one simile or metaphor.
- ❑ Does the final paragraph restate the topic and bring the narration to a satisfying conclusion?
- ❑ Are your sentences complete? Correct any run-ons or fragments.
- ❑ Do subjects and verbs agree? Do pronouns agree with their antecedents?
- ❑ Do you use transitional words to lead the reader smoothly from step to step?
- ❑ Use a dictionary to check your spelling.

B. DIRECTIONS: Begin the final copy of your essay below and continue on the back of this sheet. Write the title on the first line and indent at the beginning of each paragraph.

____

____

____

____

____

____

____

____

____

____

Name ______________________________ Date ______________

8–10. Through Someone Else's Eyes (prewriting)

DIRECTIONS: You can easily describe a normal day in your life. But how does that same day look to *someone else*? In this essay, you will describe a typical day as seen through the eyes of someone else in your family. Check whose eyes you would like to look through:

- ❑ Mother
- ❑ Father
- ❑ Brother or sister
- ❑ Pet (dog, cat, hamster, etc.)

First, prepare a **brainstorming list** below.

BRAINSTORMING LIST

A. In the first column below, list six activities that occur during a typical day in the life of your family. Include two activities for the morning, two for the afternoon, and two for the evening. In the second column, next to each activity, write words and phrases that can be used to describe this activity as seen through the special eyes you are using.

Activity	Words and Phrases
Morning 1. 2.	
Afternoon 1. 2.	
Evening 1. 2.	

B. On the back of this sheet, write a beginning sentence for your essay that will introduce the topic in an interesting way. (Example: *Have you ever tried to look at the world through someone else's eyes?*)

Name ______________________________ Date ______________

8–11. Through Someone Else's Eyes (first draft)

Are you ready to write about a typical day in the life of your family *through the eyes of someone else*? It will be easy to write a five-paragraph essay by following the guidelines below and using your brainstorming list.

- **In the first paragraph (*two to four sentences*), introduce the topic in an interesting way. Begin with the sentence from your brainstorming list.**
- **In the second paragraph (*three to six sentences*), describe morning activities through the special eyes you are using. Use words and phrases from your brainstorming list.**
- **In the third paragraph (*three to six sentences*), describe afternoon activities. Use words and phrases from your brainstorming list.**
- **In the fourth paragraph (*three to six sentences*), describe evening activities. Use words and phrases from your brainstorming list.**
- **In the concluding paragraph (*two to four sentences*), sum up the experience of seeing life through someone else's eyes.**

DIRECTIONS: Begin your essay below and continue on the back of this sheet. This is just a first draft, so concentrate on getting your thoughts down. Don't be too concerned about spelling or grammar at this point. Write the title on the first line and indent at the beginning of each paragraph.

Name ______________________________ Date ______________

8–12. Through Someone Else's Eyes (final copy)

A. DIRECTIONS: Correct and revise the first draft of your essay describing a typical day through someone else's eyes. Use proofreading symbols if you find these helpful. Read the following guidelines carefully and check off each item as you complete it.

- ❑ Does the introductory paragraph state the topic clearly? Can you add or change anything to make it more interesting?
- ❑ Do the three middle paragraphs develop the topic? Are details clearly organized into morning, afternoon, and evening activities?
- ❑ Can you add vivid language such as active verbs and sensory words?
- ❑ Add at least one simile or metaphor.
- ❑ Do you stay focused on the point of view of the person or animal who is seeing the events?
- ❑ Does the final paragraph sum up the topic in an interesting way?
- ❑ Are your sentences complete? Correct any run-ons or fragments.
- ❑ Do subjects and verbs agree? Do pronouns agree with their antecedents?
- ❑ Use a dictionary to check your spelling.

B. DIRECTIONS: Begin the final copy of your essay below and continue on the back of this sheet. Write the title on the first line and indent at the beginning of each paragraph.

Name ______________________________ Date ______________

8–13. Lost and Found (prewriting)

DIRECTIONS: Losing something can be troublesome and upsetting. Try to remember a time when something (or someone) was lost—at home, school, traveling, in a mall, or somewhere else. It might have been something belonging to you, or you could just have been helping or watching the search. Here are some examples of things that are often lost or misplaced: homework, a book, a favorite t-shirt, a family pet, a wallet, a watch, your teacher's favorite marking pen. Even people can get lost—your neighbor's three-year-old or a classmate during a class trip.

Before beginning to write about this event, first organize your thoughts by answering the questions in the **brainstorming list** below. You don't need complete sentences here, just words and phrases.

BRAINSTORMING LIST

What or who was lost?

____

When did this happen? ______________________________

Where did this happen? ______________________________

List three people who were present during the search. Next to each name, write words and phrases you can use to describe the person and what that person did. (Omit this if you were alone.)

____

____

____

List the places that were searched. Next to each place, write words and phrases to describe it.

____

____

____

Write a list of words and phrases to describe your feelings during this time.

____

____

What was the result of the search?

____

Name ______________________________ Date ______________

8–14. Lost and Found (first draft)

You are going to write an essay of three or more paragraphs about something or someone that was lost. Use your brainstorming list and follow these guidelines.

- **In the first paragraph (*two to four sentences*), introduce the topic in an interesting way. (Example: *I was frantic! I had spent two hours writing my book report the night before. Now, it was time to go to school and the report was nowhere to be found.*)**
- **In the middle paragraphs (*three to six sentences each*), tell the details of the search moment by moment. Describe the places that were searched. Describe who was there and what they did.**
- **In the concluding paragraph (*two to four sentences*), tell the result of the search and your feelings about it.**

DIRECTIONS: Begin your essay below and continue on the back of this sheet. This is just a first draft so concentrate on getting your thoughts down. Don't be too concerned about spelling or grammar at this point. Write the title (*Lost and Found*) on the first line. Indent at the beginning of each paragraph.

Name ________________________________ Date ______________

8–15. Lost and Found (final copy)

A. DIRECTIONS: Correct and revise the first draft of your essay about something that has been lost. Use proofreading symbols if you find these helpful. Read the following guidelines carefully and check off each item as you complete it.

- ❑ **Does the introductory paragraph state the topic clearly? Can you make it more exciting by using a question or a startling statement?**
- ❑ **Does the middle paragraph (or paragraphs) develop the topic in a logical order?**
- ❑ **Can you add interesting details about the people and places? Can you describe some of their feelings to make it more suspenseful?**
- ❑ **Add vivid language such as active verbs and colorful adjectives.**
- ❑ **Add at least one simile or metaphor.**
- ❑ **Does the final paragraph sum up and conclude the topic?**
- ❑ **Are all your sentences complete? Correct run-ons or fragments.**
- ❑ **Do subjects and verbs agree? Do pronouns agree with their antecedents?**
- ❑ **Use a dictionary to check your spelling.**

B. DIRECTIONS: Begin the final copy of your essay below and continue on the back of this sheet. Write the title on the first line and indent at the beginning of each paragraph.

Name ______________________________ Date ______________

8–16. Writing Stories: Developing the Plot (prewriting)

> "Nobody ever escapes from Misery Island!"
>
> My brother Luis and I stared at the huge, gorilla-like guard. It wasn't our fault that the plane we were on had crashed into the jungle here. We were lucky to be the only survivors. Now, as the black-clad thug led us to a dank, dark cell, we no longer felt so fortunate.

DIRECTIONS: Isn't this a chilling beginning for a story? Writing stories is fun. You can use your creativity and let your imagination soar. However, no matter how fantastic, the plot (what occurs in the story) and details must make sense within the context of the narrative and not wander off into irrelevant details that will confuse a reader. You are going to finish this story. First, organize your ideas in the **brainstorming list** below.

BRAINSTORMING LIST

1. Write a brief summary of how you think the plot will develop. (Example: *The prisoners will be treated badly. No food. They will try to escape three times. But they'll be caught each time. Punished. Looks hopeless. Finally, they figure out a way to dig a tunnel leading to the water. Find a boat. Get picked up by search planes.*) You don't need complete sentences here—short phrases will be enough.

____

____

____

____

____

____

Name ________________________________ Date ______________

8–16. Writing Stories: Developing the Plot (PREWRITING) *(continued)*

2. List the characters in this story with descriptive words about each one. The first three have already been introduced. Name any others who will appear.

Character's Name	Description
Narrator (I)	
Luis	
Guard	

3. Write vivid words and phrases below that will bring your story to life, such as active verbs, colorful adjectives, and sensory words.

____

____

____

____

____

____

____

____

____

Name ______________________________ Date ______________

8–17. Writing Stories: Developing the Plot (First Draft)

You are going to write the first draft of your story. Keep your brainstorming list handy and follow these suggestions:

- **Make up a title and write it on the first line.**
- **Copy the beginning of the story from Activity 8-16.**
- **Use the summary on your brainstorming list to tell what happens next. Use strong, active verbs.**
- **Use colorful adjectives and sensory words to describe the characters and the setting in which they find themselves.**
- **Be sure the plot develops in an exciting, but logical way.**
- **Use lots of realistic details to convince the reader this story is actually happening.**
- **End the story in a satisfying way.**

DIRECTIONS: Begin your story below and continue on the back of this sheet. This is a first draft, so don't be concerned about spelling or grammar at this point.

Name ______________________________ Date ______________

8–18. WRITING STORIES: DEVELOPING THE PLOT (FINAL COPY)

A. DIRECTIONS: Correct and revise the first draft of your story. Follow these guidelines, and check off each one as you complete it.

- ❑ Re-read the story carefully. Does the plot develop in an exciting, believable way? Revise any point at which it does not make sense.
- ❑ Can you add any details that will make the plot stronger?
- ❑ Can you add any details to the descriptions of the characters that will make them come to life?
- ❑ Add active verbs, colorful adjectives, and sensory words to make the writing more exciting.
- ❑ Are sentences complete? Correct any run-ons or fragments.
- ❑ Do you capitalize all proper names and sentence beginnings?
- ❑ Do you use transitional words to make connections?
- ❑ Do you bring the story to a satisfactory conclusion?
- ❑ Check spelling with dictionary.

B. DIRECTIONS: Begin the final copy of your story below and continue on the back of this sheet. Put the title on the first line and indent at the beginning of each paragraph.

Name ______________________________ Date ______________

8–19. Writing Stories: Using Dialogue (prewriting)

> Sue opened the door. "You must be Mr. Bowker," she said. "Come in."
>
> Sam Bowker was short and stocky. He had a round face and a humorous, bushy moustache. He didn't look at all like an agent. "You know why I'm here." His voice sounded like a bark.
>
> Sue nodded. "Do you have the contract?" Her heart was pounding.
>
> Bowker pulled a large brown envelope out of his briefcase. "Here it is."

This is a story that begins with dialogue (conversation) between two people. Dialogue is fun to write and read. Here are some ways to make it effective.

1. Combine it with descriptions, such as the description of Sam Bowker above.
2. Combine it with action (*Sue opening the door, nodding, heart pounding. Bowker pulling the envelope out of the briefcase*)
3. Begin a new paragraph every time someone starts to speak.

DIRECTIONS: You are going to finish this story, which is called "How to Become a Teenage Star," by continuing the dialogue and then writing the rest of the story. First, complete the **brainstorming list** below.

BRAINSTORMING LIST

1. On the back of this sheet, write a few more lines to add to the above dialogue. Use description and action along with the conversation.
2. Write a brief summary of your ideas for the plot.

   ____

   ____

   ____

3. List the characters and their descriptions.

Name of Character	Description

Name ______________________________ Date ______________

8–20. WRITING STORIES: USING DIALOGUE (FIRST DRAFT)

Get ready to write the first draft of a story called "How to Become a Teenage Star." Keep your brainstorming list handy and follow these suggestions.

- **Copy the beginning of the story from Activity 8-19.**
- **Continue the dialogue between Sue and Sam Bowker. Intersperse the dialogue with action and description. Use the dialogue and action here to tell what the story is about.**
- **Continue writing the story. Follow your plot ideas from the brainstorming list. (Sue can become any kind of "star" you choose—film, TV, music, sports).**
- **Use lots of dialogue to make the story fun to read. Be sure to include action and description with the dialogue.**
- **Write a satisfying conclusion. Try to make it funny or exciting or surprising.**

DIRECTIONS: Begin your story below and continue on the back of this sheet. Write the title on the first line and indent at the beginning of paragraphs. This is a first draft, so don't be too concerned with spelling or grammar.

Name ______________________ Date ____________

8–21. Writing Stories: Using Dialogue (final copy)

A. DIRECTIONS: Correct and revise the first draft of your story "How to Become a Teenage Star." Use the following guidelines and check off each one as it is completed.

- ❑ **Read the story all the way through. Does the plot develop in a clear, logical way? If not, change or delete unclear or irrelevant passages.**
- ❑ **Do you use dialogue to move the plot along?**
- ❑ **Do you combine the dialogue with action and description?**
- ❑ **Do you use exciting details to make the story come to life?**
- ❑ **Is your conclusion satisfying, funny, or surprising?**
- ❑ **Are your sentences complete? Correct any run-ons or fragments.**
- ❑ **Do subjects and verbs agree? Do pronouns agree with their antecedents?**
- ❑ **Do you vary sentence length, using both short and long sentences?**
- ❑ **Add more active verbs, colorful adjectives, and sensory words.**
- ❑ **Check spelling with a dictionary.**

B. DIRECTIONS: Begin the final copy of your story below and continue on the back of this sheet. Indent at the beginning of paragraphs. (In a dialogue, you should begin a new paragraph every time someone different begins to speak.)

Name ______________________________________ Date ________________

8–22. Writing Stories: Developing the Characters (Prewriting)

The characters in a story are just as important as the plot. The reader must be able to *see* and *understand* the characters in order to care about what happens to them. The writer can do this by showing: what the character **does** (*action*), what the character **says** (*dialogue*), what the character **looks like** (*description*), and what the character **thinks**.

DIRECTIONS: Think about the characters that will appear in a story you are going to write called "Lost in the Woods." Organize your thoughts by completing the **brainstorming list**. In the first column, list the names of two important characters in this story. In the second column, next to each name, write words and phrases describing what the character looks like. (Include colorful adjectives and a simile.) In the third column, write words and phrases to show what this character does. (Include active verbs.) In the fourth column, write words and phrases that this character might think. In the fifth column, write something this character might say.

BRAINSTORMING LIST				
Name	**Appearance**	**Actions**	**Thoughts**	**Sayings**

(Continue your brainstorming list on the back of this sheet.)

Name ______________________________ **Date** ______________

8–23. Writing Stories: Developing the Characters (First Draft)

Are you ready to write the first draft of a story called "Lost in the Woods"? Use your brainstorming list to develop the characters by showing what they do, say, look like, and think. The suggestions below will help you get started and develop the story.

- **In the first paragraph, introduce the story in an exciting way that will grab the reader's attention. Example:**

  "We're lost! We'll never find our way out." Shauna's pretty face was smudged with dirt and tears.

  "Don't worry," Alexis assured her. "They'll be sending a search party to look for us."

- **In the middle paragraphs, develop the plot. Show what the characters are like by what they do, say, look like, and think.**
- **In the concluding paragraph, bring the story to an end.**

DIRECTIONS: Begin your story below and continue on the back of this sheet. This is a first draft, so don't be concerned about spelling and grammar at this point. Write the title on the first line and indent at the beginning of each paragraph and new dialogue.

Name ______________________________ Date ______________

8–24. Writing Stories: Developing the Characters (Final Copy)

A. DIRECTIONS: Correct and revise the first draft of your story "Lost in the Woods." Follow the guidelines below and check off each item as you complete it.

- ❑ Does the introductory paragraph grab the reader's attention? Can you make it more exciting?
- ❑ Do you stay focused on the plot and develop it logically, step by step? Take out any irrelevancies.
- ❑ Do you develop the characters by showing what they do, say, look like, and think? Can you add anything else about them to make them more real?
- ❑ Does the story conclude in a satisfying way?
- ❑ Can you make the writing more vivid by adding active verbs, colorful adjectives, and sensory words?
- ❑ Are your sentences complete? Correct any run-ons or fragments.
- ❑ Do subjects and verbs agree? Do pronouns agree with their antecedents?
- ❑ Do you capitalize the beginnings of sentences and proper nouns?
- ❑ Check spelling with a dictionary.

B. DIRECTIONS: Begin the final copy of your story below and continue on the back of this sheet. Put the title on the first line and indent at the beginning of paragraphs and new dialogue.

____

____

____

____

____

____

____

____

____

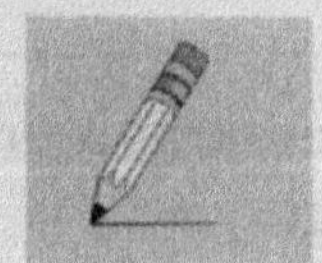

EIGHTH-GRADE LEVEL

NARRATIVE WRITING PRACTICE TEST

Name ______________________________ Date ______________

PRACTICE TEST: NARRATIVE WRITING

DIRECTIONS: Imagine this! *One night you are awakened by a loud noise. You look out the window and see a spaceship. The door of the spaceship slides open, and a space creature comes out. What does the ship look like? What does the creature look like? What does it do? What do you do?* Write a story about what happens.

Follow these four steps to write your story:

- FIRST, on the page labeled PREWRITING, follow the directions for brainstorming and organizing ideas for your story.
- SECOND, write the first draft of your story on a separate sheet of paper. Write your name and date at the top, and a title for the story.
- THIRD, revise and edit your first draft. Refer to your list of proofreading symbols if you wish to make use of these. Use the checklist as a guide, and check off each item when it has been revised to your satisfaction.
- FOURTH, write your final copy on a separate sheet of paper with your name and date at the top.

CHECKLIST

- ❑ **Does your introductory paragraph introduce the story in an exciting way?**
- ❑ **Do the middle paragraphs relate what happened step by step in a logical order?**
- ❑ **Do you stay focused on the plot? Take out any irrelevancies.**
- ❑ **Do you offer some description of background and setting to show the reader where this story is taking place?**
- ❑ **Do you bring the characters to life by showing what they do, say, look like, and think?**
- ❑ **Be sure to use dialogue. Don't forget to begin a new paragraph whenever a different person starts to speak.**
- ❑ **Do you use lots of active verbs, colorful adjectives, and sensory words? Can you add one simile to make your writing more vivid?**
- ❑ **Are sentences complete? Correct any run-ons and fragments.**
- ❑ **Do subjects and verbs agree? Do pronouns agree with their antecedents?**
- ❑ **Do you capitalize proper nouns and the beginning of sentences?**

Name ______________________________ Date ______________

PRACTICE TEST: NARRATIVE WRITING *(continued)*

Prewriting

Plan out your story and organize it below in any way that is useful to you. *Here is one suggestion:* Write a brief, step-by-step summary of the plot, including how it will end. List the characters. Next to each, write words and phrases that describe this character.

Name ______________________________ Date ______________

PRACTICE TEST: NARRATIVE WRITING *(continued)*

Student Samples

STORY A

Well, the the creature is big and green with a big head and big huge eyes in his head he/she has short arms and has big long legs with no toes. Then he shot laser beams into my eyes I guess so he could read my mind and that is why he did that. Then I invited him into my house so we could play games.

Score ______________

STORY B

Crash! A noise awakened me from my midnight slumber. I looked about frantically wondering where the noise had come from. At a sound like gas escaping from a soda can I leap out of the bed and dash to the window. Slowly I part the curtains and what I see almost makes me scream.

Standing about 20 ft. from my window is an alien bathed in purple-blue light. It reminded me of an "X-Files" alien. At first glance, I noticed its prominent black eyes, large flat nose, well-proportioned lips, high cheekbones, and small, slightly protruding ears. It was also bald. When I looked at it more thoroughly, other details came to mind. It looked to be about 5'7" with greenish-white skin, and a strong and limber body. I can only guess as to what its real body was like under its peach-colored spacesuit.

Slowly it raised its hand and waved to me. I wondered if I should wave back or not and decided to even though I was scared enough to turn and run screaming down the hallway, but I waved instead.

As I stood there, waving like a fool, I began to think really weird things. Things like "Help me save your planet" and "You must help us." On some subconscious level I realized it was communicating telepathically. I tried as hard as I could to reply and found I could.

Through our telepathic communication I found out I was supposed to help him save Earth. I noticed he was now suited in full Armani attire.

I deliberated with myself and decided to help it. Now as I look back, it seems so weird to me. But then I remember all the fun we had and reflect upon how we saved Earth. It was one of the best times of my life.

Score ______________

Practice Test: Narrative Writing *(continued)*

Scoring Guide

SCORE	Unsatisfactory—1	Insufficient—2
Content	Attempts to respond to prompt, but provides little or no clear information; may only paraphrase the prompt	Presents fragmented information OR may be very repetitive OR may be very undeveloped
Organization	Has no clear organization OR consists of a single statement	Is very disorganized; ideas are weakly connected OR the response is too brief to detect organization
Sentence Structure	Little or no control over sentence boundaries and sentence structure; word choice may be incorrect in much or all of the response	Little control over sentence boundaries and sentence structure; word choice may often be incorrect
Grammar, Usage, and Mechanics	Many errors in grammar or usage— such as tense inconsistency, lack of subject–verb agreement—spelling, and punctuation severely interfere with understanding	Errors in grammar or usage—such as tense inconsistency, lack of subject–verb agreement—spelling, and punctuation interfere with understanding in much of the response

SCORE	Uneven—3	Sufficient—4
Content	Presents some clear information, but is list-like, undeveloped; little attempt is made to present details in logical order	Develops information with some details presented in logical order
Organization	Is unevenly organized; the narrative may be disjointed	Narrative is organized with ideas that are generally related but has few or no transitions
Sentence Structure	Exhibits uneven control over sentence boundaries and sentence structure; may have some incorrect word choices	Exhibits control over sentence boundaries and sentence structure, but sentences and word choice may be simple and unvaried
Grammar, Usage, and Mechanics	Errors in grammar or usage—such as tense inconsistency, lack of subject–verb agreement—spelling, and punctuation sometimes interfere with understanding	Errors in grammar or usage—such as tense inconsistency, lack of subject–verb agreement—spelling, and punctuation do not interfere with understanding

SCORE	Skillful—5	Excellent—6
Content	Develops and shapes information with details in logical order in parts of the narrative	Develops and shapes information with well-chosen details presented in a logical order across the narrative
Organization	Is clearly organized, but may lack some transitions and/or have lapses in continuity	Is well organized with strong transitions
Sentence Structure	Exhibits some variety in sentence structure and some good word choices	Sustains variety in sentence structure and exhibits good word choice
Grammar, Usage, and Mechanics	Errors in grammar, spelling, and punctuation do not interfere with understanding	Errors in grammar, spelling, and punctuation are few and do not interfere with understanding

SECTION 9

WRITING LETTERS

Standardized Testing Information

It is not unusual for the prompt in a writing assessment test to require a response in letter form. These can be informative/expository, persuasive, or (rarely) narrative.

Letter responses in these assessments do not require accepted personal and/or business letter format except for the greeting and salutation.

National and state rubrics do not differentiate between letter and essay form responses. New Jersey's scoring guidelines, for example, are the same for essays or letters. They are scored on a scale of 1 to 6, with 1 being the lowest and 6 being the highest. Here are some excerpts from New Jersey's scoring rubrics.

SCORE SCALE POINT 2 indicates a **limited command** of written language. The writing samples in this category are scored on:

- **Content/organization:** May not have an opening and/or a closing. These responses will exhibit an attempt at organization. In other words, there will be some evidence the writer attempted to control the details. The responses relate to the topic, but in some papers, the writer drifts away from the primary focus or abruptly shifts focus. In other papers, there is a single focus, but there are few, if any, transitions, making it difficult to move from idea to idea. Details are presented with little, if any, elaboration—highlight papers.
- **Usage:** May have numerous problems with usage, but they are not totally out of control.
- **Sentence construction:** May demonstrate excessive monotony in syntax and/or rhetorical modes. There may be numerous errors in sentence construction.
- **Mechanics:** May display numerous serious errors in mechanics.

SCORE SCALE POINT 4 indicates an **adequate command** of written language. The writing samples in this category are scored on:

- **Content/organization:** Generally will have an opening and a closing. The responses relate to the topic. They have a single focus and are organized. There is little, if any, difficulty moving from idea to idea. Ideas may ramble somewhat and clusters of ideas may be loosely connected; however, an overall progression is apparent. In some papers, development is uneven, consisting of elaborated ideas interspersed with bare, unelaborated details.
- **Usage:** May display some errors in usage, but no consistent pattern is apparent.

- **Sentence construction:** May demonstrate a generally correct sense of syntax. They avoid excessive monotony in syntax and/or rhetorical modes. There may be a few errors in sentence construction.
- **Mechanics:** May display some errors in mechanics, but these errors will not constitute a consistent pattern, nor do they interfere with the meaning of the response.

SCORE SCALE POINT 6 indicates a **superior command** of written language. The writing samples in this category are scored on:

- **Content/organization:** Have an opening and closing. The responses relate to the topic and have a single, distinct focus. They are well-developed, complete compositions that are organized and progress logically from beginning to end. A variety of cohesive devices are present, resulting in a fluent response. Many of these writers take compositional risks resulting in highly effective, vivid, explicit, and/or pertinent responses.
- **Usage:** Have few, if any, errors in usage.
- **Sentence construction:** Demonstrate syntactic and verbal sophistication through an effective variety of sentences and/or rhetorical modes. There will be very few, if any, errors in sentence construction.
- **Mechanics:** Have very few, if any, errors in mechanics.

The classroom teacher should keep these and other state rubrics in mind when leading students through the letter-writing exercises in Section 9.

Teacher Preparation and Lessons

There are six letter-writing activities in this section, three each of informative and persuasive. Because narrative writing is rarely (if at all) included in assessments, it is omitted here as well. Although state and national assessments do not require knowledge of correct letter form, samples of personal letter models are offered to acquaint students with a useful skill. As in the other essay-writing activities in this resource, each activity in this section has three parts.

- **Part One** consists of **prewriting** activities such as **brainstorming, clustering,** or **outlining** to be done individually, in small groups, or with whole class participation, at the teacher's discretion. Students should be advised to use this step of the writing process to provide an organizational framework for their writing. Personal and business letter models will also be introduced in some of these prewriting activities.
- **Part Two** is the **writing of a first draft.** Students should be encouraged to write freely at this point without too much concern about grammar, spelling, and punctuation in an effort to overcome blocks that are all too common when students face a writing assignment.
- **Part Three** offers directions for **revising and writing a final copy.** The revision and editing process can be done by the individual student-writer alone, in association with the teacher, or with class participation (exchange of papers). Each revision activity includes a checklist for students to refer to during the editing process. It will be helpful to review the proofreading symbols on page 360.

These letter-writing activities offer an opportunity for a discussion of the concept of "readership." Even more so than other essay-writing assignments, a letter is usually intended for the eyes of one particular recipient. A class discussion of this subject will help students learn to focus on the ultimate reader, not only when writing letters, but in other writing activities as well. At the beginning of the first letter-writing activity, therefore, the teacher could ask the questions:

1. Who is meant to read this letter?
2. What can the writer do to focus the message for that particular reader?

The discussion can then be expanded to include samples of previously completed essay assignments and their intended readership. Elicit from students the ways in which letters are similar to essays, as having:

- a beginning identifying the topic
- a middle (one or more paragraphs) developing the topic
- an ending

Elicit from the students the aspects of letter writing that differ from essay composition and write these on the chalkboard:

- An essay is addressed to a general group of readers while a letter is addressed to one individual.
- The tone of a letter is more personal, resembling one part of a dialogue between two individuals.
- The structure of a letter, while having a beginning, middle, and end, is somewhat looser and more flexible than in an essay.

Practice Test: Writing Letters

The student letter samples on page 358 received ratings of 6 and 2, respectively.

Letter A succeeds in stating and sustaining an argument that lengthening the school year will subject students to additional stress and result in their losing some opportunities. The student provides a clear, connected series of reasons to argue persuasively against lengthening the school year. While there are occasional errors, overall the student is adept at varying sentence length and structure, providing evidence to back up a point of view. This letter scored a 6.

Letter B attempts to take a position and back it up with examples, but spelling, grammatical, and syntactical errors keep it from being effective. The writer does not have control over sentence boundaries and does not utilize the conventions of spelling or capitalization. This letter scored a 2.

Name ______________________________ **Date** ______________

9–1. Writing to Someone Who's Away (prewriting)

Note the form of the following personal letter.

> **25 Petticoat Lane**
> **Fashionville, OH 56987**
> **February 5, 2003**
>
> **Dear Adriana,**
>
> **How are you? I am fine, but I miss you very much. So does everyone here in Fashionville.**
>
> **I hope you are having a good time in Europe and enjoying the designer shows. I can hardly wait until next month when you get back and can tell me all about them.**
>
> **I am looking forward to seeing you then.**
>
> **Your friend,**
> *Jocelyn*

The first three lines on the upper right are called the **return address**. The first line shows the street address of the writer. The second line indicates the writer's city, state, and ZIP Code. The third line contains the date.

The **greeting** is written at the left margin. It begins with a capital letter and is followed by a comma (Dear ____,).

The **body** of the letter contains your message in paragraph form.

The **closing** appears at the bottom right. Only the **first word** is capitalized. The closing is always followed by a comma (Your friend,).

DIRECTIONS: Write a letter to someone you know who is on a trip or vacation, or has moved away, using the personal letter form above. (If you don't know anyone who fits this description, use a pretend person.) First, prepare a **brainstorming list.**

Name ________________________________ Date ______________

9–1. Writing to Someone Who's Away (PREWRITING) *(continued)*

BRAINSTORMING LIST

1. Write the name of the person to whom you are writing and his or her relationship to you (friend, aunt, neighbor, etc.). ____________________

2. Write a list of things happening in your life that you can describe in the letter.

____

____

____

____

____

____

____

3. Write a list of things happening in your school or community that you can relate.

____

____

____

____

____

____

____

Name ______________________________ **Date** ______________

9–2. Writing to Someone Who's Away (first draft)

Write a letter to someone you know who is on a trip or vacation, or has moved away. Follow the personal letter form and organize your thoughts around the notes you made on your brainstorming list. Be sure to:

1. Write the three-line return address (your street address; your city, state, ZIP Code; today's date) at the upper right of the paper.
2. Write the greeting at the left margin. Put a comma after the greeting.
3. Indent each paragraph in the message.
4. Introduce the topic of the letter in the first paragraph.
5. Describe what is happening in your life in the second paragraph.
6. Describe what is happening in your school and/or community in the third paragraph.
7. Bring the letter to an end in the last paragraph.
8. Write the closing at the right. Capitalize the first word only.
9. Follow the closing with a comma.
10. Sign your name under the closing.

DIRECTIONS: Begin your first draft here and continue on the back of this sheet.

Name ______________________________ Date ______________

9–3. Writing to Someone Who's Away (final copy)

A. DIRECTIONS: Revise and correct the first draft of your letter. Follow the guidelines below, and check off each item as you complete it.

- ❑ Did you write the three-line return address (your street address; your city, state, and ZIP Code; today's date) at the upper right of the paper?
- ❑ Did you write the greeting, followed by a comma, at the left margin?
- ❑ Did you indent at the beginning of each paragraph?
- ❑ Did you write the closing, followed by a comma, at the bottom right?
- ❑ Did you sign your name under the closing?
- ❑ Are your sentences complete? Correct any run-ons or fragments.
- ❑ Do subjects and verbs agree? Do pronouns agree with antecedents?

B. DIRECTIONS: Begin the final copy of your letter here and continue on the back of this sheet.

Name ______________________________ **Date** ______________

9–4. Writing a Fan Letter (prewriting)

DIRECTIONS: Have you ever written a fan letter to someone you admire? The person could be a sports star, a TV or movie personality, the author of your favorite book, or someone else. On the line below, write the name of the person to whom you would like to write a fan letter.

____

First, organize your thoughts by completing the **brainstorming list** below.

BRAINSTORMING LIST

1. In the box below, write words and phrases you can use to describe the things you admire about this person. Include active verbs, vivid adjectives, and sensory words.

2. In the box below, write words and phrases you can use to describe who *you* are and why you are writing.

3. On the back of this sheet, write an attention-getting opening sentence(s) for your letter, such as *Who is your number-one fan? It is definitely me!*

Name ______________________________ Date ______________

9–5. Writing a Fan Letter (first draft)

Are you ready to write the first draft of a fan letter to someone you admire? Keep your brainstorming list in front of you, and use the correct form for a personal letter. Here are some suggestions for writing an effective letter:

- **In the first paragraph, state in an interesting and attention-getting way that this is a fan letter.**
- **In the second paragraph, describe in detail the things you admire about this person, using the vivid words from your brainstorming list.**
- **In the third paragraph, tell who you are and why you are writing this letter.**
- **In the concluding paragraph, restate and sum up the topic you introduced in the first paragraph.**
- **Use an appropriate closing, such as *Your fan, Your friend, Your admirer,* etc.**

DIRECTIONS: Begin your letter below and continue on the back of this sheet. Be sure you are using correct letter form! This is a first draft, so don't worry too much about spelling and grammar at this point. Concentrate on getting your thoughts on paper.

Name ________________________________ Date ____________

9–6. Writing a Fan Letter (final copy)

A. DIRECTIONS: Correct and revise the first draft of your fan letter. Follow the guidelines below, and check off each item as you complete it.

- ❑ Did you follow the correct form for a personal letter, with a three-line return address at the upper right, the greeting at the left margin followed by a comma, and the closing at the bottom right followed by a comma?
- ❑ Did you capitalize only the first letter of the first word in the closing?
- ❑ Did you sign your name under the closing?
- ❑ Are sentences complete? Correct any run-ons or fragments.
- ❑ Do subjects and verbs agree?
- ❑ Can you make your introductory paragraph more attention-getting?
- ❑ Do you stay focused? Take out any irrelevancies.
- ❑ Is your writing organized logically, such as using one paragraph to describe why you admire this person, and another to tell about yourself and your reasons for writing the letter?

B. DIRECTIONS: Begin the final copy of your letter below and continue on the back of this sheet.

____

____

____

____

____

____

____

____

____

____

____

Name ______________________________ Date ______________

9–7. Writing to Someone in Another Country (Prewriting)

DIRECTIONS: You are going to write a letter to someone in another country who does not know much about the United States. Can you describe the U.S. to this person, telling about its geography, history, and government? This will be easier than you think if you first organize your ideas by completing the **outline** below. The main points have already been set out for you. All you have to do is fill in as many items as you can after each main point.

I. Geography and Land

A. ______________________________

B. ______________________________

C. ______________________________

D. ______________________________

II. History

A. ______________________________

B. ______________________________

C. ______________________________

D. ______________________________

E. ______________________________

III. Government

A. ______________________________

B. ______________________________

C. ______________________________

D. ______________________________

E. ______________________________

Name ______________________________ Date ______________

9–8. WRITING TO SOMEONE IN ANOTHER COUNTRY (FIRST DRAFT)

Get ready to write a first draft of your letter describing the United States to someone in another country. Use your outline and follow the suggestions below.

- **Write your three-line return address at the upper right.**
- **Make up a name to use in the greeting, followed by a comma.**
- **In the first paragraph, introduce yourself and tell the purpose of this letter.**
- **In the second paragraph, describe the geography and land. Use colorful adjectives, sensory words, and at least one simile in your description.**
- **In the third paragraph, describe the history of the country.**
- **In the fourth paragraph, describe the country's government.**
- **In the concluding paragraph, sum up and restate the topic.**
- **Write the closing at the lower right, followed by a comma. Sign your name below.**

DIRECTIONS: Begin your letter below and continue on the back of this sheet. This is a first draft, so concentrate on just getting your thoughts on paper. Remember to follow correct letter form.

____

____

____

____

____

____

____

____

____

____

Name ______________________________ Date ______________

9–9. Writing to Someone in Another Country (Final Draft)

A. DIRECTIONS: Correct and revise the first draft of your letter to someone in another country. Check off each guideline as you complete it.

- ❑ Did you follow correct form for a personal letter?
- ❑ Did you describe the purpose of this letter in the first paragraph?
- ❑ Do each of the three middle paragraphs give details for one main topic?
- ❑ Do you stay focused on that topic? Take out any irrelevancies.
- ❑ Does your concluding paragraph restate and sum up the topic?
- ❑ Can you add colorful adjectives, active verbs, and sensory words to make your descriptions more vivid? Do you use at least one simile?
- ❑ Are sentences complete? Correct any run-ons or fragments.
- ❑ Do subjects and verbs agree? Do pronouns agree with their antecedents?

B. DIRECTIONS: Begin the final copy of your letter below and continue on the back of this sheet. Follow the correct form of a personal letter and indent at the beginning of each paragraph.

Name ______________________________ Date ______________

9–10. Applying for a Job (prewriting)

DIRECTIONS: You would like to get a summer job to earn extra money. The following jobs have been advertised. Check the one for which you would like to apply:

- ❑ The DiPalma family (mother, father, two children) is looking for a mother's helper to live with them at their summer home at the seashore.
- ❑ Alicia Ruiz, the circulation manager of the local newspaper, *The Village Watch,* is looking for people to deliver the paper daily.
- ❑ Tim Holt, the owner of Holt's Garage, wants someone to clean the premises, run errands, and learn automobile mechanics.
- ❑ Mrs. Schultz, who lives down the block, wants someone to help with mowing the lawn and small jobs around the house.

In your letter of application, you are going to persuade the person to whom you are writing to hire you for the position. First, organize your thoughts by completing the **brainstorming list** below. In the first column, list words and phrases describing your skills that you can bring to this job. In the second column, list words and phrases to describe your experience. In the third column, list words and phrases for your personal qualities that make you perfect for this job.

BRAINSTORMING LIST		
Skills	**Experience**	**Personal Qualities**

Name ______________________________ Date ______________

9–11. Applying for a Job (first draft)

Are you ready to write a first draft of your letter of application for a summer job? Use the correct form for a personal letter and use your brainstorming list to organize your ideas. Here are some helpful suggestions.

- **In the first paragraph, introduce yourself and state the subject of the letter in an attention-getting way, such as *Would you like to have a capable, conscientious, and enthusiastic person helping out in your garage? I am a thirteen-year-old student at Briggs Junior High and a lifelong automobile enthusiast.***
- **In the second paragraph, describe any skills you have that will be useful in this job.**
- **In the third paragraph, describe any experience you have that will be useful for this job.**
- **In the fourth paragraph, describe how your personal qualities make you ideal for this job.**
- **In the concluding paragraph, restate and sum up your qualifications in a positive way.**

DIRECTIONS: Begin the first draft of your letter below and continue on the back of this sheet. This is a first draft, so just concentrate on getting your thoughts on paper. Use correct letter form.

____

____

____

____

____

____

____

____

____

____

Name ______________________________ Date ______________

9–12. Applying for a Job (Final Copy)

A. DIRECTIONS: Correct and revise your letter of application for a summer job. Follow the guidelines below, and check off each item as you complete it.

- ❑ Did you write the three-line return address at the upper right?
- ❑ Did you put a comma between the city and state?
- ❑ Did you write the greeting at the left margin, followed by a comma?
- ❑ Did you write the closing at the bottom right, followed by a comma? Did you capitalize the first word of the closing?
- ❑ Did you sign your name under the closing?
- ❑ Does your letter stay focused on the topic? Take out any irrelevancies.
- ❑ Can you change or add anything to make your letter more persuasive?
- ❑ Are sentences complete? Do subjects and verbs agree?

B. DIRECTIONS: Begin the final copy of your letter of application below and continue on the back of this sheet. Follow correct letter form and indent at the beginning of each paragraph.

Name ______________________________ Date ______________

9–13. Writing to the Board President (Prewriting)

DIRECTIONS: The Board of Education is having budget problems and plans to cut either art or music from the curriculum. The president of the school board, Mr. Pitt, has asked students to write to him stating their opinions. Your opinion is: (*check one*)

❑ Art should be removed.

❑ Music should be removed.

❑ Neither art nor music should be removed.

Write a letter to Mr. Pitt, trying to persuade him that your choice is the best one. First, organize your thoughts by completing this **brainstorming list.**

BRAINSTORMING LIST

1. Briefly state one reason for your opinion.

____

In the box below, write words to support this point. Include vivid language such as active verbs, colorful adjectives, and sensory words.

2. State a second reason for your opinion.

____

In the box below, write words to support this point. Include at least one simile or metaphor.

3. State a third reason to support your opinion.

____

In the box below, write words to support this point.

Name ______________________________ Date ______________

9–14. Writing to the Board President (first draft)

Get ready to write the first draft of a letter to Mr. Pitt, the president of the school board, expressing your opinion about removing art or music from the curriculum. Be sure to use correct letter form. Use your brainstorming list to organize your thoughts, and follow these suggestions:

- **In the first paragraph, introduce the topic in an interesting way. (Example:** ***A world without music would be a terrible place. So would a school that permits no expression of musical creativity.)***
- **In the second paragraph, state and discuss the first point in your brainstorming list. Use supporting details with lots of vivid language, such as active verbs, colorful adjectives, sensory words, similes, and metaphors.**
- **In the third and fourth paragraphs, discuss your second and third points, following the same procedure.**
- **In the concluding paragraph, sum up and restate the topic.**

DIRECTIONS: Begin the first draft of your letter and continue on the back of this sheet. This is a first draft, so just concentrate on getting your thoughts on paper. Use correct letter form and indent at the beginning of each paragraph.

Name ________________________________ Date ______________

9–15. Writing to the Board President (final copy)

A. DIRECTIONS: Correct and revise the first draft of your letter to the school board president. Follow the guidelines below, and check off each item as you complete it.

- ❑ Did you write the three-line return address at the upper right?
- ❑ Did you place a comma between the city and state?
- ❑ Did you write the greeting at the left margin, followed by a comma?
- ❑ Did you write the closing at the bottom right, followed by a comma?
- ❑ Did you sign your name under the closing?
- ❑ Can you make your introductory paragraph more exciting with a question, provocative statement, or anecdote?
- ❑ Do each of the three middle paragraphs state one point and support it with strong details?
- ❑ Does the concluding paragraph restate and sum up the topic?
- ❑ Do you stay focused on the topic? Remove any irrelevancies.
- ❑ Are sentences complete? Do subjects and verbs agree?

B. DIRECTIONS: Begin the final copy of your letter below and continue on the back of this sheet. Remember to follow correct letter form.

Name ______________________________ Date ______________

9–16. Persuading Your Parents (prewriting)

DIRECTIONS: You want to get a summer job, but your parents think you are too young. Write a letter to your parents trying to persuade them to let you get this job. First, prepare a **brainstorming list.** In the first column, list words and phrases that describe the kind of summer job you are seeking. In the second column, list words and phrases that describe how this job will benefit you and your family. In the third column, list words and phrases that tell about you and describe why you are mature enough to handle it.

BRAINSTORMING LIST		
Kind of Job	**Benefits**	**About Me**

On the back of this sheet, write an opening sentence or sentences that will get your parents' attention in a positive way. (Example: *Have you really looked at me lately? Have you noticed how I've grown, both mentally and physically? There are many new ways that I can now contribute to the welfare of our family.)*

Name ______________________________ Date ______________

9–17. PERSUADING YOUR PARENTS (FIRST DRAFT)

Get ready to write a first draft of the letter to your parents trying to convince them that you are old enough to have a summer job. Keep your brainstorming list handy. Here are some suggestions for organizing your letter.

- **In the introductory paragraph, use the attention-getting opening sentences from your brainstorming list.**
- **In the second paragraph, describe the kind of job you want.**
- **In the third paragraph, describe how this experience will benefit you and your family.**
- **In the fourth paragraph, describe in what ways you are mature enough to do this job.**
- **In the concluding paragraph, restate and sum up your arguments in a convincing way.**
- **Use vivid language, such as active verbs, colorful adjectives, and sensory words, to make your letter stronger and more persuasive.**
- **Use the correct form for a personal letter.**

DIRECTIONS: Begin your letter below and continue on the back of this sheet. This is a first draft, so concentrate on organizing your thoughts and getting them down on paper.

Name ______________________________ Date ______________

9–18. Persuading Your Parents (final copy)

A. DIRECTIONS: Correct and revise the letter to your parents persuading them to permit you to have a summer job. Follow the guidelines below, and check off each item as you complete it.

- ❑ Does the first paragraph introduce the topic in an attention-getting way?
- ❑ Does the second paragraph describe the job with interesting details?
- ❑ Does the third paragraph show how this will benefit you and your family?
- ❑ Does the fourth paragraph describe in a convincing way your maturity and ability to handle a job?
- ❑ Does the concluding paragraph sum up the topic convincingly?
- ❑ Can you add anything else to make your arguments more persuasive?
- ❑ Add at least one simile or metaphor for interest and emphasis.
- ❑ Did you use correct letter form (three-line return address, greeting, closing, and signature)?
- ❑ Did you use correct punctuation in all parts of the letter?
- ❑ Are sentences complete? Correct any run-ons or fragments.
- ❑ Do subjects and verbs agree? Do pronouns agree with antecedents?

B. DIRECTIONS: Begin the final copy below and continue on the back of this sheet. Remember to indent at the beginning of each paragraph.

____

____

____

____

____

____

____

____

____

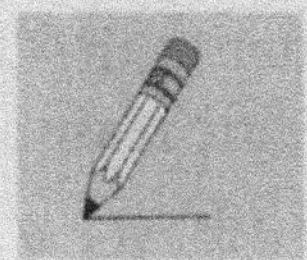

EIGHTH-GRADE LEVEL

WRITING LETTERS PRACTICE TEST

Name ______________________________ **Date** ______________

Practice Test: Writing Letters

DIRECTIONS: Many people think that students are not learning enough in school. They want to shorten most school vacations and make students spend more of the year in school. Other people think that lengthening the school year and shortening vacations is a bad idea because students use their vacations to learn important things outside of school.

What is your opinion? Write a letter to the Board of Education in favor of or against lengthening the school year. Give specific reasons to support your opinion that will convince the school board to agree with you.

Follow these four steps to write your letter:

- FIRST, on the page labeled PREWRITING, follow the directions for brainstorming and organizing ideas for your letter.
- SECOND, write the first draft of your story on a separate sheet of paper. Write your name and date at the top.
- THIRD, revise and edit your first draft. Refer to your list of proofreading symbols if you wish to make use of them. Use the checklist as a guide, and check off each item when it has been revised to your satisfaction.
- FOURTH, write your final copy on a separate sheet of paper with your name and date at the top.

CHECKLIST

- ❑ Do you follow the correct form for a personal letter?
- ❑ Do you place a comma after the greeting and after the closing?
- ❑ Does your first paragraph introduce the topic? Can you make the opening sentences more attention-getting?
- ❑ Do the middle paragraphs develop the topic clearly and logically?
- ❑ Do you support your main points with convincing details?
- ❑ Do you stay focused on the topic? Take out any irrelevancies.
- ❑ Can you strengthen your writing with more vivid language, such as active verbs, sensory words, and colorful adjectives?
- ❑ Do you use a variety of sentence sizes, varying long and short sentences?
- ❑ Are sentences complete? Correct any run-ons and fragments.
- ❑ Do subjects and verbs agree? Do pronouns agree with their antecedents?
- ❑ Do you capitalize proper nouns and the beginning of sentences?

Name ______________________________ Date ______________

PRACTICE TEST: WRITING LETTERS *(continued)*

Prewriting

Organize your thoughts on the subject of shortening school vacations by preparing a brainstorming list, outline, or cluster below. Be sure to include three or four main points. List words and phrases to use as supporting details for each main point. Include active verbs, sensory language, and colorful adjectives that will make your letter more persuasive.

Name ______________________________ Date ______________

PRACTICE TEST: WRITING LETTERS *(continued)*

Student Samples

LETTER A

To whom it may concern,

I've heard about the debate over whether or not to lengthen the school year. I decided to voice my opinion. I believe that the school year should not be lengthened. Kids are stressed out enough with homework and school without adding more. Some might say that kids aren't learning enough, and since the future of the nation rests on their shoulders they need to go to school longer and learn more. I say those who are adults now went to school the same amount, if not shorter, of time as we do and they haven't completely ruined the country.

To make the country better, you don't need to know math, English, and history; you need to know social skills like getting along with others. You learn social skills at school, but you can learn them just as easily while on vacation. If you go to another country for vacation, you learn to accept and respect other cultures. This can help extinguish prejudices.

If you add more schoolwork and homework, kids will get more stressed out. When you're stressed out, you aren't as agreeable and sometimes just give up trying and don't care about anything.

I once heard someone say that you are only a kid for a short time. When you are an adult, you have enough stress and hardly any time for fun, so why put stress on kids and make them lose their time for fun. Why turn them into adults before their time?

I completely agree with the person who said this. Let kids have fun and not be stuck in a hot school listening to a lecture, or at home doing homework when they used to be swimming or hanging out with friends.

Thank you for considering my letter.

Score ____________

LETTER B

Dear Boared of Education. It is not right trying to make our school year longer and our summer shorter. We need time out of school. We learn more out of school than we do in school stuff we need for when we get older like working on the car, Painting the house, hunting and fishing, stuff we don't learn in school and can only be taugth to us on warm suny days. So see that's why we need more time out of school than in it.

Score ____________

Scoring Guide

SCORE	Unsatisfactory—1	Insufficient—2
Content	Attempts to respond to prompt, but provides little information; may only paraphrase prompt	Presents few details OR may be very repetitive OR may be very undeveloped
Organization	Has no clear organization OR consists of a single statement	Is very disorganized; ideas are weakly connected OR the response is too brief to detect organization
Sentence Structure	Little or no control over sentence boundaries and sentence structure; word choice may be incorrect in much or all of the response	Little control over sentence boundaries and sentence structure; word choice may often be incorrect
Grammar, Usage, and Mechanics	Many errors in grammar or usage—such as tense inconsistency, lack of subject–verb agreement—spelling, and punctuation severely interfere with understanding	Errors in grammar or usage—such as tense inconsistency, lack of subject–verb agreement—spelling, and punctuation interfere with understanding in much of the response

SCORE	Uneven—3	Sufficient—4
Content	Presents a few clear details, but is list-like, undeveloped, or repetitive OR offers no more than a well-written beginning	Develops information with some details
Organization	Is unevenly organized; the letter may be disjointed; has greeting and/or closing	The letter is organized with ideas that are generally related but has few or no transitions
Sentence Structure	Exhibits uneven control over sentence boundaries and sentence structure; may have some incorrect word choices	Exhibits control over sentence boundaries and sentence structure, but sentences and word choice may be simple and unvaried
Grammar, Usage, and Mechanics	Errors in grammar or usage—such as tense inconsistency, lack of subject–verb agreement—spelling, and punctuation sometimes interfere with understanding	Errors in grammar or usage—such as tense inconsistency, lack of subject–verb agreement—spelling, and punctuation do not interfere with understanding

SCORE	Skillful—5	Excellent—6
Content	Develops and shapes information with well-chosen details in parts of the letter	Develops and shapes information with well-chosen details across the letter
Organization	Is clearly organized, but may lack some transitions and/or have lapses in continuity	Is well organized with strong transitions; follows letter format
Sentence Structure	Exhibits some variety in sentence structure and some good word choices	Sustains variety in sentence structure and exhibits good word choice
Grammar, Usage, and Mechanics	Errors in grammar, spelling, and punctuation do not interfere with understanding	Errors in grammar, spelling, and punctuation are few and do not interfere with understanding

Proofreading Symbols

¶	indent first line of paragraph
≡	capitalize
∧ or ∨	add
	remove
⊙	add a period
/	make lowercase
	move
	transpose
~~	boldface
—	italicize
. . .	stet or restore crossed-out words

APPENDIX

PREPARING YOUR STUDENTS FOR STANDARDIZED PROFICIENCY TESTS

Even as the debate over the value and fairness of standardized tests continues, standardized tests are an annual event for millions of students. In most school districts the results of the tests are vitally important. Scores may be used to determine if students are meeting district or state guidelines, they may be used as a means of comparing the scores of the district's students to local or national norms, or they may be used to decide a student's placement in advanced or remedial classes. No matter how individual scores are used in your school, students deserve the chance to do well. They deserve to be prepared.

By providing students with practice in answering the kinds of questions they will face on a standardized test, an effective program of preparation can familiarize students with testing formats, refresh skills, build confidence, and reduce anxiety, all critical factors that can affect scores as much as basic knowledge. Just like the members of an orchestra rehearse to get ready for a concert, the dancer trains for the big show, and the pianist practices for weeks before the grand recital, preparing students for standardized tests is essential.

To be most effective a test-preparation program should be comprehensive, based on skills your students need to know, and enlist the support of parents. Because students often assume the attitudes of their parents regarding tests—for example, nervous parents frequently make their children anxious—you should seek as much parental involvement in your test preparations as possible. Students who are encouraged by their parents and prepared for tests by their teachers invariably do better than those who come to the testing session with little preparation and support.

What Parents Need to Know About Standardized Tests

While most parents will agree it is important for their children to do well on standardized tests, many feel there is little they can do to help the outcome. Consequently, aside from encouraging their children to "try your best," they feel there is nothing more for them to do. Much of this feeling arises from parents not fully understanding the testing process.

To provide the parents of your students with information about testing, consider sending home copies of the following reproducibles:

- The Uses of Standardized Tests
- Test Terms
- Common Types of Standardized Tests
- Preparing Your Child for Standardized Tests

You may wish to send these home in a packet with a cover letter (a sample of which is included) announcing the upcoming standardized tests.

The Uses of Standardized Tests

Schools administer standardized tests for a variety of purposes. It is likely that your child's school utilizes the scores of standardized tests in at least some of the following ways.

- Identify strengths and weaknesses in academic skills.
- Identify areas of high interest, ability, or aptitude. Likewise identify areas of average or low ability or aptitude.
- Compare the scores of students within the district to each other as well as to students of other districts. This can be done class to class, school to school, or district to district. Such comparisons help school systems to evaluate their curriculums and plan instruction and programs.
- Provide a basis for comparison of report card grades to national standards.
- Identify students who might benefit from advanced or remedial classes.
- Certify student achievement, for example, in regard to receiving awards.
- Provide reports on student progress.

Test Terms

Although standardized tests come in different forms and may be designed to measure different skills, most share many common terms. Understanding these "test terms" is the first step to understanding the tests.

- ***Achievement tests*** measure how much students have learned in a particular subject area. They concentrate on knowledge of subject matter.
- ***Aptitude tests*** are designed to predict how well students will do in learning new subject matter in the future. They generally measure a broad range of skills associated with success. Note that the line between aptitude and achievement tests is often indistinct.
- ***Battery*** refers to a group of tests that are administered during the same testing session. For example, separate tests for vocabulary, language, reading, spelling, and mathematics that comprise an achievement test are known as the *test battery.*
- ***Correlation coefficient*** is a measure of the strength and direction of the relationship between two items. It can be a positive or negative number.
- ***Diagnostic tests*** are designed to identify the strengths and weaknesses of students in specific subject areas. They are usually given only to students who show exceptional ability or serious weakness in an area.
- ***Grade equivalent scores*** are a translation of the score attained on the test to an approximate grade level. Thus, a student whose score translates to a grade level of 4.5 is working at roughly the midyear point of fourth grade. One whose score equals a grade level of 8.0 is able to successfully complete work typically given at the beginning of eighth grade.
- ***Individual student profiles*** (also referred to as *reports*) display detailed test results for a particular student. Some of these can be so precise that the answer to every question is shown.
- ***Item*** is a specific question on a test.
- ***Mean*** is the average of a group of scores.
- ***Median*** is the middle score in a group of scores.
- ***Mode*** is the score achieved most by a specific group of test takers.
- ***Normal distribution*** is a distribution of test scores in which the scores are distributed around the mean and where the mean, median, and mode are the same. A normal distribution, when displayed, appears bell-shaped.
- ***Norming population*** is the group of students (usually quite large) to whom the test was given and on whose results performance standards for various age or grade levels are based. *Local norms* refer to distributions based on a particular school or school district. *National norms* refer to distributions based on students from around the country.
- ***Norm-referenced tests*** are tests in which the results of the test may be compared with other norming populations.

Test Terms *(continued)*

- ***Percentile rank*** is a comparison of a student's raw score with the raw scores of others who took the test. The comparison is most often made with members of the norming population. Percentile rank enables a test taker to see where his or her scores rank among others who take the same test. A percentile rank of 90, for example, means that the test taker scored better than 90% of those who took the test. A percentile rank of 60 means the test taker scored better than 60% of those who took the test. A percentile rank of 30 means he or she scored better than only 30% of those who took the test, and that 70% of the test takers had higher scores.
- ***Raw score*** is the score of a test based on the number correct. On some tests the raw score may include a correction for guessing.
- ***Reliability*** is a measure of the degree to which a test measures what it is designed to measure. A test's reliability may be expressed as a reliability coefficient that typically ranges from 0 to 1. Highly reliable tests have reliability coefficients of 0.90 or higher. Reliability coefficients may take several forms. For example, parallel-form reliability correlates the performance on two different forms of a test; split-half reliability correlates two halves of the same test; and test-retest reliability correlates test scores of the same test given at two different times. The producers of standardized tests strive to make them as reliable as possible. Although there are always cases of bright students not doing well on a standardized test and some students who do surprisingly well, most tests are quite reliable and provide accurate results.
- ***Score*** is the number of correct answers displayed in some form. Sometimes the score is expressed as a *scaled score*, which means that the score provided by the test is derived from the number of correct answers.
- ***Standard deviation*** is a measure of the variability of test scores. If most scores are near the mean score, the standard deviation will be small; if scores vary widely from the mean, the standard deviation will be large.
- ***Standard error of measurement*** is an estimate of the amount of possible measurement error in a test. It provides an estimate of how much a student's true test score may vary from the actual score he or she obtained on the test. Tests that have a large standard error of measurement may not accurately reflect a student's true ability. The standard error of measurement is usually small for well-designed tests.
- ***Standardized tests*** are tests that have been given to students under the same conditions. They are designed to measure the same skills and abilities for everyone who takes them.
- ***Stanine scores*** are scores expressed between the numbers 1 and 9 with 9 being high.
- ***Validity*** is the degree to which a test measures what it is supposed to measure. There are different kinds of validity. One, *content validity*, for example, refers to the degree to which the content of the test is valid for the purpose of the test. Another, *predictive validity*, refers to the extent to which predictions based on the test are later proven accurate by other evidence.

Common Types of Standardized Tests

Most standardized tests are broken down into major sections that focus on specific subjects. Together these sections are referred to as a *battery.* The materials and skills tested are based on grade level. The following tests are common throughout the country; however, not all schools administer every test.

- ***Analogy tests*** measure a student's ability to understand relationships between words (ideas). Here is an example: Boy is to man as girl is to woman. The relationship, of course, is that a boy becomes a man and a girl becomes a woman. Not only does an analogy test the ability to recognize relationships, it tests vocabulary as well.
- ***Vocabulary tests*** determine whether students understand the meaning of certain words. They are most often based on the student's projected grade-level reading, comprehension, and spelling skills.
- ***Reading comprehension tests*** show how well students can understand reading passages. These tests appear in many different formats. In most, students are required to read a passage and then answer questions designed to measure reading ability.
- ***Spelling tests*** show spelling competence, based on grade-level appropriate words. The tests may require students to select a correctly spelled word from among misspelled words, or may require students to find the misspelled word among correctly spelled words.
- ***Language mechanics tests*** concentrate on capitalization and punctuation. Students may be required to find examples of incorrect capitalization and punctuation as well as examples of correct capitalization and punctuation in sentences and short paragraphs.
- ***Language expression tests*** focus on the ability of students to use words correctly according to the standards of conventional English. In many "expression" tests, effective structuring of ideas is also tested.
- ***Writing tests*** determine how effectively students write and can express their ideas. Usually a topic is given and students must express their ideas on the topic.
- ***Mathematics problem-solving tests*** are based on concepts and applications, and assess the ability of students to solve math problems. These tests often include sections on number theory, interpretation of data and graphs, and logical analysis.
- ***Mathematics computation tests*** measure how well students can add, subtract, multiply, and divide. While the difficulty of the material depends on grade level, these tests generally cover whole numbers, fractions, decimals, percents, and geometry.
- ***Science tests*** measure students' understanding of basic science facts and the methodology used by scientists in the development of theoretical models that explain natural phenomena.
- ***Social studies tests*** measure students' understanding of basic facts in social studies.

Preparing Your Child for Standardized Tests

As a parent, there is much you can do to help your son or daughter get ready for taking a standardized test.

During the weeks leading up to the test . . .

- Attend parent–teacher conferences and find out how you can help your child succeed in school.
- Assume an active role in school. Seeing your commitment to his or her school enhances the image of school in your child's eyes.
- Find out when standardized tests are given and plan accordingly. For example, avoid scheduling doctor or dentist appointments for your child during the testing dates. Students who take standardized tests with their class usually do better than students who make up tests because of absences.
- Monitor your child's progress in school. Make sure your child completes his or her homework and projects. Support good study habits and encourage your child to always do his or her best.
- Encourage your child's creativity and interests. Provide plenty of books, magazines, and educational opportunities.
- Whenever you speak of standardized tests, speak of them in a positive manner. Emphasize that while these tests are important, it is not the final score that counts, but that your child tries his or her best.

During the days immediately preceding the test . . .

- Once the test has been announced, discuss the test with your child to relieve apprehension. Encourage your son or daughter to take the test seriously, but avoid being overly anxious. (Sometimes parents are more nervous about their children's tests than the kids are.)
- Help your child with any materials his or her teacher sends home in preparation for the test.
- Make sure your child gets a good night's sleep each night before a testing day.
- On the morning of the test, make sure your child wakes up on time, eats a solid breakfast, and arrives at school on time.
- Remind your child to listen to the directions of the teacher carefully and to read directions carefully.
- Encourage your child to do his or her best.

Cover Letter to Parents Announcing Standardized Tests

Use the following letter to inform the parents of your students about upcoming standardized tests in your school. Feel free to adjust the letter according to your needs.

Dear Parents/Guardians,

On ____________________(dates)____________________, our class will be taking the ______________(name of test)______________.

During the next few weeks students will work on various practice tests to help prepare for the actual test.

You can help, too. Please read the attached materials and discuss the importance of the tests with your child. By supporting your child's efforts in preparation, you can help him or her attain the best possible scores.

Thank you.

Sincerely,

(Name)

What Students Need to Know About Standardized Tests

The mere thought of taking a standardized test frightens many students, causing a wide range of symptoms from mild apprehension to upset stomachs and panic attacks. Since even low levels of anxiety can distract students and undermine their achievement, you should attempt to lessen their concerns.

Apprehension, anxiety, and fear are common responses to situations that we perceive as being out of our control. When students are faced with a test on which they don't know what to expect, they may worry excessively that they won't do well. Such emotions, especially when intense, almost guarantee that they will make careless mistakes. When students are prepared properly for a test, they are more likely to know "what to expect." This reduces negative emotions and students are able to enter the testing situation with confidence, which almost always results in better scores.

The first step to preparing your students for standardized tests is to mention the upcoming tests well in advance—at least a few weeks ahead of time—and explain that in the days leading up to the test, the class will be preparing. Explain that while they will not be working with the actual test, the work they will be doing is designed to help them get ready. You may wish to use the analogy of a sports team practicing during the pre-season. Practices help players sharpen their skills, anticipate game situations, and build confidence. Practicing during the pre-season helps athletes perform better during the regular season.

You might find it useful to distribute copies of the following reproducibles:

- Test-taking Tips for Students
- Test Words You Should Know

Hand these out a few days before the testing session. Go over them with your students and suggest that they take them home and ask their parents to review the sheets with them on the night before the test.

TEST-TAKING TIPS FOR STUDENTS

1. Try your best.
2. Be confident and think positively. People who believe they will do well usually do better than those who are not confident.
3. Fill out the answer sheet correctly. Be careful that you darken all "circles." Be sure to use a number 2 pencil unless your teacher tells you otherwise.
4. Listen carefully to all directions and follow them exactly. If you don't understand something, ask your teacher.
5. Read all questions and their possible answers carefully. Sometimes an answer may at first seem right, but it isn't. Always read all answers before picking one.
6. Try to answer the questions in order, but don't waste too much time on hard questions. Go on to easier ones and then go back to the hard ones.
7. Don't be discouraged by hard questions. On most tests for every hard question there are many easy ones.
8. Try not to make careless mistakes.
9. Budget your time and work quickly.
10. Be sure to fill in the correct answer spaces on your answer sheet. Use a finger of your non-writing hand to keep your place on the answer space.
11. Look for clues and key words when answering questions.
12. If you become "stuck" on a question, eliminate any answers you know are wrong and then make your best guess of the remaining answers. (Do this only if there is no penalty for guessing. Check with your teacher about this.)
13. Don't leave any blanks. Guess if you are running out of time. (Only do this if unanswered questions are counted wrong. Check with your teacher.)
14. Double-check your work if time permits.
15. Erase completely any unnecessary marks on your answer sheet.

Test Words You Should Know

The words below are used in standardized tests. Understanding what each one means will help you when you take your test.

all
always
answer sheet
best
blank
booklet
bubble
capitalization
check
choose
circle
column
complete
comprehension
continue
correct
definition
details
directions
does not belong
double-check
end
error
example
fill in
finish
following
go on
item
language expression
language mechanics
mark
match
missing
mistake
name
never
none
not true
number 2 pencil
opposite
order
oval
part
passage
pick
punctuation
question
read
reread
right
row
same as
sample
section
select
stop
topic
true
vocabulary

Creating a Positive Test-taking Environment

Little things really do matter when students take standardized tests. Students who are consistently encouraged to do their best throughout the year in the regular classroom generally achieve higher scores on standardized tests than students who maintain a careless attitude regarding their studies. Of course, motivating students to do their best is an easy thing to suggest, but not such an easy goal to accomplish.

There are, fortunately, some steps you can take to foster positive attitudes on the part of your students in regard to standardized tests. Start by discussing the test students will take, and explain how the results of standardized tests are used. When students understand the purpose of testing, they are more likely to take the tests seriously. Never speak of tests in a negative manner, for example, saying that students must work hard or they will do poorly. Instead, speak in positive terms: by working hard and trying their best they will achieve the best results.

To reduce students' concerns, assure them that the use of practice tests will improve their scores. Set up a thorough test-preparation schedule well in advance of the tests, based upon the needs and abilities of your students. Avoid cramming preparation into the last few days before the test. Cramming only burdens students with an increased workload and leads to anxiety and worry. A regular, methodical approach to preparation is best, because this enables you to check for weaknesses in skills and offer remediation.

The value of preparation for standardized tests cannot be understated. When your students feel that they are prepared for the tests, and that you have confidence in them, they will feel more confident and approach the tests with a positive frame of mind. Along with effective instruction throughout the year, a focused program of test preparation will help ensure that your students will have the chance to achieve their best scores on standardized tests.

Printed and bound by CPI Group (UK) Ltd, Croydon, CR0 4YY

09/06/2025

14685919-0001